GANDHIAN APPROACH TO DEVELOPMENT PLANNING

List of books published under Gandhian Studies and Peace Research Series

1. Gandhian Model of Development and World Peace, **R.P. Misra**

   Conflict Resolution Through Non-Violence : Role of the Universities (in two Vols.), **K.D. Gangrade** and **R.P. Misra** *(eds.)*
2. Vol. 1 : Science and Ethics, **K.D. Gangrade** and **R.P. Misra**
3. Vol. 2 : Development without Destruction, **K.D. Gangrade** and **R.P. Misra**
4. The Social Philosophy of Mahatma Gandhi, **K.S. Bharathi**
5. Gandhian Humanism, **Mohit Chakrabarti**
6. Gandhian Holistic Economics, **Shashi Prabha Sharma**
7. Gandhian Spiritualism : A Quest for Essence of Excellence, **Mohit Chakrabarti**
8. Gandhian Perspective on Population and Development, **A.K. Sharma**
9. Thoughts of Gandhi and Vinoba : A Comparative Study, **K.S. Bharathi**
10. Economic Philosophy of Mahatma Gandhi, **Shanti Swarup Gupta**
11. Political Thought of Mahatma Gandhi (The), **K.S. Bharathi**
12. Gandhi and 21st Century, **Janardhan Pandey** *(ed.)*
13. Gandhian Philosophy of the Spinning Wheel, **Mohit Chakraborti**
14. Gandhian Satyagraha : An Analytical and Critical Approach, **Ajay Shanker Rai**
15. Gandhi and His Religion, **(Lt. Col.) P.A. Raju**
16. महात्मा गाँधी विचार वीथिका, एस.पी. अग्रवाल
17. Poverty of Gandhian Philosophy, **Himansu Roy**
18. Right to Equality in the Indian Constitution : A Gandhian Perspective, **Shashi Nath Saraswati**
19. Meditations on Gandhi : A Ravindra Varma Festschrift, **M.P. Mathai, M.S. John** and **Siby K. Joseph** *(eds.)*
20. Politico-Economic Ideas of Mahatma Gandhi : Their Relevance in the Present-Day, **Sukhendu Mazumdar**
21. Moral Lessons from Gandhi's Autobiography and Other Essays, **K.D. Gangrade**
22. Fire Sans Ire : A Critical Study of Gandhian Nonviolence, **Mohit Chakrabarti**
23. Gandhian Alternative (Volume 1 : Towards a Gandhian World Order), **Suresh Misra** *(ed.)*
24. Gandhian Alternative (Volume 2 : Nonviolence in Action), **Savita Singh** and **Bharati Misra** *(eds.)*
25. Gandhian Alternative (Volume 3 : Socio-Political Thoughts), **Anil Dutta Mishra** and **Sushna Yadav** *(eds.)*
26. Gandhian Alternative (Volume 4 : Economics Where People Matter), **V. K. Natraj, Kamlesh Misra** and **Neeru Kapoor** *(eds.)*
27. Gandhian Alternative (Volume 5 : Education for Human Development), **Suresh Misra** *(ed.)*
28. Gandhian Approach to Development Planning, **Ram Vinod Singh**

About the Author

Ram Binod Singh (*b* 1938) is a retired professor of Economics, C.M. College, Darbhanga (LNMU). He obtained his M.A. (Economics), B.L. and Ph.D. degrees from Bihar University, Muzaffarpur.

He worked as the founder principal of Kunwar Singh College, Laheriasarai from 1970 to 1974 and as a Research Fellow in the Institute for Rural Development, Patna from 1978 to 1981. He is a socialist by conviction and is influenced by Gandhian doctrines. His other published works include *Alternative Planning for Rural Development; Petroleum Industry in India; India's Economic Development;* and *Lohia's Thought.* Besides, he has contributed many research papers to various journals of repute, and participated in seminars and symposia organised at different levels.

Dr. Ram Binod Singh's current interest includes rural development, energy problems, Gandhian economics and current socio-economic problems.

Gandhian Studies and Peace Research Series—28

GANDHIAN APPROACH TO DEVELOPMENT PLANNING

RAM BINOD SINGH

CONCEPT PUBLISHING COMPANY, NEW DELHI-110059

All rights reserved. No part of this work may be reproduced, stored in a retrieval system or transmitted in any form or by any means, electronic, mechanical, photocopying, microfilming, recording or otherwise, without the prior written permission of the copyright owner and the publisher.

ISBN : 81-8069-265-5

First Published 2006

© Ram Binod Singh (*b.* 1938)

Published and Printed by
Ashok Kumar Mittal
Concept Publishing Company
A/15-16, Commercial Block, Mohan Garden,
New Delhi-110059 (India)

Phones : 25351460, 25351794
Fax : 091-11-25357103
Email : publishing@conceptpub.com

PREFACE

Ever since my school days, I have been impressed by the socialist thought. My temperament and my bitter experiences throughout my student life due to economic stringency confirmed my belief that emancipation of men in general and of down-trodden in particular lay in socialism. With the passage of time, it was clear that U.S.S.R. and other communist countries were deviating from the main ideology and commitment and consequences are obvious with the disintegration of the U.S.S.R. and other communist countries of Europe. In the sixties, I got an opportunity to go through Gandhian literature and was convinced that Gandhi alone offers the solutions of the ills confronting the present social order.

The traditional socialist, though being rooted in materialism, has failed to interpret history and the evolution of the human race correctly. Man is not merely matter but spirit also. Any theory of social reconstruction would fail if it overstresses the one and ignores the other. Credit goes to Gandhi who established a judicious relationship between the two. The tragedy of Marxian socialism is that it ignores totally the non-material forces. Gandhian socialism is primarily based on his ethical concept. Ashok Mehta asserted that socialism is a science of new society as well as the vision of new civilization.

The contribution of Mahatma Gandhi to the theory of economic planning and development is highly significant. It is also relevant for dealing with contemporary problems created by the process of economic development itself. It is paradoxical that while these planners talk of value that must impregnate the process of development, they do not favour the methods that Gandhi advocated as the most efficacious in realizing these values. Gandhi was a rare admixture of a great humanist, a master strategist, a veteran politician and a down to earth pragmatist.

Gandhi might have borrowed from different traditions of economic thoughts, both Eastern and Western. The influence of Tolstoy, Thoreau,

Ruskin, Romain Rolland and several other thinkers on the economic ideas of Gandhi is undoubtedly great. His scheme of economic planning and development is primarily based on his principle of micro-variability and micro-viability, which necessarily incorporated ideas of *Swadeshi,* trusteeship and bread labour. *Swadeshi* fits in with his design of self-sufficiency. Gandhi's theory of trusteeship, enunciated in reply to the socialists, is a unique scheme where accumulation of wealth and the consequent concentration of power may remain an empirical reality but it cannot become oppressive and exploitative. Gandhi is dead but his ideas are still with us.

Similarly, economic development was considered Summam bonum of life and economic man was the main focus. This lacked human consideration. There was confusion and erroneous notion about means and ends. For Gandhi, man is the focal point and all other activities revolve round him. Economic development is for the man and not *vice versa.* There is symbiotic relationship between man and society on the one hand, and man and nature on the other. True economic development not only respects this relationship rather strengthens this.

Jayaprakash Narayan also made it the focal point of the struggle against administrative lapses, corruption and democratic disruption injuring the society and the nation at large. Similarly, Cultural Revolution was also launched by Mao in China during late sixties of the last century. Gandhi rightly believed that if changes are to be brought about in society, it must start from man who constitutes the society. This is why, Gandhi claimed to be a socialist whose vision was equality, justice, freedom and complete autonomy of individual to think and decide his destiny. This led him to be anarchist who considered state as an evil representing organized and concentrated form of tyranny and violence. He finds his hope in the individual whereas he spurns the state power.

Finally, Gandhi did not support creation of wealth at the cost of spoilation of nature and its precious non-renewable resources. He warned that depletion of resources would disturb the ecological balance of the nature and ultimately life cycle will be irreparably affected. This is being witnessed in the industrial societies of the West and big urban centres in the Third World countries. Anxieties are expressed but correctives are still lacking on their part who were responsible for this disaster. One has to adjust with nature, respect its beauty and protect it to the maximum extent which is inevitable for not only peace and prosperity of mankind but for its survival as well.

I was keenly interested to know and understand Gandhi in totality. Post-independence development planning and modality for development induced me to study Gandhi. Being a student of economics I tried my best to understand the relevance and implication of Gandhian principles of planning. Shreeman Narayan's book *Principles of Gandhian Planning* fascinated me most due to its clear concept and lucid style. Subsequently, Dr. Ramashray Roy's contribution to Gandhian philosophy inspired me to do some work. It must be admitted that no single book covers all his ideas, particularly on development and planning, and I have tried my best to bring together these ideas in my research. After my retirement from service in the university as a teacher of economics, I prepared a research proposal on "Gandhian Approach to Development Planning" and submitted the same to the U.G.C. for consideration. I am thankful to the U.G.C. which awarded this major project and enabled me to work on Gandhi.

I owe my indebtedness to Dr. Ramashray Roy who guided me right from drafting the proposal to final preparation of the report. He is the main driving force for the timely completion of this project. I express my thanks to Dr. H.K. Chauhan, Senior Research Officer, U.G.C., who provided me guidance whenever I felt any difficulty during the research and preparation of report etc., as per norms of the U.G.C.

I am also grateful to Dr. Anil Dutta Mishra, Dy. Director, National Gandhi Museum, for his cooperation and support and suggestions from time to time in this endeavour.

I am grateful to Dr. V.B. Singh, Dr. R.K. Srivastava, both of the G.S.D.S. Delhi and librarian Mr. Dey for helping me with necessary informations, books and journals of the library. Mr. Dey has been very kind and considerate to me.

I am also thankful to the librarians, Central Library, Lalit Narayan Mithila University, Darbhanga, librarians, National Labour Institute, Noida, IIPA, Delhi, Gandhi Peace Foundation and other institutions. I owe a sense of gratitude to a host of friends and colleagues who helped me in various ways to complete the project in time schedule. In this respect Sri V.P. Singh, Department of Economics, Satyabati Co-educational College and Dr. R.C. Pradhan, Department of Political

Science, Ramjas College, Delhi, deserve special mention with whom I interacted frequently and discussed many things on various occasions.

I am really thankful to Dr. Kameshwar Jha and Dr. K.P. Yadav, both principals of C.M. College who cooperated me during the period of my study.

Last but not the least, I would like to thank Mr. Ashok Mittal of Concept Publishing Company for publishing this book in a very short period.

Ram Binod Singh

CONTENTS

1

Introduction

India's independence represented for its people the start of an epoch that was embued with a new vision. In 1947, the country commenced its long march to overcome the colonial legacy of economic development, gross poverty, near total illiteracy, wide prevalence of diseases and stark social inequality and injustice. 1947 was only the first stop, the first break—the end of colonial political control; centuries of backwardness were now to be overcome, the promises of freedom struggle to be fulfilled and people's hopes to be met.

Starting off with a broad social consensus on the basic contours of India that was to be built on the values of nationalism, secularism and democracy and the goal of rapid economic development and radical social change was a great advantage. These values and goals, and the road to their achievement had been mapped over the seventy years by the national movement.

The first and the most important task was to preserve, consolidate and strengthen India's unity to push forward the process of the making of the Indian nation, and to build up and protect national state as an instrument of development and social transformation. It was also clear that India's revolution had to be taken beyond the merely political to include economic and social transformation. It had to begin its upward economic climb from an abysmally low level. Moreover, the Indian economy, even while being an integral part of the world economy, was to be based on self-reliance, free of subordination to the metropolitan interest or domination by foreign capital.

The founders of the Indian Republic have the farsightedness, vision and the courage to commit themselves in two major innovations of historical importance in nation-building and social engineering; first, to build a democratic and civil librarian society among an illiterate people, and second, to undertake economic development within a democratic political structure. The many social, economic and political challenges that the country was to face were to be dealt with in a democratic manner, under democratic conditions. Economic development and a democratic political order were to be accompanied by rapid social transformation so that existing gross economic, caste and gender inequalities were rapidly eliminated, poverty was removed and the level of living raised. The national movement had also aroused expectations of a rapid rise in personal and societal prosperity, of social and economic equity and quality of the good life. This was to be on the basis of democracy, avoiding bloodshed and authoritarianism, and through a process of accommodating diverse social, economic and regional interests. It was thought that agrarian reforms, state planning and a strong public sector were to serve as the major instrument for the purpose.

Then there were left-wing parties who held that no social, economic or political development was possible without a violent revolution and that nation-building, political democracy, economic development, national unity and nationalism were mere shams meant to delude the oppressed and exploited. They argued for or anticipated a peasant-based revolution as in China or a worker peasant-based revolution as in Russia. According to them, poverty, inequality, class dominance and social oppression would, sooner or later, lead the vast majority of people on the path of revolution, putting an end not only to capitalism and feudalism but also a bourgeois democracy and the multination state.[1]

Another set of observers of the Indian scene, who were less pessimistic about the democratic political system, were puzzled by India's success in sustaining itself in the face of its failure on so many fronts—inadequacy of land reforms and existence of large scale landlessness in the rural areas, the slow growth of industry and the national income, the failure to check the high rate of population growth, persistence of gross inequalities, caste oppression, discrimination against women, a dysfunctional education system, environmental degradation, growing population in the cities, human rights abuses, factionalism in politics, chaotic party situation, growing political unrest, secessionist demands and movements, administrative decline and even chaos, police inefficiencies and brutalities, high degree of corruption at higher levels and criminalisation of politics. But what they failed to appreciate is that democracy had already been indigenized and rooted in the Indian soil by the freedom struggle and the modern intelligentsia during the previous hundred years or so.[2]

There were four basic features of the colonial structure in India. First, colonialism led to the complete but complex integration of India's economy with the world capitalist system but in a subservient position. Second, to suit British industry, a peculiar structure of production and international division of labour was forced upon India. Third, basic to the process of economic development is the size and utilisation of the economic surplus or savings generated in the economy, for investment and therefore epansion of the economy. The net savings in the Indian economy from 1914 to 1946 was only 2.75 per cent of GDP. This small size may be contrasted with the net savings in 1971-75 when they constituted 12 per cent of GNP. The paltry total capital formation, 6.7 per cent of GNP during 1914-46 as against 20.14 per cent of GNP during 1971-75 reflects this jump. Furthermore, a large part of India's social surplus was appropriated by the colonial state and misspent. Another large part was appropriated by the indigenous landlords and moneylenders. Then there was the drain, that is the unilateral transfer to Britain of social surplus and potential investible capital.

The fourth feature of colonialism in India was the crucial role played by the state in constructing, determining and maintaining other aspects of colonial structure. India's policies were decided and determined in Britain and in the interest of British economy. The colonial state devoted almost its entire income to meeting the needs of British Indian administration, making payments of direct and indirect tribute to Britain and in serving the needs of British trade and industry. The bulk of public revenue was absorbed by military expenditure and civil administration which was geared to maintenance of law and order and tax collection. As late as 1900-1901 land revenue and salt tax formed 53 per cent and 16 per cent of the total tax revenue of the government.

Colonialism became a fetter on India's agricultural and industrial development. There was a decline in per capita agricultural production which fell by 14 per cent between 1901 and 1914. The fall in per capita food grains was even greater, being over 24 per cent. An agrarian which was dominated by landlords, moneylenders, merchants and the colonial state. For most of the colonial period landlessness had been rising. So that the number of landless agricultural labourers grew from 13 per cent improvement in transport and communication led to commercialisation of agriculture but did not lead to capitalist farming

---

GDP=Gross Domestic Product
GNP=Gross National Product

or use of improved technology. During the 19th century, there was a quick collapse of Indian handicrafts and artisanal industries largely because of the competition and specially deliberate policy to hamper the growth of this sector. Modern industries did develop in India from the second half of the 19th century, but both in terms of production and employment, the level of industrial development was stunted and paltry compared with the developed countries.

An important index of India's industrial backwardness and economic dependence on the metropolis was the virtual absence of capital goods and machine and tools through imports. The underdeveloped character of this modern sector of the economy can be seen by comparing certain economic statistics for 1950 and 1984 (the figures for 1984 are given within brackets). In 1950 India produced 1.04 million tonnes of steel (6.9 million tonnes), 32.8 million tonnes of coal (155.2 million tonnes), 2.7 million tonnes of cement (29.9 million tonnes), 3 million rupees worth of machine tools and portable tools (3.8 million rupees), 7 locomotives (200), 99000 bicycles (5944000), 14 million electrical lamps (317.8 million), 33000 sewing machines (338000), and it generated 14 kwh electricity per capita (160 kwh). In 1950, the number of bank offices and branches was 5072, in 1983 the figure had risen to 33055. In 1950, out of the population of 357 million only 2.31 million were employed in modern industries.[3]

Another index of economic backwardness was high rural-urban ratio of India's population. In 1951, nearly 82.3 per cent of population was rural. While in 1901, 63.07 per cent of Indians had depended on agriculture, by 1941 this figure has gone to 70. But during the same period some major changes took place in the Indian economy. The important feature was growth of the means of transport and communication. In the forties, India had 65000 miles of paved roads and nearly 42000 miles of railway track. Roads and rails unified the country, made rapid transit of goods and persons possible. In absence of industrial revolution, commercial revolution was produced which further colonized the Indian economy.

By 1947, Indian capital had also made a great deal of headway in banking and life insurance. Indian joint stock banks held 64 per cent of all bank deposits and Indian owned life insurance companies controlled nearly 75 per cent of life insurance business in the country. The bulk of internal trade and part of foreign trade was also in Indian hands. The economy did not take off. Whatever, development occurred was not because of, but in spite of, colonialism and often in opposition to colonial policies. The net result of the colonial underdevelopment was the pauperization of the people, especially the peasantry and the artisans. Extreme and visible poverty, disease and hunger and starvation were the lot of the ordinary people. The last of the major famines in 1943 carried away nearly 3 million people in Bengal. The character of the colonial state was quite paradoxical. While it was basically authoritarian and autocratic, it also featured certain liberal elements like rule of law and a relatively independent judiciary. The colonial rulers also extended certain amount of civil liberties in the form of the freedom of the press, speech and association in normal times, but curtailed them drastically in period of mass struggle.

The colonial legacy about the unity of India was marked by a strange paradox. The colonial state brought about a greater political and administrative unification of India than ever achieved before. Building on the Mughal administrative system, it established a uniform system which penetrated the country's remotest areas and created a single administrative entity. They also evolved a common educational structure which in time produced an India-wide intelligentsia which shared common outlook on society and polity, and thought in national terms. Combined with the formation of a unified economy and the development of modern means of communication, colonialism helped lay the basis for making of the Indian nation. But fearing the unity of the Indian people to which their own rule had contributed, they followed the classic imperial policy of divide and rule. These diverse and divisive features of Indian society and polity were heightened to promote cleavages among the people and to turn province against province, caste against caste, class against class, Hindus against Muslims, and the princes and landlords against the national movement. They succeeded in their endeavour to a varying extent, which culminated in India's partition.[4]

The British ruled India through modern bureaucracy, headed by the highly paid Indian civil service. Bureaucracy was rulebound, efficient and, at the top, rather honest. Following Indian pressure, the different services were gradually Indianised after 1918. By 1947, nearly 48 per cent of the members of the I.C.S. were Indian, but positions of control and authority were upto the end retained by the British. Indians in these services too functioned as agents of British rule.

Referring reproachfully to the legacy bequeathed by colonialism, Rabindranath Tagore wrote just three months before his death in 1941:

> "The wheels of fate will someday compel the English to give up their Indian empire. But what kind of India will they leave behind, what stark misery? When the stream of their centuries administration runs dry at last, what a waste of mud and filth will they leave behind them."

A meaningful appraisal of India's development experience after independence would have to place it both in historical and comparative contexts. The level and stage from which the beginning was made and the efforts to undertake economic transformation within a democratic framework need to be taken into account: the achievements should be measured with other countries at a comparable stage of development. Besides this, the real yardstick to evaluate the level of development should be what was possible to be achieved and what actually has been achieved under the democratic framework. It is a fact that colonial legacy has to be undone so that conditions could be created for rapid economic development. It cannot be denied that irreparable damage was caused to Indian economy during the colonial era but it must be admitted that it had some positive aspects also which have been discussed above.

The concept of economic planning was advocated and discussed by many thinkers in the beginning of the twentieth century. With the end of *laissez-faire,* economic planning has assumed special significance in all countries. Before the First World War, planning touched national life only at a few points like labour welfare, housing and unemployment. But in the post-war period, planned economy has become much more comprehensive, embracing almost all aspects of national life. The Five Year Plan of Soviet Russia was the first in the field and it set the fashion for planning throughout the world. President Roosevelt inaugurated his New Deal in America with a view to tiding over the great depression. Hitler launched his Four Year Plan mainly to prepare Germany for the Second World War. The Beveridge Plan of Social Security was, however, a systematic attempt in this direction.

In India, Sir Visvesvaraya was, perhaps, the first to address himself to the task of economic planning on Western lines. At a time when the nationalist voice of India was hushed and strangled, the distinguished industrialists had rendered a positive service to the country by presenting a Fifteen Year Plan of economic development, popularly known as Bombay Plan. There is no point in questioning the sincerity and patriotism of these able and competent businessmen even if they conceived the concept of capitalist plan on Western lines. M.N. Roy had also published a People's Plan which contemplated a total expenditure of fifteen thousand crore of rupees in ten years.

It is to be remembered that National Planning Committee was also constituted under the chairmanship of Pandit Nehru to prepare a plan for economic reconstruction of India. When India attained freedom in 1947, Planning Commission was created by the Government of India to assess and evaluate the existing resources of the country and to plan their fuller utilisation for solving the problems of unemployment, backwardness and unutilisation and underutilisation of available resources within the economy. First Five Year Plan was launched in 1951-52 and since then development of the Indian economy has taken place under the policies and programmes formulated and executed under the planned process of development.

It is mentioned that by independence, India had, in spite of and in opposition to colonialism, developed an independent economic base from which to attempt a take-off into rapid economic growth. A mature indigenous entrepreneurial class which could serve as the agency for carrying out a substantial parts of the post-independence planned development was an asset to India. Industrial class was there to take care of Industry, trade, banking, transport and so on. Moreover, India was fortunate to have a broad societal consensus on the nature and path of development to be followed after independence. For example, the Gandhians, the socialists, the capitalists as well as the communists were all, more or less, agreed on the following agenda:

> "A multi-pronged strategy of economic development based on self-reliance, rapid industrialisation based on import substituion including capital goods industries; prevention of imperialist or foreign capital domination, land reforms involving abolition of *zamindari,* tenancy reforms, introduction of cooperatives, especially service cooperatives, for marketing, credit, etc., growth be attempted along with equity, i.e. the growth model being reformist with a welfare, pro-poor orientation; positive discrimination or reservation, for a period, in favour of the most oppressed in Indian society, the scheduled castes and tribes; the state to play a central role in promoting economic development, including through direct state participation in the production process, *i.e.* through the public sector and so on".

As early as the late 19th century, in the economic thinking of the early nationalists such as M.G. Ranade and Dadabhai Naoroji, the state was assigned a critical role in economic development of India. This trend of seeking state intervention and not leaving economic forces entirely to the market got further crystallized and acquired widespread acceptance in the interwar period, partly due to Keynesian economic ideas, the experience of the New Deal in the U.S. and Soviet Union experiment. In 1934, N.R. Sarkar, the President of the Federation of Indian Chambers of Commerce and Industry (FICCI), the leading organisation of Indian capitalists, proclaimed: "The days of undiluted *laissez-faire* are gone for ever." Voicing the views of the leadership of the capitalist class, he added that, for a backward country like India, a comprehensive plan of economic development covering all aspects of the economy, agriculture, industry, power, banking, finance and so on chalked out and coordinated by a high powered National Planning Commission, was essential for her to make a structural break with the past and achieve her full potential.[5]

Apart from the recognition of the need for state planning, there was a wide consensus among different shades of opinion around the nation that the role of the state would not only involve the proper use of fiscal, monetary and other instruments of economic policy and state control and supervision over the growth process, but would also have to include a certain amount of direct participation in production process through the public sector. Plan of economic development for India, popularly known as Bombay Plan, was authored by business leaders in 1945. In 1947, when the Economic Programme Committee, appointed by AICC and headed by Nehru not only laid down the areas, such as defence, key industries and public utilities which were to be started under public sector but also added that in respect of existing undertakings the process of transfer from private to public ownership should commence after a period of five years.[6] Capitalists were alarmed and protests were ensued. Signs of accommodation were seen in the 1948. Industrial Policy Resolution, which while delineating specific areas for the public and private sector, added that the question of nationalising any existing industry would be reviewed after ten years and dealt with on the basis of circumstances prevailing at that time. 1956 Industrial Policy Resolution, and the Second Plan considerably expanding the scope of the public sector, made no mention of nationalising existing industries.

This was the perspective with which the Planning Commission, established on 16th of March 1950, functioned. The First Plan 1951-56 essentially tried to complete projects at hand and to meet the immediate crisis situation following the end of the war. Independence had come along with the dislocation caused by the partition.

Considerable progress on several fronts was made during the first phase of development efforts spanning first three Five Year Plans. The overall economy performed impressively compared to the colonial period. India's GNP grew at an average rate of about 4 per cent per annum. The rate of growth achieved by India after independence compared favourably with the rates achieved by the advanced countries at a comparable stage i.e. during their early development. To quote Prof. K.N. Raj[7] :

> "Japan is generally believed to be a country which grew rapidly in the latter part of the 19th century and first quarter of the 20th century; yet the rate of growth of national income in Japan was slightly less then 3 per cent per annum in the period 1893-1912 and did not go upto more than 4 per cent per annum even in the following decade. Judged by criteria such as these, the growth rate achieved in India in the last decade and half (1950-65) is certainly a matter for some satisfaction."

Higher growth requires substantial increase in the rate of investment. Higher rates of savings and investment were achieved during this period. On the basis of the data available, the Draft Outline of the Fourth Plan estimated that domestic savings and total investment in the Indian economy were both 5.5 per cent of national income in 1950-51, rising savings of 10.5 per cent and investment was met partly by liquidating the foreign exchange reserves and partly through foreign borrowing and aid.

On the agrarian front, the comprehensive land reform measures initiated soon after independence, the setting up of a massive network of agricultural extension and community development work at the village level, the large infrastructure investment in irrigation, power, agricultural research and so on had created condition for considerable agricultural growth in this period. During the first three plans, Indian agriculture grew at an annual rate of over 3 per cent, a growth rate 7.5 times higher than achieved during the last half century or so of the colonial period. The growth rates achieved compared very favourably with what was achieved by other countries in a comparable situation. However, the commendable agricultural growth achieved during this period was not sufficient to meet the growing demand of agricultural produce, necessitating increasing imports of foodgrains throughout the first three plans. Since 1956, India had to rely heavily on food imports from the U.S. under the P.L.480 scheme. It was only after the process of the Green Revolution took off, since the late sixties, that this dependence on imports ceased.

Industry, during the first three plans, grew even more rapidly than agriculture, at a compound growth rate of 7.1 per cent per annum between 1951 and 1965. This growth pattern went a long way in reducing India's near total dependence on the advanced countries for basic goods and capital equipment, which was necessary for investment or creation of new capacity. At independence, to make any capital investment, virtually the entire equipment had to be imported. For example in 1950, India met 89.8 per cent of its needs for even machine tools through imports which came down to 43 per cent in 1960 and mere 9 per cent in 1974. India could meet indigenously more than 90 per cent of her equipment requirements for maintaining her rate of investment. This was a major achievement and it considerably increased India's autonomy from the advanced countries in determining her own rate of capital accumulation or growth.

Dependence on external resources, foreign aid, foreign private investment, was kept quite low. Net aid utilisation by India was only 0.4 per cent of the Net National Product during the first plan which increased to 2.25 and 3.17 per cent during second and third plan periods and again falling drastically since the mid-sixties. Apart from industry and agriculture, the early planners gave utmost priority to the development of infrastructure, including education and health, areas greatly neglected in the colonial past. The average actual plan expenditure during first three plans accounted for an average of about 26 per cent of the total plan expenditure in each plan. The corresponding figures for social community services and power were 19.9 per cent and 1.6 per cent respectively.[8]

In 1965-66, as compared to 1950-51, installed capacity of electricity was 4.5 times higher, number of towns and villages electrified was 14 times higher, hospital beds 2.5 times higher, enrolment in schools was little less than 3 times higher and very importantly admission capacity in technical education at degree and diploma levels was higher by 6 and 8.5 times respectively.[9]

Research and development was also accorded priority and apex bodies were created to initiate and monitor the process of research with quality. That India can even think of participating in the globalisation process in today's world of high technology with any degree of competitiveness and equality, is largely due to the spadework done since independence, particularly the great emphasis laid on human resources development in the sphere of science and technology.

Despite the significant achievements during the first three plans, the Indian economy was in the grip of a massive crisis in many respects by the mid-sixties which rapidly changed India's image from a model developing country to a basket case. Two successive monsoon failures of 1965 and 1966 added to the burden on agriculture which was beginning to show signs of stagnation, and led to a fall in agricultural output by 17 per cent and foodgrain output of 20 per cent. The rate of inflation which was kept low not exceeding 2 per cent rose sharply to 12 per cent per annum between 1965 and 1968 and food prices rose nearly at the rate of 20 per cent per annum. The inflation was partly due to the droughts and partly due to the two wars of 1962 and 1965 which led to a massive increase in defence expenditure. The governments' consolidated (state and central) fiscal deficit peaked in 1966-67 at 7.3 per cent of GDP.

The balance of payments situation though fragile since 1956-57, deteriorated further with the foreign exchange resources, enough to cover only less than two months of Imports. Dependence on foreign aid which has been rising over the first three plans, now increased sharply due to food shortages as well as weakness in balance of payments utilisation of external assistance, which was .86 per cent of NNP in 1950-51, increased to 1.05 per cent in 1956-57, 2.37 per cent in 1957-58, 2.86 per cent in 1960-61 or 3.8 per cent in 1965-66. Amortization and interest payments as percentage of exports rose sharply from 0.8 upto the end of first plan to 3.9 during the second, 14.3 during the third to 20.6 in 1966-67 and whopping 27.8 in 1966-67.

This was the most vulnerable time for the Indian economy, with high inflation, a very low foreign exchange balance, food stock so low as to threaten famine conditions in some areas, calling for large imports, and nearly half the imports having to be met through foreign aid, that the US, the most important donor at that time, decided to suspend its aid in response to Indo-Pak war and refused to renew PL 480 agreement on long-term basis. Also, the US, in President Johnson's, words, wanted to keep India on a short leash, so that she did not stray too much from the policies preferred by it which they now sought to pressurise India to accept.

The US, the World Bank and the International Monetary Fund (IMF) wanted India to (a) liberalise its trade and industrial controls, (b) devalue the rupee, and (c) adopt a new agricultural strategy. Government of India conceded on the above points but these policies were condemned before their long-term effect could be realised. The post 1967 period saw launching of series of radical economic policies which were to have long-term effects on India's development efforts. Some of these policies accentuated the shortcomings that had begun to emerge during the first phase of planning itself in the fifties and early sixties, others created new distortions. The nationalisation of 14 commercial banks and passage of MRTP Act severely restricted the activities of large business houses. After 1971, series of further such measures increasing government control and intervention were introduced with the active support of leftists. The insurance was nationalised in 1972 and the coal industry was nationalised in 1973. A disastrous effort was made to nationalise wholesale wheat trade in the same year, which was abandoned after a few months. FERA was passed in 1973 which put several restrictions on foreign investment and functioning of foreign companies in India.

Between mid-sixties and the end eighties, economic achievements took place and the economy faced formidable internal and external shocks. There was a genocide in East Pakistan resulting in huge financial burden for maintaining over ten million refusees, the 1971 war with Pakistan, two droughts of 1972 and 1974, the major oil shock of 1973 leading to a quadrupling of international oil prices hence cost of oil import, the oil shock of 1979 when oil prices doubled, the disastrous harvest of 1979-80 caused by the worst drought since independence, and wide-spread successive droughts of 1987 and 1988. Concerted efforts were made after the mid-sixties to improve the balance of payment situation, create food security, introduce anti-poverty measures and reduce dependence on imports for critical inputs like oil. This enabled India to weather the impact of droughts, war and oil shocks without getting into a debt crisis and recessionary spin as happened in case of a number of developing countries, especially Latin America in eighties. On the food front, the situation improved rapidly. Green Revolution paid commendable dividends. Between 1967-68 and 1970-71, foodgrain production rose by 3.5 per cent and food import was substantially reduced and food availability increased from 73.5 million tonnes to 89.5 million tonnes over the same period. It continued to increase to 110.25 million tonnes in 1978 to 128.8 million tonnes in 1984. In short, economy was able to absorb the shocks of successive droughts of 1987-88. In fact, rural poverty index continued to show a decline in these crisis years as rural employment and incomes were maintained through government programmes using the surplus food stock.

Apart from food self-sufficiency, certain other features emerged that pointed towards a greater autonomy of the Indian economy and increased self-reliance. The fiscal deficit was brought down from 7.3 per cent of the GDP in 1966-67 to 3.8 per cent in 1969-70. The balance of payment situation improved with reduced food and other imports and particularly with the surge in remittances made by Indian workers from oil rich Middle East.

Given the arm twisting of the donors, self-reliance was seen as the need to reduce dependence on foreign aid. Partly as a result of this shift in perspective, foreign aid began to decline rapidly. Net aid as a proportion of NNP, which has peaked to an average of 4.2 per cent during the third plan came down to 0.35 per cent in 1972-73 and rose slightly after 1973 oil crisis but yet averaged not more than 1 per cent of NNP till 1977-78. The debt service ratio, i.e. the annual outflow of interest and repatriation of principal due to existing debt as a proportion of exports of goods and services, fell to a low and easily manageable 10.2 per cent in 1980-81 from an estimated 23 per cent in 1970-71 and 16.5 per cent in 1974-75. Due to rapid expansion in the indigenous capital goods, industry has greatly reduced India's dependence on the external world for maintaining her rate of investment as the share of equipment needed to be imported had fallen from 43 per cent to 9 per cent between 1960 and 1974.

Private foreign investment continued to be very low in proportion to total investment. Thus, while the volume of foreign private investment remained marginal and foreign aid declined and the ratio of foreign saving to total investment fell, the rate of domestic savings and investment increased rapidly. From an average savings rate of 10.58 per cent and the rate of gross domestic capital formation or investment of 11.84 per cent in fifties, the savings and investment rates doubled to 21.22 per cent and 20.68 per cent respectively between 1975-76 to 1979-80. The eighties and nineties saw further increases in the rates of savings and capital formation, making them comparable to several high growth economies.[10]

The new feature of the eighties was the phenomenal increase in new stock market, the stock market thus emerging as an important source of fund for industry. It has been estimated that in 1981 the capital market accounted for only 1 per cent of the domestic savings, whereas by the end of the eighties this proportion increased by about seven times. The new stock issue in 1989 was Rs. 6,500 crore, which was about 7.25 per cent of gross domestic savings of 1989-90. Another estimate shows that in 1990 Indian companies raised an unprecedented Rs. 12,300 crore from the primary stock market.

The early eighties saw a highly successful breakthrough in oil sector. ONGC made a tremendous progress. In 1980-81, domestic production of oil was 10.5 million tonnes and imports 20.6 million tonnes. The oil import bill was 75 per cent of the total export earnings of India. With a new finds at the Bombay High Oil fields, by the end of the Sixth Plan (1980-85), the target of indigenous production of 29 million tonnes was achieved. As a result in 1984-85, the net import of oil and oil products was less than a third of the domestic consumption and the oil import bill was also down to a third of export earnings.

By the mid-seventies, the industrial growth rate also started picking up from a low of about 3.4 per cent between 1965-75 to about 5.1 per cent between 1975-85. In the eighties, as a whole, the industrial growth rate maintained a healthy average of about 8 per cent per year. Again, it was in the eighties that the barrier of the low, so called "Hindu rate of growth" of 3 to 3.5 per cent that India had maintained over the previous two decades was broken and the economy grew at over 5.5 per cent. By one estimate, the average real GDP growth rate between 1980 to 1989 was an impressive 6 per cent.[11]

While on the one hand, the economy in the eighties seemed to be doing quite well, on the other hand, there were certain long-term structural weaknesses building up which were to add up to major crisis by 1991, when the country was on the verge of defaulting. Broadly speaking, there were sets of problems which had gathered strength in the Indian economy overtime and which needed urgent reform.

The first set of problems related to the emergence of structural features that bred inefficiency. Import substitution and protection to indigenous industries helped in deepening and widening India's industrial base but overtime, the excessive protection through import restrictions started leading to inefficiency and technological backwardness in Indian industry. This situation was further accentuated by the so-called Licence Quota Raj, a whole plethora of rules, regulations and restrictions which stifled entrepreneurship and innovation. The MRTP Act, and the reservation of sectors for small-scale industry are cases in point. The MRTP Act went against the basic principle of economies of scale. It also punished efficiency. Reservation of certain areas for small scale industries made the sector internationally uncompetitive, leading to India losing out to its competitors in many areas.

The large public sector in India, which controlled the commanding height of the economy, also began to emerge as a major source of inefficiency. Initially, it succeeded in creating required infrastructure and base for industrial advancement but, over time, the political and bureaucratic pressure on public sector gradually led to most of them running at a loss. They were overstaffed, often headed by politician who had to be given sinecures, became victim of irresponsible trade unionism and were unable to exercise virtually any efficiency and accountability on their employees. State-run utilities like electricity boards and road transport corporations were notorious for enormous losses. Apart from rampant corruption, inefficiency and lack of accountability, these enterprises, under populist pressure, often charged rates that did not cover even a small fraction of actual costs. Many nationalised banks started running at a loss and the insurance sector remained inefficient and covered only a fraction of its enormous potential market.

While licensing, MRTP, small-scale reservation and the like made entry or expansion of business very difficult; since the mid-seventies virtually no exit was possible for inefficient loss-making companies as they could not close down or retrench without government permission. The government ended up taking over many sick companies which otherwise needed to be closed down. All this led to the investment efficiency in India being very low or the capital-output ratio (ICOR) kept rising, it being a little over 2.0 during the 1st plan and reaching 3.6 during the third plan. According to one estimate between 1971 and 1976 the ICOR had touched a high of 5.76. This explains why despite substantial increases in the rate of investment, there was an actual decrease in overall rates of aggregate output or GDP between fifties and seventies. The ICOR started declining in eighties though it remained around 4 in the nineties. Even during the eighties, one estimate shows that average rate of financial return on employed capital in public sector enterprises was as low as 2.5.

India was thus unable to use the opportunities provided by the changing world situation to rapidly industrialise and transform its economy, increase income levels and drastically reduce poverty levels as did many of the East Asian countries. South Korea provides the best example. Even China changed track in 1978 opening up its economy, participating in the globalisation process, welcoming foreign investment, pushing up its export and so on leading to a current growth rate much higher than India's. Between 1980-89, China's real GDP, by one estimate, grew at an average rate of 9.4 per cent considerably faster than did India's over the same period.

The third set of problem, which overtook the Indian economy, was primarily the result of certain political imperatives which were related to the manner in which the Indian state structure and democratic framework evolved. More and more sections of people emerged which made strong, articulate demands on state resources. This resulted in the gradual abandoning of fiscal prudence from about the mid-seventies. Macro-economic balance was being slowly eroded. The macro-economic imbalance that now emerged tended to be long-term and structural in character as distinct from the short-term imbalance created by shocks such as those of the mid -sixties or the seventies, related to oil.

The gradual erosion of fiscal prudence was reflected in government expenditure rising consistently, mainly because of the proliferation of subsidies and grants, salary increases with no relationship to efficiency or output, overstaffing and other populist measures such as massive loan waivers. Fiscal profligacy continued through the eighties. Consequently, the consolidated government fiscal deficit rose sharply from 4.1 per cent of GDP in 1974-75 to 6.5 per cent in 1979-80, 9.7 per cent in 1984-85, peaking at 10.4 per cent in 1991.

It must be noted that the eighties was a period of high growth. Between 1985 and 1990, on an average, India's GDP grew at over 5.5 per cent per year, industry at over 7 per cent, capital goods at 10 per cent, consumer durables at 12 per cent and so on. However, this growth was not a result of any step up of savings and investments; in many ways, it was a result of over-borrowing and overspending. The growth was both debt-led and the result of an explosion of domestic budgetary spendings. This kind of growth was naturally not sustainable as the macroeconomic imbalances were bound to reach a point where a crash could no longer be postponed as happened in Latin America in the eighties and in India almost a decade later.

The deteriorating fiscal and balance of payment situations had led to a mounting debt problem, both domestic and foreign, reaching a critical point by the end of eighties. Total government (Centre and State) domestic debt rose from 31.8 per cent of GDP in 1974-75 to 45.7 per cent in 1984-85 to 54.6 per cent in 1989-90. The foreign debt situation also became very precarious. The debt-service ratio, which was still a manageable 10.2 per cent in 1980-81, rose to dangerous 25 per cent in 1990-91. Moreover, the proportion of concessional debt to total debt also fell from over 80 per cent to 40 per cent in this period. Inadequate returns on the borrowings led to an unsustainable debt service burden.

Foreign exchange reserves fell drastically. India's credit rating was sharply downgraded and it became difficult to raise credit abroad. In addition, NRI deposits in foreign exchange began to be withdrawn rapidly. In such a situation, where foreign lending has virtually dried up, the government was forced to mortage/sell 20 tonnes of gold to Switzerland in March 1991, to meet the payment obligations.

The long-term constraints, that were building up over a few decades and debilitating the Indian economy combined with certain more recent and immediate factors, led to a massive fiscal and balance of payment crisis that climaxed in 1991. This crisis pushed India into initiating a process of economic reforms and structural adjustment. Reform of the dirigiste, controls-ridden and inwardlooking Indian economy was long overdue. As early as the early sixties, Manmohan Singh had argued that India's export pessimism at that time was unjustified. He advised more openness and less controlled economy.[12] Other eminent economists such as Jagdish Bhagwati were among those who urged reform in the early stages. Indira Gandhi, particularly after her return to power in 1980, tried to bring in liberalisation measures, mainly in the area of deregulation of industrial licensing and reduction of restrictions on large monopoly enterprises. Rajiv Gandhi, when he took over in 1984, attempted reform at a relatively quicker pace towards industrial deregulation, exchange rate flexibility and partial lifting of import control. The major issues of emerging macro-economic imbalance calling for stabilization of the fiscal and balance of payment deficit was, however, left unattended. Though the need for reforms has been recognised early enough, its implementation could not occur for various reasons. A strong ideological opposition from the orthodox left strangely oblivious to the changing global reality, continued to play a role in obstructing reforms. The crisis of 1991 enabled the government to breakthrough the traditional mindset and initiate a process of reform at a quicker pace with Manmohan Singh at the helm of financial management of the economy.

The process of reforms, started in 1991, involved an immediate fiscal correction, liberalisation of trade and industrial control, considerable dismantling of licensing system and abolition of MRTP, reform in public sector including gradual privatisation, reform in capital market and financial sector, etc. The record of the first few years of reform was creditable by any standard, though a lot of problems and challenges still remained. India recovered from a deep macroeconomic crisis.

For example, the growth rate of Indian GDP which had fallen to 0.8 per cent in the crisis year 1991-92 recovered quickly to 5.3 per cent by 1992-93 and rose further to 6.2 per cent in 1993-94. Over the next three years, the Indian economy averaged an unprecedented growth rate of over 7.5 per cent, a rate closer to the high performers of East Asia. The Eighth Plan (1992-97) averaged a growth rate at nearly 7 per cent. Gross Domestic Savings averaged over 23 per cent between 1991 and 1997, higher than Seventh Plan average of 20.6 per cent. Gross Domestic Capital Formation between 1992 and 1997 also maintained a respectable average of 25.2 per cent and 22.3 per cent of GDP respectively.

Industrial production which showed a dismissal, less than 1 per cent, growth rate in 1991-92, picked upto 2.3 per cent in 1992-93 and 6 per cent in 1993-94, peaking at an 12.8 per cent during 1995-96. The capital goods sector, which demonstrated negative growth rates for a few years, bounced back to nearly 25 per cent growth in 1994-95. The central government's fiscal deficit, which had reached 8.3 per cent of GDP in 1990-91, was reduced to roughly 6 per cent between 1992-97. Even export sector performed well. The debt situation had also started moving away from a crisis point. The overall external debt/GDP ratio for India fell from a peak of 41 per cent in 1991-92 to 28.7 per cent in 1995-96. The debt-service ratio also fell from the peak of 35.3 per cent in 1990-91 to 19.5 per cent in 1997-98. It is, however, still quite high compared to China, Malaysia and South Korea, who all had till 1997 debt service ratio below 10 per cent.

Reform and liberalisation of the stock market since the eighties, and particularly after 1991, produced dramatic results. The total market capitalisation on Indian stock markets as proportion of GDP rose from mere 5 per cent in 1980 to 13 per cent in 1990 and it rose to

60 per cent of GDP by the end of 1993. By 1995, the Indian stock market was the largest in the world in terms of the number of listed companies. The amount of capital Indian companies could raise in the primary market in India increased from Rs. 923 million in 1980 to Rs. 2.5 billion in 1985 and Rs.123 billion in 1990. By 1993-94, the figure had reached Rs. 225 billion, nearly 250 times increase since 1980.[13] Even foreign investment responded favourably during this period as a result of reforms and liberalisation.

Critics of reforms, mainly from the orthodox left, made the charge that reform was anti-poor. However, studies of a large number of countries have shown that barring a few exceptions, rapid economic development has been associated with fall in poverty levels. India too witnessed significant fall in poverty levels with the relatively faster economic growth of the eighties. The proportion of population below the poverty line fell from 51.3 per cent in 1977-78 to 38.9 per cent in 1987-88. Countries like China and Indonesia, which had much higher poverty ratios of 59.5 and 64.3 in 1975 compared to India's 54.9 in 1973-74, were able to reduce their poverty levels to much below India's in the span of twenty years. These countries maintained a much higher rate of growth than India during this period and their poverty ratios had fallen drastically to 22.2 and 11.4 respectively by 1995, while India's had fallen only to 36 by 1993-94.[14] Calculations based on several different indicators of poverty show poverty, mainly rural poverty, marked a significant rise only in 1992-93 and its causation was linked mainly to a drought and fall in foodgrain output in 1991-92, leading to rise in food prices, and very weakly to the stabilisation programme. Even this was avoidable to a great extent. However, all the poverty indicators showed that by the 1993-94 there was much improvement in the poverty situation. The poverty levels, both rural and urban, were significantly lower in 1993-94 than in 1992 by nearly six percentage points, and were lower than the pre-reform average of the five years 1986-87 to 1991-92.[15] Thus, it may be noted that the stabilization under the reforms had little negative impact, if any, on poverty levels. Other aspects of structural reforms, it is generally agreed, do not threaten the poor and in fact would improve their conditions by releasing the full growth potential of the economy. The shortfall and deficiency are due to political instability and populist measures adopted under political pressure and duress. Due to political constraint, real/imaginary, no serious efforts were made to increase public savings and reduce government expenditure, and problem of high fiscal deficit continued. The public saving investment gap remained at a very high average of 7.1 per cent of GDP between 1992-96. The foodgrain subsidy increased from Rs. 28.5 billion in 1991-92 to Rs. 61 .14 billion in 1996-97. The fertilizer subsidy also increased from Rs. 32.01 billion in 1988-89 to Rs. 45.42 billion in 1989-90 and to Rs. 62.35 billion in 1995-96. C.H. Hanumantha Rao, an eminent agricultural economist, noted in 1992, the annual subsidy on fertilizer alone amounts to nearly as much as the annual outlay on agriculture by the centre and states put together.[16] A similar example was the government subsidy on diesel, kerosene and cooking gas amounting to Rs. 93.6 billion in 1995-96. The oil pool deficit in 1996-97 was Rs. 98 billion making the cumulative deficit in that year about Rs. 155 billion. The result was that the oil companies were unable to make the absolutely necessary investment in the oil sector.

Similarly, little has been achieved with regard to the reform of public sector, particularly state owned utilities like electricity and transport etc. Therefore, state electricity boards and transport corporations run at huge losses at a time when availability of power and proper transport infrastructure threaten to be critical bottlenecks, slowing down the projected rate of growth of the economy. The situation reached a point where, given the serious fiscal slippage, even the Economic Survey of the Government of India of 1998-99 was constrained to argue the time has perhaps come to reconsider the issue of constitutional limits on the deficits.[17] Slowing down of the economy since 1996-97 was partly because of East Asian crisis with Japan in recession and South Korea, Indonesia, Thailand and others showing negative growth rates. Other parts of the world such as Russia and Brazil were also facing crisis situations. World trade was slowed down and flow of capital was affected. There was fall in the receipt of foreign capital and declaration of Indian export. Poor infrastructure, archaic labour laws, etc. were responsible for the slowing down of the economy. Economic sanctions were also imposed because of the nuclear test.

The consensus is suggestive of the fact that economic reforms or liberalisation did not mean a change of goals set out at independence by the Indian people, such as rapid growth, industrialisation, self-reliance, removal of poverty and so on. On the basis of the experience with various controls and state intervention at home, of changes occurring in the world such as collapse of the socialist bloc and experience of various fast growing economies in the recent past, the aspirations towards the same goals set out at the independence required changes in the strategy.

There is, in other words, a growing recognition in India of the imperative to be responsive to the external changes and internal experiences and changed strategy so that this great country is able to come into its own and realise its enormous potential rather than fritter away the considerable achievement made since independence.

The present picture of the Indian economy presents a mixed picture of hopes and despairs. Hope in the sense that in many fields and sectors, it has made a satisfactory progress during post-independence period but it has failed to achieve the objectives set by the leaders and enshrined in the constitution. Micro-analysis of certain sectors may be assuring while the macro-analysis frustrates the hopes and aspirations of the people who thought that their problems would be taken care of and they would be in a position to live a life of dignity and their needs would be fulfilled. But things had gone astray on this score. Poverty, starvation, unemployment and deprivation continued, and these issues were wilfully sidetracked in the name of the economic growth and still faster growth. Let us examine some of the indicators of the real economic development for the country as a whole.

It is argued and claimed that India not only attained self-sufficiency in respect of goodgrain production but surplus has been created. The right to food is not just a basic human right but also a basic human need. It essentially requires the state to ensure at least that the people do not starve. The states have to take all necessary steps towards fulfilling the right to adequate food. Under the Indian constitution, there is no fundamental right to food but the fulcrum of justiciability of the right to food comes from a much broader "right to life and liberty" as enshrined in Article 21 of Constitution of India.

India does not seem to have any problem in terms of physical availability as the foodgrain production is more than adequate as evident from overflowing godowns. Accessibility is the problem. It has two aspects: physical accessibility and economic accessibility. There is a network of half a million fair price shops to make foodgrain physically available to the Indian households. Investigation reveals that large number of persons are ignorant of their entitlement.

The principal constraint in realising the right to adequate food is economic accessibility or affordability. This brings to fore two main issues: (i) price of the foodgrain, and (ii) economic means to exercise command over food. The food subsidy bill of the centre and states together exceeds Rs. 3000 crores a year, but the subsidy is inherently biased towards the producer and does not cater to the needy consumers in the form of reduced prices of food grains.

Another important issue is the interface between right to food and the right to health on the notion of adequacy. The latest N.S.S. Report shows that the calorie intake of the poorest 30 per cent of the population falls short of the dietary intake recommended by the Indian Council of Medical Research. The National Family Health Report, 1998-99[18] shows that 47 per cent of Indian children are under-nourished, and that 36 per cent and 52 per cent of Indian women suffer from chronic energy deficiency and anaemia, respectively. These deficiencies have multiple implications for newly born babies and children who are supposed to be the future hopes of the nation. Supreme Court was constrained to intervene and direct the states to fulfil their constitutional obligation to see that people do not starve for want of accessibility or proper governance.

Moreover, there should be due recognition of the fact that all pivotal rights such as the right to food, right to health, right to education or any economic and social rights, for that matter, are interdependent. For example, providing sufficient food to do away with undernutrition will not really eliminate the chronic health disorders that have already set in. Providing adequate healthcare is necessary. Similarly, to realise the right to food people should have access to education and information. But last not the least, the process of realisation of the right to adequate food should not violate any other socio-economic or civil and political rights. On the question of economic means, the realisation of right to adequate food involves the right to work. Short-term and temporary relief measures fail to deliver the good.[19]

Now relevant question arises why this dualism, i.e. overflowing godowns and starvation go together? The main cause for this state of affairs in India is our outdated low-yielding agriculture. For want of purchasing power among farmers and poor people, demand for industrial goods has slackened. The Planning Commission in its mid-term appraisal of the Ninth Plan had stated: In the 1990s, the growth rate in availability of food grain per capita has come down to minus 0.28 per cent per annum, as compared to a growth rate in per capita availability of (+) 1.20 per cent per annum during 1980s. The food consumption of the poor in India has gone down in the last 10 years.

Yet another bleak feature has been sharp decline in employment generation in the country. It has been reported, "Against the growth rate of job seekers of 2.3 per cent per annum, the rate of job creation has dropped from 2.1 per cent in the 1980s to mere 0.8 per cent in 1990s. So far as the private sector is concerned, while jobs grew at an unprecedented rate of 3.1 per cent per annum in the brief golden years from 1994 to 1997, the rate of job growth has fallen to a miserable 0.11 per cent in 2000-2001. Since public sector is bankrupt and facing disinvestment is creating no more job, it is hardly surprising that the rate of job creation in the last three years has been below 0.6 per cent per annum. Our undernourishment is not due to our huge population. On per capita basis, areas under cereals in China is 29 per cent less than in India, yet its per capita availability of food grains is 50 per cent more than ours.

Yet another reason for widespread poverty in our country is the lack of relevant education which improves work efficiency, reduces population growth, opens new avenues of employment, promotes social justice, inhibits fanaticism, and stabilises democracy. Realising the essential need of education for national progress, it was laid down in the constitution within 10 years of its coming into effect, it shall be the duty of the state to make education free and compulsory for all children between age groups of 6 and 14. How indifferent our politicians are towards education is evident from the fact that they have not implemented this directive even 50 years after its adoption.

The concept of balanced growth demands that all sectors of the economy move ahead in the same direction and approximately at the same speed. If service and industry sectors are enabled to move ahead at a faster rate, leaving the farm sector behind, particularly in a country like India, the process of growth will be stranded for want of support from below. This has already happened in India, where for want of purchasing power among farmers and rural people, demand for industrial goods has slackened and industries are stagnating.[20] Roughly, composition of the GDP indicates the level of development but sometimes development is very skewed and unbalanced. India is facing the same situation when agriculture contributes 24 per cent of the GDP in 2000-2001 which was 25.2 per cent in 1999-2000. The rate of growth of agriculture was 0.2 per cent in 2000-2001, while in 1999-2000 it was 0.7 per cent. During the 2000-2001, share of service sector was 49 per cent which increased from 47.9 per cent in 1999-2000. During 2000-01, the share of industry in GDP was 27 per cent while it was 26.9 per cent in 1999-2000. Superficially, it appears to be very healthy indicator of growth but this presents the weakness of the economy where agriculture is declining, the industry is stagnant. Similar situation is also prevailing in Pakistan and Bangladesh where service sector constitutes the major component of the GDP. If these countries are presenting a very optimistic picture, then India is also to rejoice the same situation.

These structural shifts are mainly due to liberalisation, globalisation and privatisation and boom in information technology, and not due to resilience in agriculture and industry which provide the final support base for the service sector. Infrastructure sector consisting of power, transport, medicare, education and family welfare and social security nets are either stagnant or have been sliding down due to reduced public investment. Foreign investment is slack due to the deficiency in infrastructure sector and mainly on account of bad governance or poor response of the authority towards peace and security which are the prime conditions for the investment, whether external or internal.

Social sector investment is to reduce poverty and improve the human development. Since the introduction of economic reforms, the expenditure on social sector and poverty alleviation programmes has been affected. States spend more than 80 per cent of the social sector expenditure in the country. If we take the centre and the states together, India spends 6 to 8 per cent of its GDP on social sector expenditure, as a percentage of GDP lower than in the late 1980s. There has been some shifts from rural development. Within the rural development outlay at the centre, there is a shift away from rural employment schemes to rural housing, water, rural road, etc. In other words, there is a shift from the traditional ways of addressing rural poverty to what we can call, human development or basic needs interventions with regard to health, not much has happened. Neither the centre nor the states increased spending on health considerably.

In education, the share of expenditure from all departments devoted to education declined from 4.1 per cent in 1990-91 to 3.8 per cent in 1998-99. The picture of states is the same. The education expenditure of the centre increased from 0.25 per cent of GDP in 1994-95 to 0.31 per cent in 1995-96 and to 0.31 per cent in 1998-99. There has been a shift towards elementary education in 1990s. Thus social sector expenditure in the 1990s was low. It was low compared to what India spent in the 1980s; it was low compared to other developing countries and certainly compared to the ratios recommended by the United Nations Development Programme. Concludingly, as a per cent of GDP, social sector expenditure has not increased if the centre and states are taken together. However, public expenditure as a per cent of GDP itself declined in the 1990s. Here we are taking about allocation and financial utilisation and not the actual achievement of these schemes. Performance is poor and dismal due to various constraints which are beyond control for the existing political system and bureaucratic attitude. What is really needed is the participation of civil society in planning, executing, monitoring and evaluating public policies relevant to the right of the people to guarantee the satisfaction of basic needs and to ensure fuller realisation of the potential for nation development. The existing situation must be avoided where godowns of foodgrains are overflowing and starvation is reported in some parts of the country.

The development process, specially after reforms, has been implemented. There has been sharp accentuation of economic inequalities among states during the 1990s which is morally unacceptable and if not collectively addressed weaken nation's fabric. Economic inequalities have further widened globally during 1990s as reported by Human Development Report. Before coming to the real picture of economic scenario in India, we have to note the challenges that have taken place during 1990s after implementation of economic reform. As far as industrial scene is concerned, the picture is dismal. In UP, 11 out of 35 sugar mills are closed and others are also in bad shape. As far as whole country is concerned, it has 700 licensed sugar mills and only 473 are in operation but not in a very satisfactory position. Upto March 31, 1991, 313 textile mills were closed and 2 lakh 11 thousand labour unemployed. In Ahmedabad, only 32 textile mills were operating out of 81 mills. Almost all textile mills of Indore, Ujjain and Gwalior are closed. Kanpur is facing the same situation where labourers have been displaced and are on the verge of starvation. Suicide cases have increased. Forty per cent to 60 per cent of the powerlooms in Maharashtra, Gujarat and Tamil Nadu are closed and remaining sick. The fate of expeller, fineries, vegetable oil mills, soyabin mills have huge investments and are working at nearly 35 per cent capacity. Economic Survey 1999-2000 reports that 2 lakh 74 thousand industrial units are closed. In the name of I.T., Wipro, Infosys, Satyam, etc. earned nearly Rs. 400,000 crore from the share market which roughly equal to total agricultural income.

The facts have emerged from discussions and protests from Seattle to Geneva which are listed below:

(i) Globally, people living in poverty has increased five per cent in the world.

(ii) Total wealth of richest 200 persons in the world increased from $ 440 billion in 1994 to $ 1 trillion in 1998.

(iii) Even World Bank has accepted the increasing poverty and inequality globally.

These things have been discussed here simply to prove that things are drifting too far and India is not an exception. But poor country like India is paying heavy price in terms of increasing poverty, inequality, unemployment, social and political disintegration. Sometimes, it is argued that this is the price which one has to pay for better and brighter future but this argument is also five decades old when five year plan was launched and promises made which were never fulfilled. Constitutional provisions were conveniently bypassed and deliberately ignored to further personal and political interest. Despite bright patches here and there, holistic view is neither very encouraging nor assuring. Situation appears to be irretrievable and political system has collapsed. The body of democracy is there without soul. It is used and misused according to personal convenience and not for the furtherance of the national interest. It may be said that present mode of production and management of economic affairs have failed to deliver the good, hence, it has lost its credibility. Now something must be done to retrieve the situation and revitalise the economy to meet the present challenges and future possibilities.

NOTES

1. Bipin Chandra (1999): *India After Independence*, Penguin Books India, New Delhi.
2. *Ibid.*
3. *Ibid.*, p. 13.
4. *Ibid.*
5. N.R. Sarkar (1934): Presidential Speech, FICCI, *Annual Report,* New Delhi, pp. 367.
6. INC, *Economic Resolution*, p. 29.
7. K.N. Raj (1962): *Indian Economic Growth Performance and Prospects*, New Delhi, p. 2.
8. Bhagwati, P. Desai (1970): *India: Planning for Industrialisation*, London, p. 74.
9. *Ibid.*
10. Calculated from *Economic Survey* 1996, GOI.
11. C. Rangarajan (1998): Development, Inflation and Monetary Policy in Isher

J. Ahluwalia and IMD Little (Eds) *India's Economic Reforms and Development : Essays for Manmohan Singh,* Delhi, p. 59.
12. Manmohan Singh's Ph.D. Dissertation at Oxford in 1961 and his book *India's Export Trends,* London, 1961.
13. Ajit Singh (1998): Liberalisation and Stock Market, and the Market for Capital Control, in Isher Ahluwalia and I.M.D. Little (Eds.) *India's Economic Reforms and Development,* Delhi.
14. *Economic Survey* 1998-99, Govt. of India, p.146.
15. Suresh D. Tendulkar (1996): Indian Economic Policy Reform and Poverty : An Assessment, in Ahluwalia and Little (Eds.), *India's Economic Reforms, 1991-2001,* Oxford, pp. 222-225.
16. C.H. Hanumantha Rao (1992): Agriculture: Policy and Performance, in Bimal Jalan (Ed) *The Indian Economy,* New Delhi, 1992, p. 132.
17. *Economic Survey* 1998-99, GOI, pp. 11-18.
18. *The National Family Health Report*, 1998-99.
19. *The Hindu* 10.02.03, Delhi.
20. *The Hindu*, 02.07.2001, Delhi.

2

Theories of Economic Development

The study of economic development is one of the newest, most existing and most challenging branches of the broader disciplines of the economics and political economy. Although one might claim that Adam Smith was the first 'development economist' and that his *Wealth of Nations* (1776) was the first treatise on economic development, the systematic study of the problems and processes of economic development in the Third World has emerged only after two World Wars. While development economics may draw upon certain principles and concepts from other branches of economics in either a traditional or modified form, for the most part it is a field of study that is rapidly evolving its own distinctive and methodological structure.

Economic development concerns problems of the economic development of underdeveloped countries. It is true that the study of economic development attracted the attention of economists right from Adam Smith down to Marx and Keynes. However, they were interested in the problems that were essentially static in nature and related to a western framework of social and cultural institutions. It is, however, in the forties of the twentieth century and specially after the Second World War that economists devoting their attention relevant to these countries and analysing the problems of underdeveloped countries and formulating theories and needs of development and growth. The main problems before the economists and planners were linked with the question of how economically backward country can overcome their backwardness and move on the scale of economic advancement. It is this question that has given benefit to development economics.

Numerous theories in this area have not only been propounded but also acted upon by different euphemistically called 'developing countries' but few have succeeded in breaking through the poverty curtain. Most of the so-called developing countries still suffer from economic backwardness, even though a rise in the standard of living can be observed in many of these countries. However, in most cases the phenomenon of maldevelopment has raised its ugly head, e.g. corruption, unstable political situation, tension, conflicts, violence, etc.

Looking to the experience of developing countries, several questions can be raised:

(1) What are the kinds of nature of different theories of economic development?
(2) Are they suitable for the developing countries?
(3) If some of these theories have helped developing countries to solve some of the glaring economic problems, what kind of society is being created?
  (a) What image of man do economic theories have in mind?
  (b) Is that image beneficial for man, society and world?
(4) If not, what is the alternative?

Bretton Wood Conference and the birth of IBRD, IMF and other allied financial institutions are the offshoot of these considerations and changed orientation. Their interest in the economics of development was further stimulated by political resurgence in Asian and African countries after they threw off the colonial yoke after the Second World War. The desire and commitment on the part of the leaders in these newly independent countries to promote rapid economic development, coupled with the realisation on the part of the developed nations that poverty anywhere is a threat to prosperity everywhere, aroused further interest in the subject.

The interest of the wealthy nations in removing poverty in underdeveloped countries is not based on any humanitarian motive. Economic development has also an export value for both the aid-giving and aid-receiving countries. In order to avoid secular stagnation, rich countries need an ever-increasing rate of development, which must be accompanied by outlet for use of their growing capital stock. Poor countries need an accelerated rate of development to increase their export potential for avoiding deficit in balance of payment.

However, a study of the poverty of nations and methods of eliminating the poverty cannot be based on the experience of rich nations. It is claimed as Rostow does that when the country attains the stage of take off, the process of economic development becomes automatic, it itself generates sufficient resources and forces to sustain the economy in achieving an onward movement for accelerated development. But this stage is very crucial and very difficult for underdeveloped countries to reach the stage on account of numerous internal and external constraints. Therefore, Myrdal argues that the underdeveloped countries formulated in the west uncritically; they should mould it to fit their own problems and interest.

The Pearson Committee defines development policy as recognition of the fact that the endeavour to achieve better living conditions is no longer divisible. In other words, aid for Third World is not a hobby for a new eccentric idealists, nor alms-giving to appease uneasy conscience, not a compulsory exercise for bored politicians but as a means of safeguarding export trade of industrial countries. The aid is an ambitious attempt to make life bearable for all on earth so that it will not be unbearable for all. There will be either a common future or no future at all.

Generally speaking, economic development refers to the problems of underdeveloped countries to be sure. However, it does not lose sight of or ignore the needs of developed countries. Maddison makes the distinction between two terms in the sense when he writes[1]: "The raising of income level in generally called economic growth in rich countries and in poor ones it is called economic development."

Seers[2] (1969) has stated the issue well: The question to ask about a country's development are therefore: What has been happening to poverty? What has been happening to inequality? If all the three of these have declined from high levels, then beyond doubt this has been a period of development for the country concerned. If one or two of these central problems have been growing worse, especially if all three have, it would be strange to call the result development, even if per capita income is doubled.

But it is difficult to imagine development without economic growth. Arthur Lewis in the *Theory of Economic Growth* writes that "Most often we shall refer only to growth but occasionally for the sake of variety, to progress or development". These terms will also be used as synonyms for all practical purposes.

One of the problems facing developing countries concerns economic growth along with the fulfilment of basic needs of the people. Basic needs are concerned with ends and economic growth is a means to these ends. As such there is no conflict between basic needs and economic growth. Goldstein found a strong correlation between economic growth and basic needs as measured by mortality rates. To him efficiency is the level of GDP required to reach the infant mortality target of below 5 per cent. Countries that spend a large percentage of GDP for public health are more efficient because they are able to reduce their infant mortality rates. Studies have found that meeting basic needs do not reduce productive investment in developing countries. They concluded that the provision for more basic needs does lead to economic growth. Norman Hicks has also shown in his study that the basic needs strategy has led to increase in the growth rate of a number of developing countries.

Since 1990, the UNDP has been presenting the measurement of human development in terms of Human Development Index (HDI) in its annual Human Development Report. The HDI is composite index of three social indicators: life expectancy, adult literacy, and years of schooling. It also takes into account the real GDP per capita. Thus, the HDI is a composite index of achievements in three fundamental dimensions: a long and healthy life, knowledge and decent standard of living. Over the past fifty years, development economics has undergone many changes. The emphasis has shifted from growth in GDP per capita to the creation of employment, redistribution of income, to basic human needs, structural adjustment and sustainable development.

Appropriate strategies have been evolved to tackle the problems of economic development over strategies that are supposed to meet the requirements in the changing circumstances. Mercantilism and physiocracy underlined the need of encouraging foreign trade and creation of net wealth in agriculture, respectively. But credit goes to Adam Smith who was primarily concerned with the problem of economic development. He believed in the doctrine of 'Natural Law' in economic affairs. He regarded every person as the best judge of his self-interest who should be left to pursue it to his own advantage. The invisible hand, the automatic equilibrating mechanism of perfectly competitive market, tended to maximize national wealth. He advocated the policy of *laissez-faire* in economic affairs. Division of labour is the starting point of Smith's theory of economic growth. He, however, emphasized that the process of capital accumulation must precede the introduction of division of labour. According to Smith, farmers, producers and businessmen are the agents of economic development.[3] Smith's theory has the great merit of pointing out how economic growth came about and what factors and policies impede it. He pointed out the importance of parsimony in saving and capital accumulation, of improved technology, division of labour and expansion in the market in production, and of process of balanced growth in the interdependence of farmers, traders, and producers. According to Smith, farmers, producers and businessmen are the agents of economic progress. It was free trade, enterprise and competition that led farmers, producers and businessmen to expand the market which, in turn, made economic development possible. The functions of these three are interrelated. But his assumptions are unrealistic. The political, social and institutional assumptions under the stationary state are not applicable to the conditions prevailing in underdeveloped countries. Naturally, *laissez-faire* has lost its significance in such economies. Competition has been gradually replaced by monopoly which has tended to perpetuate and strengthen the vicious circles of poverty.

Ricardo published his book, *The Principles of Political Economy and Taxation* in 1917. Ricardo never propounded any theory of development. He simply discussed the theory of distribution. Ricardian theory is based on margin and surplus principles. The marginal principle explains the share of rent in the national output and the surplus principle explains the division of remaining share between wages and profit. Ricardian theory is based on the various assumptions, e.g. supply of land is inelastic, law of diminishing returns operates on all land, workers are paid subsistence wages and capital consists of circulating capital etc.

In the Ricardian system, the whole economy consists of one huge farm fixed in supply which is engaged in producing only by applying homogeneous units of labour and capital. It grows on the basis of interrelations of three groups in the economy. They are landlords, capitalists and labourers, among whom the entire produce of land is distributed. The total national output is distributed among the three groups as rent, profits and wages respectively. Rent per unit of labour is the difference between the average and marginal product, or to put it differently, total rent equals the difference between the average product and the marginal product of labour multiplied by the quantity of labour and capital applied on land. The wage rate is determined by wage fund divided by the number of workers employed at the subsistence level.

Thus out of total corn produced and sold, rent has the first right and the residual is distributed between wages and profits, while interest is included in profit. Capital accumulation is the outcome of profits because profits lead to savings of wealth which is used for capital formation. Capital formation depends on two factors. First, it depends on the capacity to save, and second, on the will to save. Landlords and capitalists invest through this surplus. The size of this surplus of net income depends on the rate of profit. So long the rate of profit is positive, capital accumulation will continue. The labour force will grow proportionately and the total wage fund will also increase. In reality, profits depend on wages, wages on the price of corn and the price of corn depend on the fertility of the marginal land. In this way, there is an inverse relation between profits and wages and wages rise or fall in keeping with the price of corn. Taxation is a source of capital accumulation.

The fact, however, cannot be ignored that Ricardo was the forerunner of modern economists who adopted his ideas on economic development. He emphasized the importance of raising savings and profit rate for capital accumulation. But his notion of stationary state is not a reality. According to him, there is a natural tendency for the profit rate to fall in the economy so that it reaches stationary state. As population increases inferior grades of lands are cultivated to meet the increasing demand for corn. Rents on superior grades of land rise and absorb a greater share of the output produced on these lands. This reduces the share of capitalists and labourers. Profits decline and wage fund falls to the subsistence level. This process of rising rent and declining profits continues till the output from the marginal land just covers the subsistence wage of the labour employed. The profits are reduced to zero. Ricardian theory, therefore, suffers from a grievous fault.[4]

Malthus did not regard the process of economic development as automatic; he was insistent that it required consistent efforts on the part of the people. He did not conceive of any movement towards the stationary state but emphasized that the economy experiences slump many times before attaining the optimum level of development. According to Malthus, the process of development was one of ups and downs of economic activity rather than it being smooth. He was concerned with the progress of wealth of a country. By progress of wealth, he meant economic development which could be achieved by increasing the wealth of a country. The wealth of the country depends partly upon the quantity of produce obtained by its labourforce and partly upon the valuation of the produce.

Malthus showed a great amount of realism in his analysis of population growth in the context of economic development than in his essay on population. According to him, population growth by itself is not sufficient to bring about economic development, rather it is the result of the development process. He argued that "an increase of population cannot take place without proportionate increase of wealth". As the rate of capital accumulation increases, the demand for labour also increases. This encourages population growth. But mere population growth does not increase wealth. Population growth increases wealth only when it increases effective demand and it is the effective demand that leads to increases in wealth.

Malthus regarded production and distribution as the two grand elements of wealth. If they are combined in right proportions, they can increase the wealth of a country in a short period. Malthus, therefore, emphasized maximum production and optimum allocation of resources for increasing the wealth of a country in the short run. According to him, the size of potential gross national product depends upon land, labour, capital and organization. When these factors are employed in right proportions, they maximize production in the major sectors of the economy, viz. agricultural and industrial sectors. It is the accumulation of capital, fertility of the soil and technological progress that lead to increase in both agricultural and industrial production. Besides these, Malthus also emphasized the importance of non-economic factors in economic development "which come under head of politics and morals". They involve security of property, good constitution and excellent laws properly administered, and hard working and regular habits and general rectitude of character.[5]

Of all the factors, it is the accumulation of capital which is the most important determinant of economic development. The source of capital accumulation is higher profits. He suggested optimum propensity to save but he concludes that "savings, pushed to excess, would destroy the motive to production". This view of Malthus is based on his denial of Say's Law of Market and belief in the deficiency of effective demand. He does not agree with Say that there cannot be a general overproduction or glut in the market. There may be general overproduction and glut of commodities in the market due to deficiency of effective demand or underconsumption. This leads to fall in prices, profits, savings, investment and capital accumulation.

Supply of labour is inelastic in the short run but the supply of capital can be increased faster than the increase of population. As capitalists invest on productive labour to increase the supply of capital, wages rise due to competition. This may not result in increased effective demand because workers may prefer leisure to increased consumption. So there is general glut of commodities. As a result prices fall, profits decline, investment falls, and both the power of accumulation and the motive to accumulation are strongly checked. Thus gluts and underconsumption would lead to economic stagnation.

It is clear than that in Malthusian theory of consumption or deficiency in effective demand leading to glut is the main cause of underdevelopment. Development of a country requires maximization of output in agriculture and industry. This requires technical progress, equitable distribution of wealth and land, expansion of internal and external trade, increase in unproductive consumption and increase in employment opportunities through public works schemes. Besides, there are non-economic factors like education, moral standards, hard working habits, good administration and efficient laws which help in increasing production in the two sectors of economy. As such these economic and non-economic factors must be given adequate attention so that economic development can be guaranteed.

J.S. Mill was greatly influenced by Ricardo. He regarded economic development as a function of land and labour and capital. While land and labour are the two original factors of production, capital is a stock previously accumulated out of the products of former labour. Increase in wealth is possible only if land and capital help increase production faster than the labourforce. It is productive labour that is productive of wealth and of capital accumulation. The rate of capital accumulation is a function of the proportion of the labourforce employed productivity. Mill believed in Malthusian theory of population. By population, he meant only size of the working class. He believed that population control was essential for improving the conditions of working class so that they might enjoy the fruits of technological progress and capital accumulation. He propagated birth control as against moral restraints.

According to Mill, the elasticity of supply of labour is very high in response to the rise in wages. The rate of capital accumulation depends upon the amount of fund from which saving can be made or the size of the net produce of industry. It also depends upon the disposition to save. Capital is the result of savings and savings come from the abstinence from the present consumption for the sake of future goods. Mill was in favour of the policy of *laissez-faire* which should be general rule: "Every departure from it, unless required by some great good, is a certain evil". He, therefore, assigned the minimum role of the state in economic affairs. For instance, he thought it a necessary intervention by the state to reform the distribution of ownership of the means of production with such schemes as a ceiling on inheritance, peasant proprietorship, profit sharing and cooperation. Even as a believer of *laissez-faire,* Mill favoured reforms in the institutional framework of market. He also favoured the regulation of working hour. He was in favour of free trade and against protection but defended the imposition of protective duties temporarily in the case of infant industries. Mill's theory of economic development based basically on the concept of *laissez-faire* system cannot be accepted uncritically in the changed situations, particularly when the concept of welfare state is being recognized universally. Despite limitations, his theory has essential ingredient of the relevant theory of development. As a matter of fact, no development is possible in underdeveloped countries without assigning effective role to the state, whether implicitly or explicitly.

In a nut shell, the classical theory of economic development can be briefly explained as follows:

> The classical economists believe in the existence of an automatic free market, perfectly competitive economy which is free from any government interference. *Laissez-faire* policy was supported and it is the 'invisible hand' which maximizes the national income. Profits induce investment. The larger the profits, greater the accumulation and investment. Capital accumulation is key to economic progress. But profits do not increase continuously. They tend to decline when competition increases for larger capital accumulation among the capitalists. All the classicists visualize the stationary state as the end of the process of capital accumulation. In the classical model, the end result of capitalist development is stagnation. This stagnation resulted from the natural tendency of profit to fall and the consequent choking of capital accumulation. When this happens, capital accumulation ceases, population becomes constant and stationary state sets in.[6]

The Marxian Theory

Karl Marx, the author of *Das Kapital,* is one of the few celebrities who influenced millions across the globe. As Schumpeter wrote,

"Marxism is a religion". To the orthodox Marxists, as any believer in a faith, the opponent is not merely in error but in sin.[7]

Marx predicted the inevitable doom of the capitalism and it was on this prediction that communism built its edifice. The Marxian analysis is the most penetrating examination of the process of capitalist development. It casts the greatest influence in shaping policies in the USSR, China and other communist countries. Here our main concern is to examine the Marx's concept of economic development and not the Marxist system as a whole.

Marx contributed to the theory of economic development in three respects, namely, in broad respect of providing an economic interpretation of history, in the narrower respect of specifying the motivating forces of capitalist development, and in the final respect of suggesting an alternative path of planned economic development.

The materialistic interpretation of history attempts to show that all historical events are the result of a continuous economic struggle between different classes and groups in society. The main cause of this struggle in the conflict between 'the mode of production' and 'the relation of production'. The mode of production refers to a particular arrangement in a society that determines the entire social, political and religious way of living. The relations of production relate to the class structure of a society uniquely characterized by the following components: (i) the organisation of labour in a scheme of division and cooperation, the skills of labour, and the status of labour in the social context with respect to degree of freedom and servitude; (ii) the geographical environment and the knowledge of the use of resources and material; and (iii) technical means and process and state of science generally.[8]

According to Marx, every society's class structure consists of the propertied and non-propertied classes. Since the mode of production is subject to change, a stage comes in the evolution of society when forces of production come into clash with the society's class structure. The existing property relation turns into fetters on the forces of production. Then comes the period of social revolution. This leads to the class struggle between the haves and the have-nots which ultimately overthrows the whole social system.

Marx uses his theory of surplus value as the economic basis of the class struggle under capitalism and it is on the basis of his theory of surplus value that he builds the superstructure of his analysis of economic development. Capitalism, according to Marx, is divided into two great protagonists, the workers who sell their labour power, and the capitalists who own the means of production. Labour power is like any other commodity. The labour sells his labour for what it is worth in the market. The value of labour power is the value of means of subsistence necessary for the maintenance of the labour which is determined by the number of hours necessary for its production. According to Marx, the value of the commodities necessary for the subsistence of the labour is never equal to the value of produce of that labour. If a labourer works for ten hours a day, but it takes 'him six hours' labour. The extra labour that a labourer puts in and for which he receives nothing, Marx calls "Surplus Labour".

It is surplus labour that leads to capital accumulation. The capitalist's main motive is to increase the surplus value which goes to swell his profits. He tries to maximize his profits in three ways: (i) prolonging the working day in order to increase the working hours of surplus labour; (ii) diminishing the number of hours required to produce the labourer's sustenance. It also tantamounts to a reduction in the subsistence wages; and (iii) by the speeding up labour, i.e. increasing the productivity of labour. This requires technological change that helps in raising the total output and lowering the cost of production. Out of the three methods, according to Marx, increase in productivity of labour is the likely choice of capitalists, since other two methods of extending working hours and reduction of the wages have their own limitations. Therefore, in order, to make improvement in the productivity of labour, the capitalists save the surplus value, reinvest it in acquiring a large stock of capital and thus accumulate capital.

One of the consequences of capital accumulation is the concentration of capital in gigantic enterprises. Competition forces capitalists to cheapen their products. Capital accumulation and concentration involve increase in constant capital and decline in variable capital which implies relative decline in the demand for labour. This process of supplanting labour by machines creates an industrial reserve army which increases as capitalism develops. The capitalists are also able to cut down wages to a semi-starvation level and appropriate more and more surplus value. This is the law of the increasing misery of the masses under capitalism.

But when the capitalists are replacing the workers by machines, they are killing the goose that laid the golden eggs. There is continual reduction of surplus value. Marx believes that technological progress tends to increase the organic composition of capital the former tends to decline with accumulation. This is called falling rate of profit. In order to counteract this tendency of falling rate of profit, the capitalist increases the degree of exploitation by reducing wages, lengthening labour-saving and cost-reducing devices, the ratio of labour to total output falls still further. The rate of profit declines all the more. Capitalist crisis begins from this point which appears in the form of overproduction of commodities, acute difficulty in finding market, a fall in price and sharp curtailment in production.

In a period of crisis, stronger capitalists expropriate the weaker capitalists and along with it grows the indignation of the working class. Centralisation of the means of production and socialization of labour at last reach a point where they become incompatible with their capitalist integument. This integument is burst asunder. The expropriators are expropriated. This is the historical tendency of capitalist accumulation. Marx provides the economic explanation of the necessity and inevitability of the revolutionary transformation from capitalist to socialist society. Capitalism leads to the proletarian revolution whereby the 'dictatorship of the proletariat' is established. Poverty will disappear. The state will wither away and each receives according to his needs. Socialism replaces capitalism. Now adequate empirical evidences are available to repudiate most of the arguments advanced by Marx all over the world.

To start with, Schumpeter assumes a perfectly competitive economy which is in stationary equilibrium. In such a stationary state, there is perfectly competitive equilibrium, with no profit, no interest rates, no savings, no investment and no involuntary unemployment. This equilibrium, characterized as 'circular flow' by Schumpeter, continues to repeat itself in the same manner year after year, similar to the circulation of the blood in an animal organism. In the circular flow, the same products are produced every year. For every supply awaits somewhere in economic system a corresponding demand. In other words, all economic activities are repetitive in a timeless economy. The circular flow is a stream that is fed from continually flowing savings of labour power and land, the flow in every economic period into reservoir which we call income, in order to be transformed into the satisfaction of wants.[9]

Development, according to him, is spontaneous and discontinuous change in the channel of circular flow, disturbance of equilibrium, which for ever alters and displaces the equilibrium state previously existing. The spontaneous and discontinuous changes in economic life are not forced upon it from without but arise by its own initiative from within the economy and appear in the sphere of industrial and commercial life.[10]

The new combination comes about in the form of innovations. Innovation may consist of: (i) introduction of a new product; (ii) introduction of new method of production; (iii) opening up new market; (iv) the carrying out of the organization of any industry like the creation of monopoly. According to Schumpeter, it is the introduction of a new product and the continual improvement in the existing ones that lead to development. He assigns the role of an innovator not to the capitalist but to entrepreneur.

The entrepreneur is not a man of ordinary managerial ability but one who introduces something entirely new. It does not provide funds but directs their use. The entrepreneur is motivated by: (a) the desire to found a private commercial empire; (b) the will to conquer and prove his superiority; (c) the joy of creating, getting things done, or simply of exercising one's energy and ingenuity. To perform his economic function, the entrepreneur requires two things: first, the existence of technical knowledge in order to produce new product; second, the power of disposal over the factors of production in the form of credit. According to Schumpeter, untapped technical knowledge exists which he can make use of, therefore, credit is essential for development to start. An entrepreneur innovates to earn profit. Profits are conceived as surplus over cost, a difference between total receipt and total outlay. According to Schumpeter, under çompetitive equilibrium the price of each product equals its cost of production, hence, there are no profits, profits arise due to dynamic changes resulting from an innovation. They continue to exist till innovation becomes general. Innovation breaks the circular flow of Schumpeter. To him, very success of capitalism "undermines the social institutions which protect it and invariably creates conditions in which it will not be able to live and which strongly point to socialism as the heir-apparent".[11]

In the early stages of capitalism, the driving force come from entrepreneurs who dared to innovate, to experiment and to expand. But now innovation is reduced to a routine. The technological progress has become the business of teams of trained specialists. The new lords of business are the managers, depersonalized owners and private bureaucrats.

This reduces the industrial bourgeoisie to a class of wage earners and thus undermines the functions and the position of the entrepreneur. In the large concerns, the proprietors are small shareholders who are 'dematerialised' and defunctionalised by the professional and salaried managers. The intellectuals sow the seeds of doubt and discontentment in the minds of masses against the social and political framework of the capitalist order. As a result, the institutional framework upon which capitalism rests starts crumbling and there is a gradual movement towards socialism. No doubt, Schumpeter's theory is replete with brilliant reasoning and insight of a great theorist yet it is neither free from criticism nor immune from limitations and fails to solve the problems of backwardness.

The Keynesian theory does not analyze the problems of underdeveloped economies. It has relevance to advanced capitalist countries. But the question is how far Keynesian theory is applicable to underdeveloped economies. Keynes approaches the problem from macro economic points of view. The greater the national income, the greater the volume of employment resulting the reform and *vice versa.* The volume of employments depends on effective demand. Effective demand determines the equilibrium level of employment and income. The effective demand is determined at the point where aggregate demand price equals aggregate supply price. The effective demand consists of consumption demand and investment demand. Consumption depends on propensity to consume. The latter does not increase to the same extent as the increase in income. The gap between income and consumption can be made up by investment. The volume of investment depends on the marginal efficiency of capital and rate of interest. Marginal efficiency of capital is the expected rate of return from new capital assets. When profit expectations are high, businessmen will invest more. The rate of interest, the other determinant of investment, depends on quantity of money and liquidity preference of the people. Now, investment can be increased either by raising the marginal efficiency of capital or by lowering the rate of interest[12]

As a result, a given rise in investment causes a multiple increase in income via the propensity to consume. This relationship between increment of investment and of income is called by Keynes, the multiplier. The multiplier establishes a precise relationship, given the propensity to consume, between aggregate employment and income and the rate of investment. It refers to the fact that when there is an increment of aggregate investment, income will increase multiplier times of the increment of investment. Since the marginal propensity to consume falls with increase in income, it becomes necessary to inject large doses of investment for securing higher level of income and employment within the economy. In brief, this is Keynesian theory of employment. He is not a development economist in a technical sense, rather he is said to be a depression economist. Keynes has the credit to save the capitalist system from the Marxian prophecy that capitalism will dig its own grave. Keynes provides moral booster to the collapsing citadel of advanced economies from the devasting impact of great depression and debilitating consequences of wars. Communist countries are collapsing while the capitalist system is in resilient and urgent situation.

Prof. W.W. Rostow has sought a historical approach to the process of economic development. He distinguishes five stages of economic growth, viz. (i) the traditional society; (ii) the preconditions for take-off; (iii) the take-off; (iv) the drive to maturity; and (v) the stage of high mass consumption.[13] A traditional society has been defined as one whose structure is developed within limited production functions based on pre-Newtonian science and technology and as pre-Newtonian attitudes towards the physical world. This does not mean that there was little economic change in such societies. In fact, more land was brought under cultivation, the scale and pattern of trade could be expanded, manufactures could be developed and agricultural productivity could be raised along with increase in population and real income. But the undeniable fact remains that for want of a regular and systematic use of modern science and technology, a ceiling existed on the level of attainable output per head. It did not lack inventiveness and innovations, but lacked the tools and the outlook towards the physical world of post-Newtonian era.[14]

Social structure of such societies was hierarchical in which family and clan-connections played a dominant role. Political power was concentrated in regions and in the hand of landed aristocracy supported by large retinue of soldiers and civil servants. Agriculture happened to be the prime source of income for the state and employment for the people. The second stage is a transitional era in which preconditions for sustained growth are created. The preconditions for sustained growth were created slowly in Britain and Western Europe. The preconditions for take-off were encouraged or initiated by forces such as renaissance, the New Monarchy, the New World and the New

Religion or reformation. These forces led to 'reasoning and scepticism' in place of 'Faith' and 'Authority', brought an end to feudalism and led to rise of national state; inculcated the spirit of adventure which led to new discoveries and inventions and consequently the rise of the bourgeoisie elite in the new mercantile cities. These forces were instrumental in bringing about changes in social attitudes, expectations, structures and values.

The idea spreads that economic progress is possible and is a necessary condition for some other purposes, judged to be good, be it national dignity, private profit, the general welfare or better life for the children in future. Education broadens and changes to suit the needs of modern activity. Preconditions for sustained industrialisation, according to Rostow, have three non-industrial sectors. First, a build-up of social overhead capital specially in transport in order to change the market and to exploit natural resources productively and to allow the state to rule effectively. Second, a technical revolution in agriculture so that agricultural productivity increases to meet the requirements of rising general and urban population. Third, an expansion of imports, including capital import, financed by efficient production and marketing of natural resources for exports. As Rostow says: "The essence of transition can be described legitimately as a rise in the rate of investment to a level which regularly, substantially and perceptibly outstrips population growth. The spread of modern education brought about a gradual transformation in thought, knowledge and attitude of the people and growing spirit of nationalism. Under the impact of powerful international demonstration effect people wanted the product of modern industry and technology itself.

The take-off is the great watershed in the life of a society when growth becomes its normal condition and forces of modernization contend against the habits and institutions. The value and interests of traditional society make a decisive breakthrough. At another place, Rostow defines the take-off as an industrial revolution, tied directly to radical changes in the methods of production having their decisive consequence over a relatively short period of time. The requirements of take-off are the following three related but necessary conditions:

(i) A rise in the rate of production investment from, say, 5 per cent or less to over 10 per cent of national income or net national product;

(ii) The development of one or more substantial manufacturing sectors with a high rate of growth; and

(iii) The existence or quick emergence of a political, social and institutional framework which exploits the impulses to expansion in the modern sector and gives to growth an ongoing character.[15]

Thus, the take-off is initiated by a sharp stimulus, such as the development of a leading sector or a political revolution which brings as outgoing change in the production processes, a rise in the proportion of net investment over 10 per cent of national income outstripping the growth of population.

Rostow defines the drive to maturity as the period when a society has effectively applied the range of modern technology to the bulk of its resources. It is a period of long sustained economic growth extending well over four decades. New production techniques take the place of old ones. New leading sectors are created. Rate of investment is well high over 10 per cent of national income. And the economy is able to withstand unexpected shocks. When a country is in the stage of technological maturity, three significant changes take place :

(i) The character of working force changes. It primarily becomes skilled. Urbanisation increases, Real wages start rising and the workers organize themselves in order to have greater economic and social security;
(ii) The character of entrepreneurship changes. Rugged and hardworking masters give way to polished, polite and efficient managers; and
(iii) The society feels bored of the miracles of industrialisation and wants something new leading to a further change.

The last stage of economic growth is the stage of high mass-consumption characterized by the migration of suburbia, the extensive use of the automobile, the durable consumer goods and household gadgets. In this stage, the balance of attention of the society is shifted from supply to demand, from problems of production to problems of consumption and of welfare in the widest sense. However, three forces are discernible that tend to increase welfare in this post-maturity stage. First, the pursuit of national policy to enhance power and influence beyond national frontiers. Second, to have a welfare state by a more equitable distribution of national income through progressive taxation, increased social security and leisure to the working force. Last, decisions to create new commercial centres and leading sectors like cheap automobiles, houses, innumerable electrically operated household devices, etc. Very few countries have reached this stage of economic growth.

Gerschenkron, an economic historian, examined the traditional economies of Europe as they attempted to industrialize. He looked for similar characteristics and differences among countries and analyzed the process of change in each. He described some common stages through which underdeveloped countries must pass on the way to economic development. Severe tensions between economic backwardness and urgency of development necessitate a big spurt of industrial development in many directions. He categorized countries into three categories on the basis of economic backwardness: advanced, moderately backward, and very backward. For a great spurt of industrialisation, he noted that advanced nations started their first stage of development with the factory in the organisational lead, moderately backward nations with banks, and extremely backward with governments. Preconditions can be created even during the course of industrialisation. According to him, the greater the degree of backwardness, the greater the role of the state in the spurt of industrialisation. Hence, he suggests adoption of capital-intensive techniques.[16]

Finally, Gerschenkron points out the greater spurt in industrialisation could take place if five preconditions were fulfilled. First, either the old framework in agricultural organisation should be abolished or productivity of agriculture be increased. Second, an influential modern elite should be created who is interested in economic change on modern line. Third, there should be provision for material social overhead capital. Fourth, there should be a value system which favours economic change. Fifth, an effective entrepreneurship should be available.

Thus, he tried to evolve a model of development which describes the common stages through which backward economies must pass on the path to economic development.

The concept of disguised unemployment was introduced in the Theory of Underdevelopment by Rosenstein Rodan but was elaborated by Ragnar Nurkse. In its strict sense, it means that given the techniques and productive resources, the marginal productivity of labour in agriculture, over a wide range, is zero in overpopulated underdeveloped countries. It is, therefore, possible to withdraw some surplus labour from agriculture without reducing total output. Such unemployment is found where too many workers are engaged in agricultural operations because of lack of alternative or complementary employment opportunities.

Prof. Sen does not agree with this interpretation of disguised unemployment. He asks, "If marginal productivity of labour over a wide range is zero, why is labour being applied at all"? The confusion arises from failure to distinguish between labour and labour time. In Sen's view, "It is not that too much labour is being spent in the production process but too many labourers are spending it. Distinguished unemployment thus normally takes the form of a smaller number of working hours per head".[17]

Ragnar Nurkse developed the thesis that disguised unemployment in overpopulated underdeveloped countries can be a source of capital formation. According to him, the state of disguised unemployment in underdeveloped countries is 'a disguised saving potential'.[18] With existing techniques of production in agriculture, it is possible to withdraw from land a large proportion of surplus labour without adversely affecting the agricultural output and the same surplus labour can put on capital projects like irrigation, drainge, roads, railways, houses, factories, training schemes, community development, education projects, health, etc. In this way, rural disguised unemployment can be a potential source of capital formation.

Nurkse has split up the problem of mobilising the disguised unemployed as a saving potential in two parts: firstly, how to feed the surplus population transferred to the various capital projects, and secondly, how to provide tools and implements to the new workers to work with. Though the first problem can be solved to some extent by voluntary savings, by taxation and even by importing foreign capital, yet the magnitude of the problem requires that it should be 'self-financing'. At present, unproductive surplus labour is being supported by productive labour. But this is going to waste because it is being utilised in feeding the unproductive labourers whose contribution to output is zero or negligible. If the productive peasants working on land continue to feed their unproductive dependents working on capital projects, their savings would become effective savings.[19]

The second problem relates to the financing of tool to be provided to new construction project workers. Even though capital goods can be imported yet as usual an act of domestic savings is required in this case. In a densely populated agricultural economies there is not only underemployment of labour but also of capital in the forms of tool and implements. Due to fragmentation and division of land holdings most of the plough units are not viable hence of far below the economic holding to utilise available capital in a proper and optimum way. As Nurkse put it 'much simpler tools and equipments may be appropriate to relative factor endowments of the countries of this type in early stage of economic development'.

To sum up, 'Hands would move from the village to the new construction sites; with hands would also move mouths, and with less mouths to feed in the villages the possibility would be created to move out of the village to supply the needs of a swollen army of construction workers, without any fall in consumption on the part of those remaining in the villages.[20] Nurkse, thus, rightly believes that there is concealed saving potential in rural unemployment in overpopulated underdeveloped countries that can be effectively utilised as a means of capital formation. In Bihar, the wide networks of schools and colleges are the best example of private initiative and examples of capital formation.

Prof. W.A. Lewis has developed a very systematic theory of economic development with unlimited supplies of labour.[21] Like many classical economists, he believes that in many underdeveloped countries an unlimited supply of labour is available at the subsistence wage. Economic development takes place when capital accumulates as a result of the withdrawal of surplus labour from the subsistence sector to the capitalists sector. The capitalist sector is that part of the economy which uses reproducible capital and pays capitalists for the use thereof. The subsistence sector is that part of the economy which does not use reproducible capital. In this sector, naturally, output per head is lower than in the capitalist sector.

Lewis starts his thesis with assertion that the classical theory of perfectly elastic supply of labour at subsistence wage holds true in the case of number of underdeveloped countries. Such countries are overpopulated relatively to capital and natural resources, so that the marginal productivity of labour is negligible, zero or even negative. With this unlimited supply of labour available at subsistence wage rate new factories can be started, existing factories can be expanded. Unskilled labour is a 'quasi bottleneck' which can be removed providing training facilities to them.

Capitalists aim at profit maximisation. It is they who save and automatically invest what they save. Since the marginal productivity of labour in the capitalist sector is higher than the capitalist wage, this results in capitalist surplus. This surplus is again invested in new ventures. Capital formation takes place, new investment is made, naturally, more people are employed from subsistence sector. This process continues till the capital-output ratio rises and the supply of labour becomes inelastic and surplus labour disappears. According to Lewis, if technical progress is capital-saving, it may be considered as an increment in capital and if it is labour-saving, it may be considered as increment in the marginal productivity of labour.

The theory shows that if unlimited supply of labour is available at a constant real wage, and if any part of profit is reinvested in productive capacity, profits will grow continuously relatively to national income. But the process of growth cannot go on indefinitely, if as a result of capital accumulation no surplus labour is left. It may also stop if, despite the existence of surplus labour, real wages rise so high as to reduce the capitalist profit to the level where they are all consumed and nothing is left for investment.

John Fei and Gustav Ranis in an article entitled "A Theory of Economic Development" analyse the transition process through which an underdeveloped economy hopes to move from a condition of stagnation to one of self-sustained growth.[22] The theory relates to an underdeveloped labour-surplus and resource-poor economy in which the vast majority of population is engaged in agriculture amidst wide-spread unemployment and high rates of population growth. The agrarian economy is stagnant. People are engaged in traditional agricultural pursuits. Development consists of the reallocation of surplus agricultural workers, whose contribution to output is zero or negligible, to the industrial sector where they become productive at the wage equal to the institutional wage in agriculture. It is an improvement over Lewis' model as this model shows the interaction between the two sectors in initiating and accelerating development. Despite merits, it has limited significance in the practical application.

Jorgenson presented a neo-classical model of dual economy and divided the economy into traditional or agricultural sector and modern or manufacturing sector. There is asymmetry in the production relations in the two sectors. Agricultural sector is a function of land and labour alone. The labourforce available for employment in manufacturing sector grows at a rate which is equal to the growth rate of agricultural surplus. There may be wage differential in the two sectors. This differential determines the terms of trade between manufacturing and agricultural sectors.[23]

Harvey Leibenstein has developed the thesis that underdeveloped countries are characterised by the vicious circle of poverty that keeps them around a low per capita income equilibrium state. The way out of this impasse is a certain "critical minimum effort", which would raise the per capita income at a level at which sustained development could be maintained. According to Leibenstein, every economy is subject to shocks and stimulates. A shock has the impact of reducing per capita income initially, while stimulant tends to increase it. It is only when the income raising factors are stimulated much beyond the income depressing factors that the critical minimum is reached and the economy would be on the path to development. In the development process such conditions are created by the expansion of growth agents. The typical growth agents are the entrepreneur, the investor, the saver, and the innovator. The growth contributing activities result in the creation of entrepreneurship, the increase in the stock of knowledge, the expansion of productive skill of the people and increase in the rate of saving and investment.

As a result of the critical minimum effort, the per capita income would rise and tend to increase the level of saving and investment, which in turn, would lead to: (a) expansion of the growth agents; (b) an increase in their contribution to per unit of capital as the capital-output ratio declines; (c) a decrease in effectiveness of the factors inhibiting growth; (d) creation of social environmental conditions that promote social and economic mobility; (e) increased specialisation and expansion of secondary and tertiary sectors, and lastly, the development of an atmosphere that leads to changes more conducive to economic and social change.[24]

The theory of the 'big push' is associated with the name of Professor Paul N. Rosenstein-Rodan. The thesis is that a 'big push' or a large comprehensive programme is needed in the form of a high minimum amount of investment to overcome the obstacles to development in an underdeveloped economy and to launch it on the path of progress. There is a minimum level of resources that must be devoted to a development programme if it is to have any chance of success. Launching a country into self-sustaining growth is a little like an airplane off the ground. There is a critical ground speed which must be passed before the craft can become air borne. It necessitates the obtaining of external economies that arise from the simultaneous establishment of technically independent industries. The indivisibilities and external economies, flowing from a minimum quantum of investment, are a pre-requisite for launching economic development successfully. It is a minimum quantum of investment rather than price mechanism in such imperfect market that takes an underdeveloped economy towards an optimum position.

There is controversy focusing around the doctrine of balanced growth *versus* unbalanced growth. The concept of balanced growth requires balance between different sectors, i.e. consumer goods and capital goods industries. It also implies balance between agriculture and industry, on the one hand, and domestic and export sectors, on the other. This balance is also required between demand and supply sides. The theory of unbalanced growth is opposite of the doctrine of balanced growth. According to this concept, investment should be made in selected rather than simultaneously in all sectors. No underdeveloped country possesses capital and other resources in such quantities to invest simultaneously in all sectors.

The concept of unbalanced growth has been popularised by Hirschman.[25] It is his contention that deliberate unbalancing the economy is the best way to achieve economic growth in an underdeveloped country. He regards development as a 'chain of disequilibria' that must keep alive rather than eliminate the disequilibria, of which profits and loses are symptoms in a competitive economy. Social overhead capital has been defined as 'comprising those basic services without which primary, secondary and tertiary productive activities cannot function'. In social overhead are included investment on education, public health, communications, transportation, and conventional utilities like light, water, power, irrigation, drainage schemes, etc. Rostow also favours unbalanced growth and explains in terms of the leading sectors.

Gunnar Myrdal maintains that economic development results in a circular casuation process whereby the rich are rewarded more favours and efforts of those who lag behind are thwarted. The 'backwash effects' predominate and the 'spread effects' are dampened. This tends accumulatively to accentuate international inequalities and leads to regional inequalities within the underdeveloped countries. In underdeveloped countries, a circular and cumulative process also known as the 'vicious circle of poverty' operates downwards and being unregulated causes increasing inequalities. Myrdal believes that our inherited theoretical approach is inadequate to solve the problems of economic theory generally were never worked out to serve the purpose of explaining the reality of economic underdevelopment and development.[26] Myrdal builds his theory of economic underdevelopment and development around the idea of regional inequalities on the national and international planes. To explain it, he uses the notions of 'backwash' and 'spread effects'. He defines backwash effects as all relevant adverse changes of economic expansion in a locality. The spread effects refer to certain centrifugal spread effects of expansionary momentum from the centres of economic expansion to other regions. The main cause of regional inequalities has been the strong backwash effects and weak spread effects in underdeveloped countries. In these respects, Myrdal's thesis marks an important departure from other theories of underdevelopment. Even empirical evidence indicates that Myrdal's thesis has been vindicated.

Some of economists have constructed models of economic growth to indicate how growth can be generated and accelerated on the sustained basis. The Harrod-Domar models of economic growth are based on the experience of advanced economies. They are primarily addressed to an advanced capitalist economy and attempt to analyse the requirements of steady growth in such economy. Both the economists are interested in discovering the rate of income growth necessary for a smooth and uninterrupted working of the economy. Harrod and Domar assign a key role in the process of economic growth. They lay emphasis on dual character of investment. Firstly, it creates income, and secondly, it augments the productive capacity of the economy by increasing its capital stock. The former may be regarded as the demand effect and the latter the supply effect of investment. Hence, so long as net investment is taking place, real income and output will continue to expand. However, for maintaining a full employment equilibrium level of income from year to year it is necessary that both real income and output should expand at the same rate at which the productive capacity of the capital stock is expanding. Otherwise, any divergence between the two will lead to excess or idle capacity thus forcing the entrepreneurs to curtail their investment expenditure. Ultimately, it will adversely affect the economy by lowering incomes and employment in the subsequent periods and moving the economy off the equilibrium path of steady growth. Thus, if full employment is to be maintained in the long run, net investment should expand continuously. This required rate of income growth may be called the warranted rate of growth or the full capacity growth rate.[27]

Domar builds his model around the following questions: since investment generates income, on the one hand, and increases productive capacity, on the other, at what rate investment should increase in order to make the increase in productive capacity so that full employment is maintained? He answers this question by forging a link between aggregate supply and aggregate demand through investment. The demand side is expanded by the Keynesian multiplier.

Harrod model is based upon three distinct rates of growth. Firstly, there is the actual growth rate determined by the saving ratio and the capital-output ratio, secondly, there is the warranted rate of growth reflecting the full capacity growth rate of income of an economy. Lastly, there is the mutual growth rate, which is regarded as the welfare optimum by Harrod .[28]

Professor Kurihara is of the opinion that growth models have positive lesson for underdeveloped economies, that the state should be allowed to play not only a stabilising role but also a development role if these economies are to industrialise more effectively and rapidly than the now industrialised economies did in conditions of laissez faire. He further opines that because of the universal character of saving- income ratio and capital output ratio as measurable strategic variables, the growth mechanism discussed by Harrod-Domar is applicable to all economic systems. That is why, their growth models are applicable to those underdeveloped countries in which techniques, saving ratio and capital-output ratio remain constant during the plan period.[29]

Harrod-Domar models are based on the restrictive assumption of a constant saving-income ratio. The Kaldor model is an attempt to make the saving-income ratio a variable in the growth process.[30] It is based on the classical saving function which implies that saving equals the ratio of profit to national income. Kaldor concludes that warranted and the natural rates of growth are not independent of one another, if profit margins are flexible, the former will adjust itself to the latter through the consequential change in profit-income ratio. But there will not be an inherent tendency to a smooth rate of growth in capitalist economy. In fact, the cause of cyclical movements are found in disharmony between the warranted and natural growth rates, like all contemporary theoretical models of economic growth, it assumes a production function that does not allow any substitution between factors. Thus, it represents a rigid and angular picture of economic progress.

Mrs. Joan Robinson in her book *The Accumulation of Capital* builds a simple model of economic growth based on the capitalistic rules of the game. But it is not so much concerned with an automatic convergence to a moving equilibrium in a capitalist economy as with studying the properties of equilibrium growth. J.E. Meade has constructed a neo-classical model of economic growth which is designed to show the way in which simplest form of economic system would behave during a process of equilibrium growth.[31] In the economy visualised above, the net output produced depends upon four factors :

(a) the net stock of capital available in the form of machines;
(b) the amount of available labourforce;
(c) the availability of land and natural resources; and
(d) the state of technical knowledge which continues to improve through time.

Equilibrium position ultimately depends upon the rate of accumulation of capital stock. According to Meade, there is a critical growth rate of capital stock which makes the growth rate of income equal to the growth rate of capital stock. Model of technical change consists of discovering new methods of production, developing new products and introducing new techniques. Technical change is synonymous with a change in production function. Whenever there is a technical change, it leads to increase in the productivity of labour and capital. The technical change is said to be neutral when it is neither capital-saving nor labour-saving.

In 1953, Mahalanobis developed a single sector model based on the variables of national income and investment. It was further developed into a two-sector model in 1953 where the entire net output of the economy was supposed to be produced in only two sectors: the investment goods sector and the consumer goods sector. Finally, he developed the famous four-sector model in 1955, two-sector model was based on several assumptions. Mahalanobis model is not a growth model in the real sense, rather it is an allocation model. Mahalanobis model takes a four-sector economy consisting of:

(a) the investment goods sector; (K)
(b) the factory produced consumer goods sector; (C1)
(c) the small household produced consumer goods sector; (C2) and

(d) services (health, education etc.) producing sector; (C3).

In a given time period, in order to achieve a certain growth rate for the economy, the total investible fund has been divided in such a way that it leads to the required growth rate. But since the required growth rate is to be reasonably high, it can be achieved by expanding K and thereby producing larger quantities of investment goods. However, investment in sector K is bound to generate increased purchasing power and hence demand for consumer goods which require comparatively less capital but employ more labour. In this way, a balance is sought to be established between the investment goods sector and consumer goods sector. The above solution of Mahalanobis model and its practical application to India in the form of the Second Five Year Plan proves that it possesses great utility as an instrument of developing planning, but it has its own limitations and weakness.[32]

Various theories of economic development and models of economic growth have been propounded and constructed and no single theory explains the real problems of underdevelopment. Similarly, no model has succeeded in prescribing the clear-cut formula for promoting alround development of the economy. They are based on certain assumptions and hypotheses of limited relevance and applicability, hence partly efficacious especially under given conditions.

Despite the applications of these models and theories, problems of backwardness, poverty and unemployment are persisting. The mankind is confronted with various problems even for survival. Economic problems, in a limited context, have been solved in the advanced countries but other problems are still endemic. This calls for reorientation in the concept, content and procedure of development to address the afflictions facing the mankind.

NOTES

1. A. Maddison (1970): *Economic Progress and Policy in Developing Countries.*
2. D. Seers (1969): The Meaning of Development, *International Development Review,* Vol. II, pp. 2-6.
3. Adam Smith (1976): *An Enquiry into the Nature and Causes of Wealth of Nations.*
4. David Ricardo (1917): *The Principles of Political Economy & Taxation.*
5. Jhingan, *op. cit.* p. 81.

6. B. Higgins, *Economic Development*, p. 7.
7. J.A Schumpeter, *Ten Great Economists*, p. 5.
8. M.M. Bober, *Karl Marx's Interpretation of History*, p. 24.
9. J.A. Schumpeter, *Theory of Economic Development*, p. 64.
10. *Ibid.*
11. J.A. Schumpeter, *Capitalism, Socialism and Democracy*, p. 61.
12. J.M. Keynes (1936): *General Theory of Employment, Interest and Money*, pp. 113-115.
13. W. W. Rostow (1960): *The Stages of Economic Growth.*
14. *Ibid.*
15. *Ibid.*, p. 39.
16. Alexander Gerschenkron (1962): *The Economic Backwardness in Historical Perspective.*
17. A.K. Sen, *Choice of Techniques,* pp. 3-5.
18. Ragnar Nurkse. *op. cit.* chapt. 11.
19. *Ibid.*, p. 40.
20. M. Dobb (1951): *Some Aspects of Economic Development,* in one of the lectures delivered at the Delhi School of Economics.
21. This is the title of an article published by W.A. Lewis in the Manchester School, May 1954.
22. John Fei and Gustav Ranis (1961): A Theory of Economic Development, *A.E.R.* Vol. 51, September.
23. D. Jorgenson (1961): The Development of Dual Economy, E.J. 71.
24. Harvey Leibenstein (1957), *Economic Backwardness and Economic Growth, Studies in the Theory of Economic Development.*
25. A.O. Hirschman, *The Strategy of Economic Development,* Chap. 4-7.
26. Gunnar Myrdal, *op. cit.*
27. R. F Harrod (1947): "Towards a Dynamic Economics in Economies Essays, Evsey Domar, Expansion & Employment in *American Review,* March.
28. R.F. Harrod (1960): Second Essay in Dynamic Economics, *Economic Journal,* June.
29. K. Kurihara, chap. 9 &11.
30. N. Kaldor (1960): *Essays on Value and Distribution,* pp. 227-230.
31. J.E. Meade (1961): *A New Classical Theory of Economic Growth.*
32. P.C. Mahalanobis (1953): Some Observations on the Process of Growth of National Income, *Sankhya*, September.

3

Deficiencies of Economic Theory

Since the publication of Adam Smith's *The Wealth of Nations* in 1776, political economy or economics has ramified itself in a number of directions. Whatever approach is adopted, any such discussion must rest on a consideration of the nature and subject matter of economics which have undergone considerable change. If *Wealth of Nations* is taken as providing the birthday of political economy, then to use Prof. Samuelson's[1] words, 'like a baby' it was taking shape even before it was born. It was conceived in Aristotle's writing as 'the science of household management' and 'the science of supply.[2] Aristotle clearly saw that from the natural supply of household wants through exchange, unnatural practices of exchange developed. Thus, trade and commerce developed during middle ages, Saint Thomas Aquinas and other scholastic writers sought to guard against these tendencies with the help of Christian ethics — an attempt which led to development of the idea of a just price.

In the fifteenth and sixteenth centuries, the hold of the so-called Christian ethics slackened, and as the opening of the new trade routes widened the scope of trade and exchange, the mercantilists used their economic ideas for political manoeuvring of 'state-craft' to subserve their own interest. Adam Smith's ideas were a reaction not only against the 'wretched spirit of greed and monopoly'conferred upon the businessmen by the mercantilist policies in general, but also against the mercantilist economic ideas in particular.[3] This reaction led him to develop all the categories which form the contents of subsequent economic controversy.[4] It must not be forgotten that the author of the *Wealth of Nations* was also the author of *Theory of Moral Sentiments*. The philosophy of economic liberalism was an extension of his idea of natural moral law and well-balanced sympathies. Thus, though Adam Smith may not have a strong claim to being the Adam of systematic economics, as Prof. Boulding (1969)[5] envisaged, it was at his forge that economics was infused with a moral element that made it a social science.

The moral element continued to dominate the thoughts of the economists till the first quarter of the twentieth century. As Prof. Robbins pointed out, "the definition of Economics which would probably command most adherents, at any rate in Anglo-Saxon countries, is that which relates to the study of the causes of material welfare. This element was common in the definitions of Cannan, Marshall, J.B. Clark and even Pareto. Robbins thought that this definition was not only misleading but it did not also have the capacity to describe exactly the ultimate subject matter of the main generalisation of the science, a criterion which Robbins regarded as the final test of the validity of any such definition.[6] He, therefore, rejected this definition of Economics and put forward another which has since become widely popular. He defined 'Economics is the science which studies human behaviour as a relationship between ends and scarce means which have alternative uses.'[7]

He observed, it does not seem logically possible to associate two studies, ethics and economics, in any form but mere juxtaposition. Economics deals with ascertainable facts, ethics with valuations and obligations. The two fields of enquiry are not on the same plane of discourse. Between the generalisations of positive and normative studies, there is a logical gulf fixed which no ingenuity can disguise and no juxtaposition in space or time can bridge over. Here Robbins' definition of Economics may itself be open to criticism. The definition is too wide to include aspects of other subjects like engineering, political science and so on. Boulding (1969)[8] points out that the allocation of scarce resources is a universal problem which applies to political structures through coercion, threat and to love of community, just as it does to exchange. He prefers to define Economics as 'the study of that part of the total social system which is organised through exchange and deals with exchangeables'.

It is the neglect of the human behavioural aspects in society from his later discussion that had led Robbins to adopt the view of logical gulf between the positive and normative economics. If the problem is one of allocating scarce resources among given ends, the problem can be solved by activity analysis, whose economic content is nil.[9] But if we take account of the fact that man is a social animal, then we can at once see that the ends and the means are not given, but are socially determined.

In social sciences, anomalies in old paradigms of thought and institutions have often appeared. These anomalies were identified quite often from ethical considerations, and their solutions were also sought in new paradigms of thought and institutions from ethical considerations. In the field of economics, the classical paradigm was a reaction against mercantilism. Similarly, Marxian paradigm was a reaction prevailing in the classical thought. Thus, the so-called independence of positive and normative studies does not have much empirical support, particuraly in social sciences.

There was a time when philosophy and science of economics were inseparable but they were separated and the gulf between the two widened. The crisis is not merely philosophical or intellectual, it is also empirical. Scientific hypothesis cannot be verified or falsified because of enormous complexities of human problems. The tragedy of economics is that it is found weakest where it was supposed to be the strongest, i.e. in terms of its logic, methods, and empirical analysis and results. The crisis has to be seen in the historical perspective. About two centuries ago, right at the time when the science of economics was discovered, it was called a dismal science. There were two reasons for this. First, economics was torn away from moral philosophy of which it was a part in the curricula of the universities. Second, the economic situation, which was translated into economic laws, was one of unrelieved misery, on the one hand, and garish riches, on the other. But a century later, the science of economics became a matter of great optimism as it opened up tremendous vistas for the production of goods and services. Paradoxically, as life became more and more complex, holistic analysis gave way to compartmentalisation and specialism which increasingly rested on pure economic analysis. Then was born the economic man in whose name the economists played games with one another in terms of fancy theories unconnected with the problems of relationship between facts and values. Whenever the question of values was brought in, economists rejected the challenge and pushed out values as belonging to some other field of analysis. Even earlier, Adam Smith, the father of modern economics, desperately tried to deal with both but could not link the two. The questions that he asked in his *Moral Sentiment* were left out in his *Wealth of Nations,* despite the fact that he waited for years to publish the latter in order to find in it a place for ethical issues.

Just as philosophy moved from rationalism to empiricism and logical positivism, economics also shed its non-economic contents and concentrated on the so-called economic man. Whenever, economic man was found to be inconsistent in his behaviour or to give preference to non-economic considerations or seemed to violate every economic law, this was explained by the non-operation of the phrase, other things remaining the same.

Unfortunately, after Adam Smith, normative philosophy of economics gradually disappeared and for almost two hundred years positivism has a field day. In defence of their theory, the classical political economists, such as Ricardo and Malthus carried a persistent campaign against the poor and the sick. The poor had to be sacrificed in order to get the theory right and equilibrium established. Their loud opposition to the Poor Law (1819) led to the abolition of the laws in 1836 which produced the phases of worst misery, also ironically rested itself on the classical political economy and provided defence for it. No wonder, values and even simple compassion were cosidered enemies of Marxism as they had been banished from classical theory. Ricardo and Marx were the originators of pure economic theory as an autonomous logical system unconcerned with human beings except workers and capitalists.

The half century following J.S. Mill that was characteristically dominated by general optimism, notwithstanding all the predictions of Marx to the contrary, strengthened the trends towards making the science of economics free from all values except those of market. Persistent technological advances further strengthened this trend. Along with its twin sisters, science and technology gave a powerful push to industry in the direction of producing a plethora of goods meant for human consumption. But under the influence of the same science and organisation, it legitimised unlimited consumption and greed. There was quantum jump on the side of the demand. In the industrialised countries, the situation of misery that was reflected in the unfulfilment of basic needs, was transformed into a situation of unfulfilled wants of infinite variety. The science of economics ceased to be dismal, it rather became an art of rat race[9]

Rapid development in transport and communication was another push factor. It was again in the field of international economic relations that the economics of rationality and optimisation produced its worst effects. Ironically, in this field, economics could not be separated from politics and wars. Some economic issues could only be settled through wars. Imperialism was at once a system of economic expansion and a war system. Robbin's definition tightened all the loose ends of earlier definitions by insisting on the pursuits of purely material ends. The subsequent barren debates over welfare economics confirmed their trend.

In other words, no matter how rich a society is, its economic society is supposed to be materially poor because the means always remain scarce in relation to wants. However, one merit of this definition was that it was focused on the need to avoid waste. Any misallocation of resources amounted to economic waste. On the other hand, the way the economic theory came to be formulated ignored the question of social wastefulness as distinguished from market wastefulness. This resulted in private affluence and public poverty.

The great depression knocked off the assumed optimism of old economic theories and the system based on them. Keynes put forward a new theory which, he insisted, was a total critique of the neo-classical and classical theories. In reality, it was only an attempt to defend and legitimise capitalism by removing the unnecessary abstractions in the old theories. The main contribution was the new demand theory from which he derived his Macro Effective Demand function.

Both the classical and neo-classical economics were shaped by an environment of poverty, high population growth, inadequacy of production, and inequality of distribution. The Keynesian theory was shaped by all this as well as by unemployment and insecurity of incomes. The difference in the economic situation explained by the two schools is that inadequacy of production has been replaced by excess production combined with large scale unemployment. To many economists, belonging to both the schools, economic problems could be solved in view of increases in productivity, technological developments, and control of population in the developed world. Every society felt and still feels poor psychologically because of unfulfilment of some wants and others despite the fact that the rising curve of average income has made inequality look less blatant and harsh, people felt sense of relative deprivation. Besides, the continuous expansion of production produced new environmental problems which have created scarcity and threats of new kinds. Real scarcity has been replaced by contrived scarcity. In other words, the new economic problem is that of instability created by contrived wants, artificially boosted consumption through credit and instalment planning and structural inflation. Inflation and high wages have kept chasing one another without a solution.

Pure economic analysis and the concept of economic man bolstered by the demand theory created economism of many varieties. Ironically, it gripped the communist nations which had thrown to the winds the humanism of early Marx. Economism has many meanings.

The mathematical revolution in economics, which claimed to analyse every issue rigorously, produced some kind of counter revolution. Not only have the value premises been further weakened, but great controversies of political economy have also been sought to be settled via mathematics. Economic theory has been mystified as a great mathematical riddle. As Homa Katouzian has aptly remarked, 'the greatest potential threat to economic science posed by mathematics, is the real possibility for mathematical forces over technologies to determine the substance and content of economic knowledge. Mathematical economics began by the application of terrestrial mechanics to economic problems. There is no tendency to use concept and methods of Celestial mechanics.'[10]

The crisis is deepening because specific theories which held great sway and cut across competing models have proved defective and self contradictory. For instance, the role of expectation has made free competition look like silly. The self-adjusting market or other mechanisms adjust no more without serious intervention. Important theories have been exposed. For instance, the production function is found to be circular because one of its determinants, namely capital, defined in terms of marginal productivity, cannot be unless we know the production. Both unemployment and inflation have simultaneously grown up to produce stagflation. The labour theory of value and the impossibility of transforming value into prices completely upset the consistency between production and distribution.

Although economists have debated, though without definite conclusions, the problems of linkages between economic theory, economic behaviour, and policy prescription, they have refused to bring into the theory question of value explicitly. If economic theory stated that government expenditure could lead to reduction of unemployment, it also became a policy prescription. But when the same theory also proved that public investment could generate inflation and inefficiency, the policy prescription broke down. The moral question left out were: that employment is a fundamental right as well as duty, that the state is an institution of violence, and that corporate system is an institution of exploitation. Once economics begins with these questions of value, which are not falsified by scientific hypotheses, the result will be very different kind of ecomomic theory, different from the mercantilist, or liberal, or Marxist, or any other theory known so far. Perception of a society and its choices in social sciences are determined by the values which are themselves seriously influenced by environments. It has been of no help to modern economists for raising the discipline of economics to the level of a science to keep value out of their analysis. Values without philosophy lead to vulgarisation of theory and corruption of practice.

The setback to both the Keynesian and the new-classical theories, that came from their failures to meet the challenges of the last two decades followed by development decades proving a damp squib, led to an even higher level of abstraction in economic theory despite massive strides in empirical research through the use of econometric technique. One reason for this escapism was that econometrics could prove anything and establish strong but meaningless correlations.

Marxist theory, which claimed methodologically integrated treatment of philosophy, economic theory, laws of motion of capitalism, and method of socialist construction, has also let itself be reduced to the narrow scope of the other narrowly defined, in order to prove its superiority over them by choosing their methodology. A leading journal described the state of Marxism thus: 'It is commonplace now-a-days that Marxism is in crisis. Theoretically, this is apparent in the disintegration of the old orthodoxies and the failure to fill the resulting vacuum with more fruitful analysis; politically, it is evident in the ability of socialist and popular democratic forces to build upon the current crisis in capitalism as well as in the problems of actually existing socialism. The current crisis is there both theoretical and practical.[11]

At the level of practice, economics has become more and more anti-humanistic. In the name of efficiency, productivity, good management, and reasonable return on capital, the corporate sector, with its growing monopolistic and oligopolistic and transnational character, has become the centre not only of economic power but also of the draconian and violent political power. The countervailing power of the state economic sector, instead of countervailing the corporate sector, has become its ally. The alliance, however, is losing its legitimacy because it has failed to tackle the major economic issues of unemployment, poverty, inflation, inequality, etc. Besides, the rise of new problems such as pollution, ecological imbalances, exhausion of natural resources and massive diversion of resources to nuclear armament, etc. Problems which were kept separate, now demand a joint solution. However, the economic complexities and crises have not yet produced a corresponding political consciousness for a new political order that can integrate facts, problems and values.

The results of practical policies have not always been efficient and optimum. Both inefficiency and inequality have been defended and sustained by a network of restrictive practices of various kinds such as price agreements, government subsidies, monopolies and oligopolies etc. The national economies have developed behind protective walls and now feel obliged to protect their high standard of living by raising even higher protective walls.

The production philosophy of the modern industrial society is dominated by the corporate greed, technological determinism and ecological carelessness. Vast sums of money are spent in influencing government policies by companies which spread this pollution. Technological determinism includes not only high technology but large capital and energy per unit of production. The energy crisis is a direct product of this modern industrial system. Unless the modern economic and technological systems are drastically changed, the crisis will ever stay with us. But then the modern economic laws or theories do not deal with these issues.

Probably, the highest crisis of science of economics lies in the total break down of all wage price theories. The rise to power of big unions and their closed shops and then mafia like—bosses, emergence of big multinationals, credit-based consumption on a nation-wide scale, and the strength of the labour-liberal politicians continued for several decades. That coalition was the ideological hot bed for consumerism, economism and high technology. However, because of internal and structural changes, the coalition has broken down to the disadvantage of the organised labour. Prolonged unemployment has put worker against worker, employed against unemployed, men against women. The hands of buyers market are being gradually strengthened at the cost of sellers' market though, it was always imperfect and full of constraints and limitations. The opting out of labour from the unions in order to get better economic bargains and rise of political conservatism have wrecked the old comfortable arrangement under which labour market created working equilibrium and protected workers. But what has remained of the old arrangement are the craze of material gains, greed and insensitivity in workers and capitalist alike, and alliance against the rest of the community. Now that the structure of the labourforce has undergone, profound changes, workers no longer hold the central position, the power of the trade unions is broken, job security has taken precedence over better conditions of worker, and the old economic arrangement has been thrown out of gear. So far the unorganised labour has suffered, but now it is the organised labour which is at disadvantage. For the first time, workers are realising that they cannot ignore the conditions of rest of the community. Workers are slowly agreeing to become partners in ownership but powerful unions, particularly those which are controlled by communists, are resisting this change. They fail to realise that conflict oriented role of the organised labour in the developed world is no longer relevant. Trade unions will have to be replaced by wider communities, and this is what the science of economics is unable to comprehend.

Explosion of knowledge and rapid progress in technological development, instead of solving old problems, are creating new ones. Technology has taken the place of philosophy and it threatens to become the supreme value. Technology is also looked upon as the answer to crisis created by technology itself. But by changing the structure of production, labourforce and demand, technology has also eroded many old economic theories and paradigms. The crisis is getting circular and the curve of economics is a vicious circle.

Notwithstanding all the development in the field of science and technology, human organisation lags behind in capturing and controlling their essence. On the contrary, human beings are becoming victims of science and technology. The greater the thrust of new innovations, the greater the threat of human enslavement. There is bound to be a reaction towards total anti-technology which is equally dangerous. To remove an old misunderstanding, it must be affirmed that Gandhi was neither anti-science nor anti-technology. There are limits within which science and technology can be neutral. Once those limits are crossed, science and technology become monster.

Gandhi was not against science and technology, but against selfishness and want of consideration for one's neighbours, display of power and wealth, which, unfortunately, have become the accepted norms of our society. "The craze", he said, "is for what they call labour-saving machinery. Men go on saving labour till thousands are without work and thrown on the streets to die of starvation. I want to save time and labour, not for a fraction of mankind, but for all. I want the concentration of wealth, not in the hands of few, but in the hands of all. Today machinery merely helps a few to ride on the back of millions. The impetus behind it all is not the philanthropy to save labour, but greed. It is against this constitution of things that I am fighting with all my might.[12]

If economic man and economic society are so defined as to make them always feel poor, no matter how rich they are, the core of this contradiction lies in the theory of consumption and demand and not in the theory of production. Even Marshall, the master creater of the theory, was obliged to draw attention to the artificially generated wants. He wrote: 'Although it is man's wants in the earliest stages of his development that gave rise to his activities, yet afterwards each new step is to be regarded as the development of activities giving rise to new wants, rather than of new wants giving rise to new activities.' In other words, 'the purpose of economic organisation is not merely to satisfy wants but to create wants.' If new wants can be generated at the rate faster than the existing ones are satisfied, not only will there be feeling of deprivation and poverty but society would be obliged to become an arena for rat race among the human beings. This directly emanates from the accepted definition of economics, even without questioning its logic, and in turn, must inevitably create the feeling of psychological poverty, no matter how rich a society is.[13]

Thus it is not surprising that the demand theory has produced greed and vulgar consumerism. Truly the utility-disutility theory, the very basis of the demand theory as conceived by the economists included greed and craze for consumerism because human wants are assumed to be unlimited. Wasteful consumption and luxurious living have become the mainstay of the system which sustains itself on a built-in accumulation of capital and growth. In fact, this new syndrome of luxury, waste, growth and decline in public services has become the main component of new economic theory. Maintaining the rich has become the necessary cost of social production. As Harry Johnson says: 'Luxurious living, which drives the whole machine, becomes the necessary cost of production, so that the margin of resources available for social uses as defence is unduly small in relation to national income.[14]

One does not have to be a Gandhian to see the difference between material and non-material wants. Even hardened neoclassicists recognise it. To quote Johnson again, the margin of want satisfaction tends to move from the physiological to the psychological and sociological, the physiological needs are satisfied, the psychological and sociological become necessities, while the luxuries are psychiatric, hence the hidden persuaders and motivational research.

Looking at the state of the world economy, global inequalities, poverty, corruption, insensitivities of multinationals and the brutality of the super powers, one gets the impression that the economists are highest paid legitimisers of this state of affairs. The United Nations system is the central forum from which they operate. They may be neoclassicists, or Keynesian, or Marxists, but they all seem to converge on protecting the prevailing order. All the talk about new international economic order is a matter of diversionary tactics in an attempt to legitimise the prevailing order. There is no counter community of economists to challenge these establishments. Most of the people of the developing world are sinking into misery, while their ruling elites enjoy a life of luxury which is the envy of the rich even in the developed world. The Third World rulers have no difficulty in accepting or rejecting any of the prevailing models or theories emanating from the West or from the East. It is no accident that they also converge on pushing out Gandhi from the debate and curricula because of his emphasis on making ethical means, the central core of economic theory and practice.

The aforementioned problems and crises of economics are both the cause and effect of very peculiar intellectual failures. The problems are getting more and more intertwined and integrated, but the intellectual response remains fragmented. One does not have to go very deep into the great complexities to understand the issue. It is no accident that the two opposing social systems, capitalism and communism, organised in two great blocks, are similar in everything else except economics. If opposing economic theories produced the same consequences, then economics must be accepted as having ceased to be a science. The question is: can we survive economically without artificially stimulating the level of consumption, without built-in obsolescence? The political dimension of this question is clear. Can we use our productivity to eliminate poverty and inequality, national and international, and how far is high consumption the means by which the bulk of the working class are kept incorporated into the Western capitalist societies? This incorporation of the working class into middle-class culture or what is called their embourgeoisiement remains the unsolved problems of modern economics. The possibility of reform of the mainstream economics in order to make it conform to values is dim because of the methodology which is common to all schools of thought. There has to be an alternative economics and alternative paradigm if man is to survive and live by values though quite comfortably also.

According to Jayaprakash Narayan, the application of science does not depend upon science itself but upon the character of the society. Money makers are the dominant class in the society, their will has to be done. Government also, irrespective of ideologies, prefer centralised, big-scale production, because that is necessary for war or defence, and no less important, because it also concentrates great economic and, therefore, political power, in their hands.[15] What would have been the situation, had the society pursued not the aims of power, profit and war, but of peace, goodwill, cooperation, freedom, and brotherhood? Science could be equally applied to evolve such technology as would ensure these. This would have enabled science to wash its blood-stained face.

In addition to armament competition between the East and the West, the world is divided between the rich North and the poor South. The logic of the development policy with its emphasis on industrialisation has promoted an infrastructure in these countries that encourages a miniscule minority to live luxuriously in sea of mass poverty where malnutrition, hunger and lack of shelter and medical care are the rule. The UNICEF estimates that thousands of children die everyday for lack of food in a world where food production and supply far outstrip the subsistence demand. The process of development divides the country into dual societies of rich and poor. The dynamics of dual society and compulsions of international relations between rich and poor countries helps bring to power authoritarian government that rule by a police state mentality, and where the institutions that are created to uphold law and order are themselves involved in neutralising or murdering their own citizens or to use a contemporary euphemism, making people disappear. Many countries in the South thus are in a state of continuous turmoils on the edge of a violent revolution, successful or otherwise.

In the name of greater affluence for the rich and more development for the poor countries, the existing world order is involved in the extraction of ever increasing non-renewable resources to the point of reaching the very limits of our planet. Some other problems such as topsoil and its erosion, acid rain, deforestation, overfishing and grassland loss have not yet produced equally visible effects everywhere. Yet one fears that these effects are far more serious than those of all shortages since these resources form the basis both of human existence and of our civilization. All the same, the world has passed the peak levels of production and use in these resources is now showing a declining trend. In the not-too-distant future, the impacts are likely to become both more visible and more detrimental.

The unfortunate situation with these basic resources is that by the time their limits become more clearly visible, it may already be too late for any remedial action. And, compared to the case of oil, the shock to system is expected to be far more serious and damaging. Some even think that it may be beyond repair and lead to serious calamities.

The impact of all these calamities on the world economic system is tremendous. Its effects are visible on the world monetary system and international liquidity. A large number of countries of the South are already heavily burdened by foreign debt. No major relief of this debt is in sight, as much as 100 per cent of the export of a number of countries are already mortgaged to the payment of cumulative interest on this debt. Under such circumstances, this total debt has a natural tendency to increase even more which is technically known as debt trap.

With few adjustment mechanism able to reverse this trend, some confrontation between the large developing countries in Latin America and rich North appears to be inevitable. The government of Argentina has already started moving towards such a potential confrontation. The organisation of African states is now also pushing in the same direction. The persistence of high interest rates, continuing recession in European countries and the fall in the prices of raw material would not make an adjustment towards some sorts of an equilibrium any easier. All this points to a growing instability of the present international monetary system.

Such instability of the existing international order tells us much about the economic and political health of various countries, rich or poor, belonging to the East or to the West. In the rich countries, the quality of life is deteriorating even if the standard of living has phenomenally improved. The value of family life and other social values are breaking down. A substantial number of children have never lived with both their parents. The single parent household is in the process of becoming the majority of households in the United States. Kidnapping and various forms of child abuse are now a national phenomenon. The adult life is marred by anxiety and job stress. The work of a large majority of workers is both stressful and meaningless. There is growing scarcity of joy or pride in the work done. Old age is full of loneliness. Life has, no doubt, been prolonged, but the life-style in many places has become more like a nightmare. Single and old people living alone in their heavily locked apartments find themselves prisoners in their own homes. In our cities, the fear of being mugged is omnipresent, and the increase in police services seems to be to alleviate this little or not at all. Crime has become a commonplace that police often cannot even care about burglaries, even rape, being busy as they are with murders and other serious crimes. On top of it all, the availability of such basic goods as water, air and food is qualitatively deteriorating through environmental pollution.

The process of self-alienation which was described by Marx and Hegel had dealt with the concept of religious alienation but he did not explain the reasons for malady in society. This latter question haunted Marx and he discovered that the estrangement of man from his humanity and from his fellowmen was the reason. The most important is the alienation of labour. He wrote: The worker becomes poorer, the more wealth he produces, the more his production increases in power and extent. All this consequences follow from the fact that the worker is related to the product of his labour as an alien object. For it is clear on this pre-supposition that the more powerful becomes the world of objects which he creates in face of himself; it is just the same as in religion. The more of himself man attributes to God the less he has left in himself. The worker puts his life into the object and his life then belongs no longer to himself but to the object. The greater his activity, therefore, the less he possesses, only that his labour becomes an object, assumes an external existence, but that it exists independently, outside himself, that it stands opposed to him as an autonomous power. The life which he has given to the object sets itself against him an alien and hostile force.[16]

Marx did not combine himself to alienation of the workers or work. He was more concerned with man's alienation from himself, his fellowmen, and from nature.[17] Alienation creates sickness in man, it corrupts and perverts all human values.[18] Modern technology has further aggravated the process of self-alienation and stripped man of his human content. Man has become part as well as the product of the machine. This is inevitable. The machine penetrates into and permeates his life. Work ceases to be a joy, having been reduced to repetitions and mechanical movements.

Indeed, technology has brought comforts and pleasure to millions of people. Gandhi was not against science and technology. But what concerns him is that it has mentally and emotionally upset man and driven millions of people to "grinding pauperism". Some one asked Gandhi: "If you multiply individual production million times, would it not give you mass production on a tremendous scale? I understand that your mass production is a technical term for production by the fewest possible number through the aid of highly complicated machinery. My machine must be of the elementary type which I can put into the homes of the millions."[19]

In the poor countries, poverty stares into our face. The size of the poor population is unbelievably large. A visit to any big city in the South introduces to the visitors begging and starving children in very large number, as also mutilated bodies, dying old people and people living on the street without any amenities of shelter, food, medicine, etc. At the same time, the governments of those countries boast of growth in G.N.P., new industries, advanced technologies, and more and better higher education and research. All the analyses, estimates, and other evidences point to the fact that the poverty is on the increase both in terms of absolute number and proportions of total population.

The growth in poverty, deterioration in quality of life, instability in the monetary system, depletion of non-renewable global resources, disappearances of people, and production of weapons of mass destruction have been rationalised by policy of economic development. The elite economists and scientists, more often than not, ignore the existence of these facts. When informed of these matters, they refuse to see any relationship between these dire facts and the policies of economic growth and development advocated by them. When their advice is sought as to how these trends could be reversed, they typically argue for an acceleration of the rates of economic growth and development, i.e. more of the same. The public, on the other hand, recognising that the future is uncertain and the quality of life is deteriorating, is losing faith in such policies, not only in policies but also in ideas and conceptual framework from which these policies follow. Science, in general, and economic science, in particular, is no longer sacrosanct. The high priests of both of them are losing their authority. There is more and more of questioning of what we have learnt. There is even a desire voiced by some to return to the old good days with their traditional ways of dealing with problems. Needless to say, economic science itself is in a state of flux.

Not only are people in general losing faith in the effectiveness of economic policies and consistencies as well as ability of economic ideas to explain such reality, but economists themselves are recognising the deficiencies of economic theories and ideas. Today, it is being increasingly recognised that ideas based on the world views of Locke,

Hume, Descartes and Newton are incapable of explaining the present day reality. The real world is neither linear nor mechanistic; instead, it has all sorts of relativities. The relativity introduces many contradictions and ambiguities into concepts and arguments that considered from Newtonian logic, appear perfectly consistent. The Einsteinian Revolution, together with the new Quantum Physics, is slowly but surely making a large number of ideas, held sacrosanct for centuries, increasingly obsolete and irrelevant. Such a revolution in our world-view is not confined to physics only. We see it being diffused to other disciplines and thought process as well. One of its major effects is to remake relevant some of the cultural and religious issues long discarded by the rationalist empirical dogma.

The loss of faith in economics by economists, however, is of a different kind. There are three basic areas in economics: Micro-economics, Macro-economics, and International economics. Micro-economics deals with the process of decision making regarding supply, demand, prices, etc. at the level of individual, the family and the firm. The major ideas and theorems here deal with utility preference, production, cost function, and principles of maximisation. The object is to determine price and output of commodities and factor inputs. Macro-economics relates to the determination of national income and government policy. It involves monetary and fiscal policy, e.g., the determination of money supply, interest rate, government expenditures, taxes and subsidies, and budget deficits. The objective is to develop a process of non-inflationary high growth rate of the economy. The major school of thought here has been Keynesian. Finally, International economics attempts to understand the growth and composition in the global economy as it is affected by the interplay of various countries and economies. It deals with such issues as North-South dialogue, exchange rates, the theory of comparative advantage, tariffs, imports, exports, balance of payment, international debt and capital flow and transfers. The objective is to maximise the growth of the global economy and open up countries to international flows of commerce. There is no real consensus among the major schools of thought in this field. Instead, different schools of thought vie with each other for explaining the reality of the existing international economic order. As always, the method of economics seeks to rely on mathematical logic as well as quantifications of some of the economic relations by econometric techniques. There is always the hopeful expectations of establishing empirical facts that would reduce controversies and settle disputes between alternative theories and explanations.

Given these three areas of economics, a number of courses can be spun off by various combinations of concepts, principles, and relations involved in these areas. Thus, public finance analyses in-depth the implications of macro-economic policies of taxation, money growth, government expenditures, budget deficit, as well as micro-economic effects of the incidence of taxation. Industrial organisation employs the various degrees of elasticities in supply and demand functions, price determination under different market structures, nature of investment decisions in technology and its diffusion, etc. In labour economics, the implications of the price-auction equilibrium model are analysed within the context of the rigidities of supply and demand, different types of institutional make-up brought about by government regulations, and unionisation and historical events. Development economics studies the principles involved both in macro and international economics to determine why certain countries have not been able to achieve certain level of growth. Money and banking analyse primarily the impact of government monetary policy in the context of banking type institutions. Urban economics draws heavily from international economics, micro-economics, and macro-economics. There are various branches of economics which overlap each other when put to proper analysis and scrutiny.

In the *Bhagavadgita,* a large part of the manifest world is seen as illusion—*Maya Ka Jaal.* In economics, Keynes formulated an important part of his analysis on what he considered 'money illusion', rigidity in the downward movement in wages. Economists may suffer from their own illusion. The potential of such illusion manifests itself when we ask the question what is wrong with economics? A majority of economists readily admit that one thing or another is wrong with their discipline. In particular, many feel that there are serious problems with international and macro-economics. It is easily pointed out that in international economics, little, if any thing, really works. Since there is no accepted school in international economics, this is not that serious a criticism.

It appears that there are basically three things wrong with economics. First, there is no accepted or consistent body of knowledge in international economics. Opposite conclusions can be obtained from the same theoretical ideas: gains from trade or immiserising growth whether we get one or the other depends upon various factors. As presently constituted, international economics can be seen as a hodge-podge of some macro-economics and micro-economics, with many other things thrown in. Second, for some time in 1950s and the 1960s, thanks to war efforts, macro-economics seemed to have a predictive value even if it had no elegant theory. However in 1970s and onwards, with stagflation and deepening recessions, it lost much of that attribute and therewith much of its only defence. As Keynesian economics had little or no grounding in micro-economics, that was all that was needed for its downfall. Third, the relevance of micro-economics is grossly over estimated. In some respects, it is quite remote from reality.

No doubt, its greatest strength is in its mathematical elegance, one of the prime sources of economists' illusion. The reality, however, is catching up. Too many assumptions in micro-economics have been rendered unrealistic or untenable. Utility functions, assuming they exist, are neither independent nor transitive. Production functions are conceptually impossible to define and typically unknown to businesses involved in production. There is little flexibility in prices. Indeed, rigidity seems more generally the norm. Businesses are well known to discourage factor mobility, since such mobility tends to be incompatible with smooth production. Factor prices have little relationship with factor productivity. And, finally, as the experience of excellent companies of Japan confirms, marginal productivity is undefinable, much less quantifiable. Instead, it is common experience that productivity and efficiency result from team work and commitment grounded in guaranteed job security. Cultural factors in motivation seem more important than economic reward.

In view of the disappointing relevance of micro-economics, the theoretical problems of macro-economics and the ad hoc nature of the international economics, it is strongly felt that there is a basic need to reformulate the structure of economic thought. Such a reformulation would ideally involve the development of micro-economics based on more realistic assumptions, a mutually consistent macro-economics and microeconomics, and the extension of new macro-economics to international economics taking into consideration the realities of the world order. In view of the diversities and variations in cultures, ecologies and environments, this is perhaps an 'impossible task'. However, because of the failure of economics and the deficiencies of existing economic ideas, a search for such a reformulation remains most important. This is more important for a country like India which has suffered more and for a longer time than most others under the economic doctrines imported from the West.

On 22nd December 1916, Gandhi spoke before an economic society in Allahabad. The title of his address was 'Does Economic Progress Clash With Real Progress'. Right at the outset he felt it necessary to warn his audience, explaining:

Frankly and truly I know little of economics, as you naturally understand it. Only the other day, sitting at an evening meal, a civilian friend deluged me with a series of questions on my crankisms. As he proceeded in his cross-examination, I being a willing victim, he found no difficulty in discovering my gross ignorance of the matters. I appeared to him to be handling with a cocksureness worthy only of a man who knows not that he knows not. To his horror and even indignation, I suppose, he found that I had not even read books on economics by such well known authorities as Mill, Marshall, Smith, and host of other such authors. In despair, he ended by advising me to read these books before experimenting in matters economic at the expense of trusting friends. But there comes to us moments in life when about somethings, we need no proof from without. A little voice within us, you are on the right track, turn neither to your left nor right, but keep to the straight and narrow way. With such help we march forward, slowly indeed, but surely and steadily. That is my position.[20]

In the major part of his address, Gandhi first argued that material advance has a strong tendency to lead a moral decay. Then he proposed: 'You cannot serve God and Mammon' in an economic truth of the highest value. We have to make a choice. Western nations are groaning under the heel of a monster, God of materialism. He pleaded for an ideal economy where there is more truth than gold, and greater charity than love of the self. Concludingly, in his address, he admonished his audience: 'Let us seek first the kingdom of God and His righteousness, and the irrevocable promise is that everything will be added unto us. These are real economics. May you and I treasure them and enforce them in our daily life'.[21]

An examination of his above-mentioned lecture clearly points to what he knew rather than what he did know. He was not interested in the scope and method of economic science as we economists naturally understand it. Rather he worked for a whole life time on articulating the principles of an alternative and "more real" human economy centring on the themes outlined in his lecture. The lack of correlation between material expansion and genuine process, the need for an economics-cum-ethics that will enable moral growth and dignity for all, the fallacy of seeking happiness in individual acquisitive behaviour, and the need for encouraging people to seek a life rich in self-esteem and genuine meaning.

It is in this new context that the study of Gandhi, his philosophy of economics and his methods, has suddenly become relevant and urgent. Looking back, one is amazed at the acute understanding of each of the problems by Mahatma Gandhi. He dealt with some problems more intensively than others but never lost sight of anyone of them. He denounced the concept of an economic man because he refused to recognise the separation of economics from ethics. He denounced the technological determinism because it enslaved man and sanctified only those technologies that conformed to value premises. Above all, he struggled against the mightiest imperial power in terms of a non-violent theory and order. As he went long with these tasks, he discovered his own science of economics though he did not analyse it in very vigorous manner.[22]

Since every social science has dominant paradigms which are not only historically relativistic but also culture-bound, it is difficult to pin point any mature Gandhian paradigms or, for that matter, to indicate a single paradigm dominated science. But all the concepts are there and the right methods are also available. Since all the paradigms are in a state of crisis, there is an implicit recognition of the relevance of Gandhian approach. And yet one must accept that at the hands of the Gandhians, the Gandhian economics still remains immature. The word 'immature' may be defined as reflecting the numerous ill-defined paradigms. However, the superiority of Gandhian approach and concept lies in their in-built dynamics and close relations with praxis implying that once on a Gandhian path, not only is the system put on the path of steady growth, its moral legitimacy also does not remain in doubt any longer.

Gandhi's strong point was that he refused to build any systematic model because all models become static after having their full run. But he systematically went about initiating, developing, and perfecting open-minded concepts which were amenable and adequate to produce many models, that is, models for given context, situation, and society.

Gandhian method was both scientific and moral. But it was scientific only in the sense in which Thomas Kuhn has used the phrase. The critique of prevailing paradigm on the basis of its internal contradictions and empirical evidence is not enough for its rejection unless a new and alternative paradigm is conceptual and empirically assumes the force of calling for the rejection of earlier paradigm. But without a moral dimension, it is difficult to prove the superiority or greater validity of one paradigm over other. What was scientific has become vulgar empiricism. In his life and political activities, Gandhi simultaneously adopted both the approaches and only when he was convinced of the double validity of a new concept or paradigm would he call for the rejection of the old. In his case, one must always make distinction between the critique and the rejection. Yet it is undisputable that most of Gandhi's primary concepts, including the sanctity of labour, truth, self-sacrifice, justice based on fellow-feeling, trusteeship, priority for care for the poor, importance of a moral political economy and emphasis on human needs can all be found to be more relevant in the existing socio-economic scenario within and outside the nation.

NOTES

1. Prof. Samuelson, 1973. p. 830.
2. Eric Roll, 1953. p. 32.
3. Taylor, 1960. p. 81.
4. Roll, 1953. p. 173.
5. Prof. Boulding, 1969.
6. Robbins, 1932. pp. 4-5.
7. Robbins, 1932. p. 15.
8. Boulding, 1969. p. 123.
9. Baumol, 1958.
10. J. D. Sethi, Foreword, *Essays in Gandhian Economics* (Ed.) Ramesh Diwan & Mark Lutz.
11. *Ibid.,* p. XVI.
12. *Ibid.,* p. XVIII.
13. An Article entitled, "*Industrialism, Khadi Gramodyog*", Bombay, Vol. 11, May, 1965, p. 572.
14. *Ibid.* p. XXI.
15. *Ibid.*
16. Jayaprakash Narayan, *Socialism, Sarvodaya, and Democracy,* p.163.
17. Karl Marx (1961): *Economic and Philosophy Manuscript,* Moscow, pp. 95-96.
18. Erich Fromm (1963): *Beyond the Chains of Illusions,'* New York, p. 48.
19. *Ibid.,* p. 52.
20. Louis Fisher (1954): *Gandhi: His Life and Message for the World,* New York, pp. 84-85.
21. Ramesh Diwan & Mark Lutz, Introduction, *Essays in Gandhian Economics,* p. 9
22. *Ibid.*

4

Gandhian Alternative to Planning and Development

> Poverty results from increase of man's desires, not from diminution of his property.
>
> —Plato

> The best state for human nature is that in which, while no one is poor, no one desires to be richer, nor has any reason to fear being thrust back by the efforts of others to push themselves forward.
>
> —John Staurt Mill

The ultimate social order envisioned by the Gandhian Economic Theory will have as its goal the promotion of happiness of all material as well as non-material, which comes through general acceptance of higher values of life, that is subordination of self, self-realization, which consists in destroying the ego and regarding his own interest as identical with that of others. All economic and political activity will be spiritualized. The creed of the multiplication of wants as the spur to economic activity characteristic of the present day capitalist economies and materialistic outlook, state control and indifference to purity of means characteristic of socialist economies are both rightly regarded as the bane of modern civilization.[1]

The former leads, among others, to accumulation of riches and concentration of means of production in the hand of a few amidst mass poverty and deprivation in a major part of the world while the latter destroys individuality and human dignity and glorifies use of force and violence. The Gandhian Economic Theory aims at a radical reconstruction of the economy on the basis of need-based, as opposed to want-based, activities and that ensures lasting happiness and social harmony. J.K. Mehta's views that, "our life is an attempt to free ourselves from the bondage of wants and to attain *Nirwana* is the fundamental truth" and that economics is a "science that studies human behaviour as the efforts to minimize pain in the long run and endeavour to gain freedom from wants,[2] may be taken as representing the situation in the Gandhian social order. Contentment with simple ways of life and techniques of production and making virtue of curtailment of wants and austerity so long emphasized by our sages and saints are put forth as the key to human happiness, spiritual calm and welfare and, therefore, the quintessence of the new social order.

Before discussing the basic elements of Gandhian economic thinking, the background of the prevailing economic scenario becomes very important. The situation is not very encouraging either at national or global plane. The growth in poverty, deterioration in quality of life, instability in the international monetary system, depletion of non-renewable resources, police atrocities and production of weapons of mass destruction have been rationalized by policies of economic growth and economic development. The elite economists and scientists have generally ignored existence of these facts. When informed of these facts, they have found no relationship between these facts in real world and the policies of economic growth and development. When their advice has been sought as to how these trends can be reversed, they argued for the acceleration of the rates of growth. The public, on the other hand, recognizes that the future is uncertain and quality of life is deteriorating, and has lost faith in such policies, not only in policies but also in ideas, from which such policies follow. Science in general and economic science in particular, is no more sacrosanct. That high priest has lost his authority. There is questioning of the existing return to old and search for new ideas.

Not only are people in general loosing faith in the effectiveness of economic policies and the consistency as well as capacity of economic policies to explain such reality even economists themselves are recognizing the deficiencies of economic theories and ideas. The public perceptions about failure of economics arise from such phenomena as high deficits, high inflation, high interest rates, high unemployment and recession, and visible decline in the standard of living. Even economists agree that there is something wrong with economics. The problems were highlighted by J.K. Galbraith, who talked about private affluence and public poverty as the central crisis of the developed capitalist system.

The global crisis led to the realization that some alternatives to existing economic thoughts and theories may be evolved to provide relief to the suffering masses all over the world, which is characterized by an oasis of affluence in the vast desert of poverty. Here it becomes relevant to consider Gandhian concept of economic ideas afresh.

The real world is full of real people, people of flesh and blood, people who have good nature and bad nature, people who care for others and cooperate. Love, affection, compassion, sentiment are vital aspects of human personality. People are not only physical existence or reality, they are also manifestation of psychological, mental aptitudes. Families are bound by ties of love, so are groups of people, tribes and nations. Self and society are inseparable. Harmonious relationship is required. Symbiotic relationship between man, society and nature is essential to impact harmony and cohesion.

In Gandhi's words, "I claim that even now, though the social structure is not based on conscious acceptance of nonviolence, all the world over mankind lives and men retain their possession on the sufferance of one another. If they had not done so, only the fewest and the most ferocious would survive".[3] What is more, people make sacrifices; just as opposite of self-interest. It is common for parents to make sacrifices for their children and *vice versa.* Hardly a day passes when people do not discover, even in the urban getto and jungles, the human kindness. Conventional economics misses this reality. No wonder it is out of touch.

What is needed is to formulate a different economics, an economics based on love, sharing the truth instead of the conventional economics based on greed, envy, hatred and falsehood. Gandhi laid the basic ideas of such an economics of love, truth and non-violence. It starts from the fundamental assumptions that human beings are good, decent, moral, cooperative and nonviolent. The objectives of such economics are to build on the brotherly and sisterly love for each other to the extent the love of the family to the love of humanity. There is now growing literature on Gandhian Economics. This literature is based on the idea that the thought and practices of Gandhi provide a complete, if not fully, articulated basis of economic theory. Two points need to be emphasized at this stage. Gandhian economics and thought, in spite of its emphasis on local level, relate to the global economy. It is universal. The global issues are highly related to the local issues. This inter-relationship follows from Gandhian propositions regarding the existing reality; namely (i) there is an elite-mass contradiction in every society; and (ii) in this elite mass division the national elites exploit national masses and international elites exploit masses all over the world. Elite mass contradiction is fundamental to Gandhian thought and analysis. So long as this contradiction exists anywhere it can disrupt and destroy a Gandhian economy and society. Secondly, analysis in Gandhian economy is based on a theoretical construct. This theoretical construct is similar to theoretical construct in neo-classical economics. Such as "equilibrium", "Pareto optimality", i.e. theoretical constructs do not relate directly to existing reality. Theoretical construct is an unrealistic assumption. In view of the general lack of familiarity with the ideas of Gandhian economics, one might argue that this theoretical construct is an unrealistic assumption. It is an idealized Gandhian society.[4] The arguments, however, would be similar if one were to say that equilibrium, perfect competition, etc. are unrealistic. Yet, in neo-classical economics, one would hardly go very far without these assumptions.

From the elite mass contradiction it follows, the society is divided into two sub-societies, (i) the elite society, and (ii) the mass society. The elite society is made up of a small part of the population. Its members are elites, economically rich, politically powerful, urbanized, educated in elite institutions, etc. The society defines its own class. The elite society has the control of instruments that give this society the power to make all sorts of decisions, economic and non-economic, such as to arm some groups and disarm others, to prosecute certain crimes while ignoring others, to produce certain goods and not others, to invest, to tax, to subsidize, etc. Even though the elite society controls the instruments of decision making power, it cannot exist by itself. In this regard, it is parasite. It needs the other, the mass society, fundamentally to maintain its status and privileges.

The mass society is made up of the bulk of the population. These are politically powerless, economically poor and mostly exploited. Yet, this is the society, which provides manpower for production of all goods and services, for military and police etc. Generally, this mass society suffers from the lack of all sorts of goods and services and opportunities. These two sub-societies are distinguished by four characteristics: economic, political, elitism and exploitation. These may also be distinguished by the possession or lack of privilege; the elite society is the privileged society. Obviously, there is a lot of interaction between these two sub-societies. These interactions promote its own dynamics which further sharpens the elite-mass contradiction.

The objective of Gandhian economics is to understand the forces and interrelationships that would lead a society or economy towards the idealized Gandhian society. This idealized Gandhian society is one in which the mass-elite condition is ultimately resolved. In other words, in this Gandhian society there are no elites and no masses. Furthermore, social and economic institutions promote the movement towards the idealized society and help maintain it in its idealized form.

Any attempt to understand the Gandhian perspective, in general, and also his economic views in particular, will have to fully appreciate two books so profoundly influenced his world view and continued to shape his ideas throughout his life. One is the *Bhagavadgita,* a sacred text of Hinduism. To him, the *Gita* was not a description of a real battle scene but of the struggle between the two natures in us, the good and the evil. It is the description of the eternal duel going on within ourselves given so vividly as to make us think for the time being that the deeds therein were actually done by the human being. In the eyes of Gandhi, the text provides a complete and reasoned moral code which satisfies the intellect as well as the heart. To him, *Gita* meant the realization that "life is given to us for service and not for enjoyment". We have all, by virtue of being human beings, an innate duty *(Swadharma)* to serve Truth by serving our fellowmen and the life process in general such action *(Karmayoga)* is to be performed detached from the consequences and expected results to the agent. It involves self-sacrifice *(Yajna)* for the welfare of others. By so rising above self-interest, we fulfil our cosmic destiny and become integrated with the true self within us.[5]

The other book that deeply influenced Gandhi was *Unto This Last* by John Ruskin. This book in his own words "brought about an instantaneous and practical transformation in my life". Ruskin was humanistic critic of John Stuart Mill, whose utilitarian orientation Ruskin relentlessly attacked. It is undisputable that most of Gandhi's primary concepts, including sanctity of labour, truth and self-sacrifice, justice based on fellow-feeling, trusteeship, priority of care for poor, importance of moral political economy, and emphasis on human needs, can all be found in one form or another in *Unto This Last.*[6] It was, however, left to Gandhi to really develop these concepts into full-fledged system of human economy.

Gandhian perspective of economics can be divided into four basic domains. There is emphasis on economics as a moral science, there is reconstruction of economic foundation, there is the novel contribution to economic theory, and finally, there are the more practical insights into economic policy.

Economics as a Moral Science

Many conventional economists rooted either in neo-classical or the Marxist tradition still take pride that economics is a positive science meaning that it observes and describes what is rather than engaging in supposedly unscientific methods have learnt to question this traditional doctrine and readily grant the meaninglessness and impossibility of presenting a supposedly value-free-science. Whether we like it or not, values are always present either in an explicit or in an implicit form. Good sciences, therefore, need to operate with good values.

Gandhi involved himself with the construction of a new normative economics. At one time he claimed: " That economics is untrue which ignores or disregards moral values". A normative economics of Gandhian style that intertwines economics and ethics into one inseparable whole reflects a vertical, multidimensional image of man where both material and spiritual forces need to embrace each other in the human quest for unity and wholeness.

This integrated and holistic perspective in economics boils down to this simple injunction;[7] never advocate actions or policies that lead to material advancement at the cost of social, moral or spiritual impoverishment. Instead, the economist as the holistic economist should ascertain that his organisational principles and policies enable, possibly even encourage, a higher or overall quality of life for all.

Reconstruction of the Economic Foundations

The first principle of economics is that very agent is actuated only by self-interest. Economist took it for granted for a pretty long period. Once it is recognized that the public good is at times not secured by maximization of private self-interest, but by self-restraint or even self-sacrifice. Adam Smith's legacy of the invisible hand loses much of its glamour. At the same time, economists are pushed to entertaining new thoughts on what kind of action does lead to social welfare, Gandhian economics had to be seen as an attempt to go beyond self-interest-based economics.

Just as building economic theory around the notion of utilitarian self-interest, mobility and competition, so does a non-self-interest economics emphasizes the social virtues of loyalty and cooperation. No other Gandhian concept illustrates this better than that of Swadeshi, "the spirit in us which restricts us to the use and service of our immediate surroundings to the exclusion of the more remote". Clearly, then, Gandhian economics is not built around the abstract notion of atomistic rational economic man who ceaselessly calculates the pros and cons of actions to determine when his own advantage is maximized. The concept of economic man is even more unfitting with the framework of normative economics. Gandhi replaced the utilitarian guide articulated by Bentham during nineteenth century, which called for "the greatest happiness of the greatest number", by the welfare of all, Sarvodaya, expressing what Ruskin tried to communicate through his *Unto This Last*. A more literal translation would have been *Antyodaya* rather than *Sarvodaya*. Yet, to Gandhi, the latter subsumed the former and something more, the need to give the rich uplift too.

Sarvodaya is a full-fledged alternative to the utilitarian goal of using an existing resource base for the output of goods available for consumption. No doubt, deep in Gandhian economics we find the implicit notion that every human being has the right to live decently. The special fundamental feature of Gandhian economics to promote higher human capacities was also eloquently recognized by late EF Schumacher, the author of *Small is Beautiful,* when he wrote in a foreword to a book on trusteeships: "If you want a good society, you must appeal to the goodness that is in people, provoke it, stimulate it, take it for granted and acclaim it".

It has been focused on the basic transformation that economics undergoes with the fresh metaphysical outlook of Gandhi. There are six basic elements that are essential in Gandhian economics. These are all related to each other. There is no hierarchy among them. They are *Swadeshi,* bread labour, non-possession, trusteeship, non-exploitation and equality. Of all these elements, *Swadeshi,* no doubt, attracts the greatest attention.

Practical Insights into Policy Issues

What is also necessary to discuss Gandhi's insight into macro-economic issues more specifically the economics of employment and growth, development and international trade, as well as his insights into intrinsic limitation of the Marxian alternative. Much of Gandhian economics discussed so far is only thoroughly understandable once its metaphysical and spiritual ground is fully appreciated. But it needs to be stressed that several of Gandhi's other contributions can also be understood and found meaningful without a direct reference to his spiritual ethical outlook. This is also true of his economic theory of growth and development as well as his theory of structural unemployment.

The conventional development strategy emphasises that development is to occur by means of capital-intensive technologies replacing the traditional labour-intensive activities and with it the gradual elimination of the limited exchange system of traditional village economies. It is here that the Gandhian perspective differs radically and sheds much additional light. Rather than focusing on the growth of the urban sector, he foresaw the central and ever-worsening problem of the stagnation and decay of the traditional sector resulting directly from such modernization and the single minded stress of urban capital-intensive development. By what is today known as the "backwash effect" much of the indigenous skills and crafts get destroyed by the new market competition of mass-produced consumption goods, whether foreign or domestic. Gandhian macro-economics has to be seen as the giving priority to investment in labour-intensive occupations of the traditional sector. 'Production by the masses replaces mass production. Gandhi ardently advocated the 'appropriate technology' as distinct from the conventional stress on 'least cost technology'. In the process, he outlines the several conditions that make a technology 'appropriate', i.e. both nonviolent and non-exploitative.[8]

Absolutely central to Gandhi was his notion of the essential difference between man and what he called 'the brute'. Human beings do not only have the need to survive, employing the needs for food and shelter, but they also have the need to exercise their capacity to care for others. Above all, there is an inborn quest that characterizes everyman as man, a quest for life fulfilment, a quest for Truth. Gandhi elevated absolute Truth to the status of the highest value by equating Truth with the concept of God.

There are certain axioms on which foundations of Gandhian economics stand:

(a) Truth *(Satya)* exists in and beyond man in an absolute eternal, and living sense. Nothing else exists besides it. Truth, not man, is the measure of all things.

(b) The purpose of all life and evolution is to realize Truth. For mankind, this translates into biological need for self-realization, to know one's self.

(c) Truth is the end, and *ahimsa,* i.e. self-giving one, is the means; Truth and love are ultimately two sides of the same coin.

(d) Human truth is always relative. Truth, as we can apprehend it, is always personal, subjective, and to that extent, relative to our individual context of culture and history.[9]

From these four basic philosophical axioms emphasizing self-giving love as the key to the realization of Truth. The following fundamental premises are given below which pertain to Gandhian economic thought:

(a) Economics, ethics, politics and religion constitute an indivisible whole. In the words of Gandhi:

> "True economics never militates against the highest ethical standard, just as all true ethics to be worth its name must sometimes be also good economics. An economics that inculcates Mammon worship, and enable the strong to amass wealth at the expense of the weak, is false and dismal science. It spells death."[10]

(b) Economics is the science of human welfare. Its goal ought to be *Sarvodaya,* the welfare of all.

(c) The supreme consideration has to be man. Economic theory that ignores the human element of social affection is meaningless.

(d) Human welfare economics focusing on what Gandhi called the 'human element' implies the crucial importance of a decentralized social economy. The ideal is a community economy allowing for a living interaction, mutual access, and voluntary cooperation of all its members.

(e) Economics has to respect the law of *Swadeshi.*

(f) At the very core of Gandhian economics is the concept of rationality. Gandhi broadens the concept to involve harmonious action of body, mind and soul. Rational action is guided by the inner faculty of conscience which he calls inner voice.

Within the context of these foundational premises, we can easily derive the principles of Gandhian economic thought. They have to be seen in relation to each other and to their background of foundational premises and axioms in order to have relevant meaning.[11]

There are six basic concepts that are essential in Gandhian economics. They are all equally important. They are: (i) *Swadeshi,* (ii) bread-labour, (iii) *aparigrah* or non-possession, (iv) trusteeship, (v) non-exploitation, and (vi) equality.[12]

The basic elements in *Swadeshi* principle can be stated in the following two propositions; one, an individual consumer will reduce his/her wants and reorder preference function such that it is made up mostly of goods produced in the neighbourhood defined in terms of community. Two, the consumer will cooperate with neighbour producer/workers to produce the goods efficiently. The emphasis here is on cooperation between producer and consumer. Contrary to the existing situation where efficiency is determinded by competition between producers, in *Swadeshi* efficiency is ensured via cooperation between the producer and consumer neighbour. The *Swadeshi* principle leads to a downward shift in the cost functions.

Swadeshi may be translated as self-reliance. It follows from the concept of *swaraj.* There are various interpretation of *Swadhshi.* Some interpret it narrowly as "autarky" or self-sufficiency.[13] The question is: how some apply the concept of *Swadeshi* to a nation? The problem and misunderstanding arise from this question itself. A more meaningful question is: how would *Swaraj* look like without *Swadeshi*? If *Swadeshi* is essential to *Swaraj,* then how does one go about introducing it in the transitional state? The interpretation of *Swadeshi* as "self-reliance" provides a clue to this question. Macro-economic implications of *Swadeshi* are obvious in reality. *Swadeshi* principle involves that the consumer neighbour encourages the producer neighbour to produce goods efficiently. If one adds the activities of all such producers in community two conclusions follow: (i) The community as a whole is able to produce virtually all the goods needed by it; unless, of course, such production is not possible for either technical or resources reasons. (ii) The community as a whole would reproduce all it can at the least social cost. After all, the producer neighbour has to ensure that the consumer neighbour can obtain the goods. The total effect is that the community will have a surplus production. The validity of this fact is corroborated by a visit to such community anywhere in the world. It is no mere accident that peasants and simple communities are able to share their production freely with the outsiders and visitors who visit them. The anthropologists have been particularly impressed by this fact and have commended them regularly.[14]

If we translate this idea in the language of trade, we find that *Swadeshi,* at the micro-economic level, implies two propositions. One, the country needs to import little. It imports only those goods it cannot produce. Two, it has an exportable surplus. Many critics of *Swadeshi* have misinterpreted this concept as autarky because they have concentrated on propositions one only and missed proposition two completely.

Bread-labour provides the ethical dimension to *Swadeshi* at the level of personal action. One cannot be self-reliant if one cannot produce the necessities of living by one's own labour. It is possible that one cannot obtain one's necessities from other person. However, this is possible only under two different conditions; (a) one can become dependent on others; or (b) one can exploit others. Both are unacceptable since they involve violence, alienation and dehumanization. Hence, the importance of bread-labour is self-evident. The question is: What is bread-labour? Is it the time spent by one person in obtaining goods that can be later exchanged for the desired necessities themselves? Bread-labour defines a particular composition of the production in the country. In its purest form, the production in a country following principle of bread-labour will consist of value-in-use only. Production for the value-in-exchange will get place where it is technically necessary and socially viable. There will be little, if any, value-in-threat. It is, again, no accident that such economies have regularly suffered attacks from outsiders. Since these communities and countries did not produce value-in-threat, they were not in a good position to fight back a well-organized enemy. This is true even today. The poor producers who produce value-in-use only are the most vulnerable in the modern society; what they have and produce is desired and needed by everyone. Since they do not produce value-in-threat, they remain vulnerable.[15]

It is again no accident that victors impose the production of value-in-use on their victims, partly because the victors need them, (Indigo Cultivation in Champaran), partly because victims cannot mount back a threat. Thus, after Second World War, both Germany and Japan were not allowed to develop their war machines, euphemistically called defence department. In view of this, bread-labour is a global principle. If the world community as a whole adopts it, the value-in-threat are not produced and the question of victor and vanquished or enemies does not arise.

The rejection of the individual dictum: I own, therefore I am as John Dewey calls it. *Aparigrah* means possession by all. The principles implied in the concept of *aparigrah* are as follows: (i) the welfare of an individual person depends not only on consumption of commodities but also on service to other fellow beings, (ii) the utility apace, defined by consumption of goods alone is limited. On the other hand, welfare obtainable from service is limited, (iii) the object is not to maximize utility or consumption goods. Being limited, maximization of utility is not a meaningful objective. The objective, instead, is to obtain a certain level of utility. The underlying principle is 'contentment' or 'enough' as against greed and 'more and more.'

Accordingly, *aparigrah* defines a demand relationship between price and consumption. However, this demand function is somewhat different from that of a neo-classical demand function. In this demand function there are two limits given by a maximum and minimum consumption. There is certain level, beyond which consumption of a commodity will not increase. There is certain level of consumption that everyone will obtain whether the person has income or not.[16]

Aparigrah or non-possession follows from the truth and non-violence. It involves that a person should not possess anything that one does not need. The Gandhian concept of theft is based on *aparigrah.* Accordingly, anyone who possesses things and objects not needed by oneself but needed by others is a theft. There is an essential concept of *Swaraj,* because it brings it to the most coveted state: 'to each according to his need'. This also implies institutional reforms. The whole concept of private ownership of property—where property is distinguished from tools—comes under sharp questioning. It becomes obvious that non-possession is not compatible with capitalism. Gandhian has been misunderstood and misinterpreted by Marxist as a defender of private property and as being soft on capitalism. Clearly, the concept of *aparigrah* is the strongest denunciation of capitalist system.

Aparigrah relates to consumption. The object is not maximum consumption but 'enough'. It imposes maximum level of consumption for the community or economy. Thus, consumerism is not consistent with *aparigrah.* In view of the limits to consumption, the economy would exhibit a high rate of savings. Growth will be promoted through capital accumulation which will result into more saving than to more consumption. The rate of growth of savings will increase the growth of output, unless, of course, one is starting from a very low level of consumption which does not satisfy even the basic minimum needs of the society. The principle of *aparigrah* will lead to a redistribution of total output between public and private consumption. Private consumption based on primarily material goods will reach a limit while public consumption would grow. The effect is to create a society where there is private and public affluence.

Trusteeship follows from and is built on the concept of non-possession. Non-possession may also be considered as a form of nonviolence; if possession involves violence. By trusteeship is meant that all those people who possess things as well as capabilities, abilities or other natural gifts, must hold these possessions as trustees for all others. In others words, they should not derive the benefits from these possessions for themselves. On the contrary, the possession brings immediately an obligation. Possession is a burden.

The concept of trusteeship is derived from the highest moral principles of service to others. In Gandhi's own words, "what belongs to me is the right to an honourable livelihood; no better than enjoyed by millions of others. The rest of my wealth belongs to the community and must be used for the welfare of community".[17]

In other words, the endowments of better ability and larger resources do not allow the person the privilege of using these for personal gain. Instead, these are obligations to the community. The ethical proposition is that these endowments are given to a person as a 'trust' and these have to be used for the benefit of all. As can be appreciated, this principle is contrary to the principle of 'incentives' and places major limitations on property rights. In this respect, trusteeship involves a relationship between privilege and access to power. This relationship is negative, the greater the access to power, trusteeship principle implies a lower level of privilege and vice versa. In view of this, trusteeship implies decentralization.[18] Decentralization follows from the fact that trusteeship imposes a negative relationship between economic privilege and political or other power. The more power one has to exploit, the less privilege one obtains till one becomes economically underprivileged. Trusteeship, thus, poses a limit to power and its use.

E.F. Schumacher's foreword to the *Equality Through Trusteeship and Full Employment* holds that the theory of capitalism and private enterprise suggests that the only way to run an economy efficiently is to let everyone pursue mainly, if not exclusively, his own advantage. The theory of communism is that the economy works best when everybody acts according to central plan for the public interest. Both the theories are plausible enough, but in practice they work badly. Hence, Mahatma Gandhi put forward his trusteeship model in 1945 in which he proposed, the individual will be free to make as much money as he likes but will not be free to hold or use his wealth for selfish satisfaction or in disregard to the interest of the society. To make these possible, the character of production at the same time would be determined by social necessity and not by personal whims of greed.

Schumacher illustrates few of his sayings on this subject:

— Earn your crore by all means but understand that your wealth is not yours, it belongs to the people. Take what you require for your legitimate needs and use the remainder for the society.
  Those who own money now are asked to behave like trustees holding their riches on behalf of the poor.
— Absolute trusteeship is an abstraction like Euclid's definition of points and is equally unattainable. But if we strive for it, we shall be able to go further in realizing a state of equality on earth than by any other means.
— The rich man will be left in possession of his wealth he will use what he reasonably requires for his personal needs and will act as a trustee for the remainder to be used for the society. In this arrangement honesty on the part of the trustee is assumed.
— By the non-violent method we seek not to destroy capitalist. We seek to destroy capitalism. We invite the capitalist to regard himself as a trustee for those on whom he depends for the making the retentions and the increase of his capital.
— Wherever we may be situated, we cannot go on with warfare, confrontations and the prevailing separations of economics and politics from any kind of ethical responsibility. The attempt to operate a social system on the basis of no other principles than those of GAINS and POWER has failed and can never succeed. It is not possible to desire a system which will produce good results without goodness on the part of the people within it.[19]

Non-exploitation involves the reduction and eventual elimination of privilege. These three types of privileges may be distinguished:

(i) privilege of non-accountability, (ii) privilege of easy opportunities, and (iii) economic privilege. These three privileges, though analytically distinct, are not independent of each other. On the contrary, these are highly interrelated, one promoting the other. The basis of elite-mass contradiction lies in the concept of exploitation. Non-exploitation, thus, involves the reduction in this elite-mass contradiction.[20]

The concept of non-exploitation and trusteeship determines the nature of institutions that generate the environment conducive to Gandhian economic principle. Non-exploitation involves eliminating privileges of all kinds. Trusteeship can refer to management techniques and style. The Japanese management seems to incorporate some of the principles of trusteeship. The level of hierarchy is less, the job in the corporation is secure and for life, the emphasis is on team and cooperative work, specialization is discourged, security is respected. In other words, Japanese management is based on the family system where the senior members consider it a trust rather than a source of income and privilege.

Non-exploitation follows straightforwardly from the concept of nonviolence. One cannot exploit without doing violence. It is both a simple and complex concept. The complexity arises particularly from the nature of society all the world over today. Some people maintain that both the Marxist and capitalistic societies, as constituted today, have institutionalized exploitation, particularly in the production of goods and services. In view of the inequalities and the prevalence of alienation, the very concept of market may be exploitative.

Equality follows from and ensures non-exploitation. Exploitation among equals is not possible. Questions have been raised; what is equality? Is it equality of opportunities only? Looking at the other concepts, we feel that equality in the Gandhian system involves "all possible achievable equality". It is something more than equality of opportunity. It does accept differences in natural gifts. But this is a part of diversity and not a question of equality.

Equality is an objective social policy. Not only do principles of *Swadeshi,* bread-labour and *aparigrah* promote equality, the society itself formulates redistribution policies that bring about equality. In Mondragon, the formula is 3:1, i.e. the maximum range of earnings differentials is set at three to one. In other words, the gross earnings of the highest paid cooperation can never be more than three-folds of those of the lowest paid. In modern society, on the other hand, inequality is the rule and is encouraged. The difference between the lowest paid is many thousand times. In India, a rich person can spend in one evening what it may take a four persons to earn in a life time. Japan and Sweden are considered to be economies where inequalities are less; the bottom 20 per cent of the population has 10 per cent of total income, while top 20 per cent have 30 per cent of total income. In other market economies, it is worse, top 20 per cent account for approximately 50 per cent of the total income, which has crossed 70 per cent in the last decade. If India should be able to move along the path of equality through trusteeship, she could be a beacon to the world. By bringing in to life again the best of her marvelous traditional teachings, she could become the most modern nation while remaining faithful to her. In the context of economic development, this means that the conscious striving for equality through trusteeship must be matched and paralleled by an equally conscious striving for the evolution of appropriate technologies. It is a grave error to assume that technology is neutral factor in socio-political affairs; that there is a simple way of distinguishing 'better' from 'worse' and that the latest is always likely to be the 'best'. Technology is anything but 'neutral'. It is the most powerful political force, shaping and moulding society into its own image. Technologies evolved during the last century are now the strongest force pressing all societies to adopt them into the mould of Western capitalism. They are opposite of what Gandhi considered good for the people at large. If we are interested in 'economics as if people matter', we must work for technologies as if people mattered or you might say technologies with a human face. Once created they will try trusteeship and pave the way towards equality. To create them swiftly and effectively requires the ethical climate of trusteeship.[21]

Contemporary society is characterized by a growing distrust of technology. The many social benefits which technology has helped bring about are being increasingly counter balanced by the social problems associated with its use. These range from the oppression and manipulation of the individuals to the wide spread destruction of the natural environment and the depletion of the world's finite supply of natural resources. At the same time, man's technological skills have so far failed to provide effective solutions to many of the world's major problems, in particular those of mass poverty, starvation and international conflicts, rather they have aggravated the situation. Technology is no longer seen as the omnipotent God to take care of all the problems of mankind.[22]

Technology is never value neutral. It plays a political role in society, a role intimately related to the distribution of power and the exercise of social control. In both the senses, i.e. material and ideological fashion, technological development is essentially a political process. At material level, technology sustains and promotes the interest of the dominant social group of the society within which it is developed. At the same time, it acts in a symbolic manner to support and propagate the legitimating ideology of the society, the interpretation that is placed on the world and on the individual's position in it. Both material and ideological factors play an important part in determining the nature of technology itself.[23]

Thus, it becomes imperative to evolve alternative technology popularly known as appropriate technology to resolve the outstanding problems of poverty, unemployment, exploitation and alienation. This technology would embrace the tools, machines, and techniques necessary to reflect and maintain non-oppressive and non-manipulative modes of social production, and a non-exploitative relationship to the natural environment.

In the simple terms the basic principles of Gandhian economic programme are the following:

(i) Avoidance of mechanization and encouragement of cottage industries, specially spinning and weaving;
(ii) improvement of rural small-scale agriculture;
(iii) making the village community as much self-sufficient and self-reliant as practicable;
(iv) decentralization of administrative and economic structure;
(v) reducing income inequalities by raising the income level among the poor and by changing the attitude and motivation of the rich; and
(vi) ensuring that the capitalist and big business men serve as trustees.[24]

One of the significant contributions of Gandhi to Indian economic thought is in the area of the development strategy, he has recommended for countries like India which is based on his understanding of the phenomenon of poverty and the possible solutions for the removal of poverty. In this connection, his ideas on modernization, urbanization, industrialization, investment planning, foreign trade and technology are quite valuable. At the level of economic analysis, Gandhi identifies the cause of growing mass poverty in underdeveloped economies as the result of two kinds of errors in the decision making of the elite, which controls the mobilization and allocation of investment resources. The first error consists in an attempt to technology modernize faster than the conditions of the economy permit. This error is further compounded by an attempt to use the international trade mechanism in an accumulationist pattern thus increasing the capital intensity of the investment mix. These two errors lead to a situation in which the available resources for investment prove insufficient to generate sufficient new employment. Less developed countries like India have the necessity of breaking from the development strategy of the rich country and following the basic ideas behind the Gandhian development strategy, viz. (i) redirection of investment flows towards the more labour-intensive sectors of activities and the adoption of certain criteria concerning technological innovations; and (ii) making progress towards a collaborative economic order.[25]

Gandhian approach to investment planning is superior to the conventional system since it avoids the problems involved in choice between the present and future, it may be said that there are significant contributions of Gandhi to economic theory in terms of both the content and the methods as well as towards policy making which is relevant in the context of economic development in India.

NOTES

1. J.K. Mehta, *Gandhian Thought,* p. 137.
2. J.K. Mehta, *Advanced Economics,* p. 17.
3. Mahatma Gandhi (1966): *Socialism of My Conception,* Bharatiya Vidya Bhawan, 866, p. 15.
4. Diwan Ramesh & Mark Lutz (1985): *Essays in Gandhian Economics.*
5. *Op. cit.,* p. 11.
6. *Ibid.,* p. 12.
7. *Ibid.,* p. 13.
8. *Ibid.,* p. 24.
9. Mark Lutz, Human Nature in Gandhian Economics in *Essays in Gandhian Economics* (Ed), Diwan & Mark Lutz, p. 38.
10. *Collected Works of Mahatma Gandhi,* Vol. VI, 1968, pp. 321-322.
11. *Ibid.*
12. Diwan & Gidwani, Elements of Gandhian Economics, In *Essays in Gandhian Economics* by Diwan & Mark Lutz, p. 56.
13. J.D. Sethi (1978): *Gandhi Today,* Vikas Publishing House, Delhi.

14. Romesh Diwan in *Relevance of Gandhian Economics* (Ed), D.S. Awasthi, p. 26. .
15. *Ibid.*
16. Romesh Diwan, *The Economics of Love, An Attempt at Gandhian Economics,* Vol. XVI No. 2, June 1982, pp. 574-575.
17. Mahatma Gandhi, *Socialism of My Conception, op. cit.*
18. Romesh Diwan, Trusteeship and Decentralization, *Gandhi Marg,* January 1980, pp. 652-659.
19. E F. Schumacher (1978): Foreword, *Equality Through Trusteeship and Full Employment,* Bharatiya Vidya Bhawan, Second Ed., Bombay.
20. Romesh Diwan (1983a): Mahatma Gandhi and Economics of Non-Exploitation, *Journal of Social Science.*
21. E.F. Schumacher, *Small is Beautiful.*
22. David Dickson, Alternative Technology, *Fontana,* 1974.
23. *Ibid.*
24. Bhahtosh Dutta (1980): *Indian Economic Thought,* Tata McGraw Hill, New Delhi.
25. A. Das (1979): *Foundations of Gandhian Economics,* Allied, New Delhi pp. 95-96.

5

Gandhian Concept of Man and Society

The crisis of modern civilization is the crisis of man. Any worthwhile solution to the problem of man's predicament must start with man himself. But what does "starting with man himself mean?" On the most basic plane, it means a radical departure from what modern civilization presupposes man to be and the type of relationship it deems appropriate between man and his external world. The advisability of radical departure will be evident if we consider the fact that if we reduce man to history and culture his redemption, his rising above the shackles of history and culture becomes problematic. The modern concept of man reduces him to an entity which is completely determined by certain biological, psychological and sociological laws. History ought to be the most important determinant of man's nature.

If history is a very powerful force in the making of man, it is itself a product of man's actions. Historical laws are nothing more than constructions about reality, they do not deal with reality *per se.* As a construction, these laws are nothing more than description of patterns created by certain factors and their interaction that produce a particular outcome. Constructions about reality, they are partial, tentative and ideological. Such as, they are incapable of providing reliable guidelines for man to emancipate himself from the conditions he has himself created. Moreover, man cannot hope to escape the consequences of his actions by an attempt to control the consequences. To escape certain consequences, it becomes necessary to change the pattern of action which means far going modification in the concept of man.

The phenomenal world was considered simply on the reflection of the conceptual world as constituted by the world of ideas or forms. In Christianity, the conceptual world coincides with a divine order. In both these conceptions, the conceptual world contains the true models of things phenomenal of everything that exists in the real world. The test of perfection of things phenomenal lies in the extent to which they conform to their models in the conceptual world.

In both these conceptions, man is conceived not as self-complete and self-sufficient subjects who defines for themselves their own ends and ways to attain them. It is conceptual order that is the locus of norms and values that shape man's ideas, customs and institutions. True, the conceptual world is separated from the real world, however, man has the capacity—reasons, faith or both to apprehend the structure of the conceptual world. To act according to this structure is both rational and natural. Morality and freedom consist in conforming to and shaping one's behaviour according to the model extant in the conceptual world. In both these formations, the real world in itself does not have any inherent moral order. It lacks substantive moral and spiritual attributes. Norms and values are in this respective, transcendent, not immanent.

In the absence of a trans-human anchor for grounding the search for truth and reality, such a search focused on man himself and yielded what Iris Murdoch calls "broken totality". This splits between reason and desire, man and society, and man and nature are the manifestations of this "broken totality". With the denial of trans-human source of norms and values, man emerged as a self-complete and self-defining subject. However, uniqueness of being human now reduced to biological, psychological and sociological considerations. With this, man emerged as nothing more than individual society interaction.

This view of man yields two polar foundations of man and his relation with external world. First, individuals are considered as self-defining subjects endowed with and driven by impulses and equipped with reason to work for release from the fetters of constraining institutions. The necessity of upholding the social order requires the pursuit of individual happiness compatible with others, to be sure.

Second, man may simply be treated as a byproduct of social relations. On this view, community takes precedence over individual, and social institutions provide not only the ground for individual identity but also norms and values for acting on and interacting with the external world. Such a perspective puts emphasis on order and links the preservation of individual freedom with the performance of social roles. The person is equated with personal, that is, the masks of social roles he puts on.

Both of these views are unacceptable. On the first view, the dichotomy between individual and society reduces society to a secondary entity, a shadow, so to speak, of the social reality of the individuals. The second perspective, on the other hand, abolishes the individual altogether. He reincarnates in certain social roles and finds solace in the hierarchic or functional organisation of society. In the first perspective, the individual cannot make anything of his freedom because of the impingement on his life of numerous forces beyond his control, in the second perspective the question of freedom does not arise.

Gandhi steers clear of the pitfalls inherent in either perspective on man. However, before we discuss Gandhi's concept of man and society, it is fruitful to examine the various formulations extant in the tradition of Western thinking. It is only against the background of such an appraisal that true significance of Gandhi's concept can be fully appreciated.

Tradition of Western Thought

Perspectives on man and society in the tradition of Western thinking are numerous. It is not at all possible to discuss them all here. It is proposed here to examine briefly four formulations, which, for the sake of convenience, can be labelled (a) atomist or representational approach, (b) rationalist approach, (c) significance approach, and (d) human needs approach.

Atomist or Representational Approach

The approach is predicated upon the rejection of the ideal of intelligible essences. It treats mind as tabula rasa. On this view, there is no fixed impression of self. As such there can be no idea of self. Mind is a bundle or collections of different perceptions, which succeed one another with an inconceivable rapidity, and are perpetual flux and movement, a kind of theatre where several perceptions successively make their appearance, pass, repass, glide away and mingle in an infinite variety of postures and situations.[1]

The successive perceptions constitute the mind. In this perspective, self does not seem to have any positive role to play. It is simply a synonym for whatever perceptions register on the screen of the mind at particular moments. What then does self-identity consist of ? It is true that self is passive and has no independent role in organising stimuli coming from the outer world through the medium of senses.

The distinctiveness, stability and continuity of self in the midst of rapidly moving perceptions derive from the principle of pleasure and pain. The concept of self-interest gradually came to be equated with the augmentation of fortune. This transition came about gradually and in response to the problem of keeping under leash violent and turbulent passions of men.[2] Convinced of the futility of harnessing this wide world by brain spun terminology such as philosophy and religion came to be viewed as poor instrument of controlling violent and destructive passions of men. The passion which was formerly looked down upon and denounced as the deadly sin of avarice, thus came to be assigned the crucial role of containing and controlling unruly and destructive passions of man. Even more important, it was seen as something which not only cultivated "the spirit of frugality, of economy, of moderation, of work, of wisdoms, of tanquility, of order, and of regularity", as Montesquieu, saw it, but also as instrumental in checking despotism, as Sir James Stewat argued. Thus, the pursuit of self-interest came to occupy a central position in not simply controlling violent passions but, more importantly, in conducting the cultivation of finer qualities that sustain refined and ordered social life.

Once interest was equated with augmentation of fortune and considered the most dominant passion capable of taming other passions, man was reduced to nothing more than an "externalised" creature, an object. Interest in effect replaced man's inner being, and man became simply the reflective creature of external, largely material objects which attracted or repelled him, his relation to those objects, of course, being to a great extent determined by his class and economic position. Man became, in essence, a receptacle for interest.[3]

Freedom, then, consists in being disengaged from the outer world, to drain it of its significance and to control it and to bend it to one's own will to serve one's ends. These ends are given, they originate in natural desires and taking the shape of self-interest, gets fulfilment in the improvement of one's own worldly conditions. In other words, one's location in the socio-economic space, class and economic position moulds self-interest which, in turn, determines self's relationship with the outer world. The aggrandisement of will, understood in terms of acquisitiveness and possessiveness, untrammelled by any external constraints, becomes freedom. As Marx characterises it, freedom consists in "the right to the undisturbed enjoyment of accidents of fortunes".

The achievement of self-identity through appropriation, that is defining of "I" through the "My" constitutes the foundation of the atomist society that emerges out of aggregation of autonomous, self-defining subjects. In such a society, possession in the words of Dewey, "shapes and consolidates the "I" of philosophers. I own, therefore, I am 'expresses a true psychology than the Cartesian' I think, therefore, I am.[4]

One important source of threat to individual freedom lies in the fact that vast technological, economic, political and social systems have emerged and carved for themselves an autonomous realm of functions, decisions, and principles of their operation. As a result, the individual wishes either to do what other people do (Conformism) or do what he is told to do (Totalitarianism). This promotes facelessness and paves the way for exploitation, domination and consequent alienation.

Rationalist Approach

The conception of self-sketched above constitutes the central component of modern world view. However, for various reasons, this dominant worldview is under attack. This conception, it is argued, not only truncates the totality of man and his existence, but also makes man into the slaves of his inclination. If freedom lies in rising above nature, then surely inclinations have to be curbed and mastered for man to enjoy freedom. To curb inclinations is to reject desires as the basis of freedom. Reasons they must provide such basis. This is the line rationalist approach takes.

In the empiricist tradition, experience is said to be the organising element of impression involving direct action of objects on the subject. In this scheme, mind is passive and receptive. For Kant, the contents of knowledge are derived from experience, to be sure, however, mind plays an active role in organising whatever it receives from the outer world via the senses. It thinks its experience, conceives them according to its nature, *a priori,* that is rational ways. The function of understanding is to use rational or logical preconditions of transcendental origin of endowing uniformity and intelligibility to experience of phenomena.

Kantian subject is thus active and creative. Experience of the world is, therefore, in part experience of oneself. The receiving of reason from the empirical onslaught permits. The self not only to constitute the outer world but also to attain freedom as a moral entity. This is possible only when will is liberated from the coercion of sensuous impulses, from the tyranny of inclination and is made subject to transcendental reason itself. Man is a part of nature and, therefore, subject to the law of nature, the chain of cause and effect. However, he is also an intelligent or moral being in which capacity he can originate acts and hold himself responsible for his actions. Freedom requires not only grounding action in reason but also reason to be a creative and spontaneous; that is, there should be no antecedent to the determination of man's will except the laws which he gives to himself through reason. It is in this sense that every voluntary act is the direct expression of man's intelligible character, of pure, spontaneous reason, hence, man is a free agent, he is not a link in the chain of natural causes.

The emergent society, a rational realm of spirit, contains persons who are both sovereign and subject; they lay down and acknowledge the law. And in doing so, they recognise the ideal world as the highest good we have moved from self-interest as the imperial governor of passion to reason as sovereign.

Significance Approach

Taylor makes a distinction between consciousness as a representation and consciousness as commitment to certain standards of action. He concedes that one must have an original point of view in order to fulfil the basic condition of being a respondent. However, he insists that something more is needed to distinguish person from agent. As he argues, "Consciousness in characteristically human form can be seen as what we attain when we come to formulate the significance of things for us. We then have an articulate view of ourselves and world."[5]

To be moral agent is to be sensitive to certain standards. Morality requires some recognition that these are higher demands on one and hence the recognition of some distinction between kinds of moral. More agency, in other words, requires some kind of reflective awareness of the standard one is living by.[6] Consciousness is essential to man. But consciousness is more than representation. It is more than the power to depict the outer world clearly; in a very important sense, it is constitutive of matters of significance. This means that man as a moral being is open to concerns of right and wrong to certain standards of action.

Such a view of self takes us far beyond the realm of instrumental reason and restores the importance of role of emotions in human valuation. However, it rains more questions than it settles. First, how does the sense of significance inhere? Presumably not in rationality itself because then, it brings about a distinction between reason and emotion, which is unacceptable in this perspective. Second, if it is not innate, it must be acquired. If so, then self may not become anything else than the product of social relations.

The Adequacy of Human Needs Theory

True, the significance theory is an improvement on the two other approaches discussed earlier. However, it raises questions whose answer it fails to provide. If standards of action are grounded in the significance of things social institutional patterns became the locus as well as determinant of significance. This reduces individual to the status of the moment of social order who fulfils himself only by reflecting, protecting and promoting the spirit contained and actualised in a particular community. It is against such a view that need theory rebels.

The needs theories widely differ in substantive approaches and emphases. This endeavour finds an anchor in biological needs which provide a firm empirical grounds for the certitude of needs theories. They articulate certain needs the fulfilment of which leads to a proper development of human personality. In this perspective, rationality cannot fully explain human action. Motives are said to have a universal structure that channel human actions in certain directions. Various versions of needs hierarchy exist, but they all being with lower physiological needs and end with some notion of self-actualization at the top. Human growth is generally defined as movements away from dependency and towards the fulfilment of potential.

To develop potentiality is self-actualization. These potentialities can be actualised at stages. Each of these stages of development path is related to other and all of them constitute the system.[7] Naturalism treats nature as self complete. Man is an integral part of nature and subject to all its laws. But when man is supposed to be the measure of all things and considered to be the ground of truth and reality, humanism takes over. Even while man is biologically, psychologically and sociologically determined, he has implanted in his natural tendency towards unfolding of certain potentials which, when fully realised, develop his power fully. This primary need of self-realisation creates other needs whose satisfaction, either sequentially or otherwise, is *sine qua non* for primary need fulfilment.

Needless to say that needs theories stand on four major props of dubious nature. In the first place, needs theories claim to provide a firmer ground for defining human welfare as well as a well defined set of purportedly objective and universally valid criteria for understanding and improving human condition. In the second place, needs theories transform supposedly empirical fact into teleological necessity. This is to say, the future is implicit in the past. In the third place, it is assumed that past achievements and advances, both at the individual and social levels, concatenate to make possible further advances towards psycho-social maturity and freedom.

Needs theories emphasize the fulfilment of certain needs as the precondition of the full-flowering of self. However, they do not stop here, they go a step further and insist that these needs must be fulfilled in a certain way if human felicity is to be assured. The satisfaction of needs and the way their satisfactions are culturally conditioned. The meanings of love, trust, competence, relatedness, etc. vary from culture to culture.

Society can be treated simply as an aggregate of self-defining subjects. Society is merely a collection of self-defining individuals, not an entity over and beyond individuals that compose it. It will be good if individuals are good, and bad if individuals are so. But then, it is quite out of the question to blame society for the ills individuals may suffer from. Social pathology can only mean the aggregation of individual pathologies. Society can be sick not in the sense that society as an entity, over and apart from individuals, is sick but only in the sense that numerous members of society are sick.

Even if we accept the idea of social causation of individual pathology and certainly there is ground to accept it, we are told in general terms that a society characterised by equality, fairness, justice, participation, etc. will create a good society and good life for its citizens. In short, the living of good life depends on each individual releasing his potential, on the one hand, and on the constitution of society in such a way that it is prepared to meet and invite, and to safeguard and encourage the process of the actualisation of potentiality, on the other. A life not dedicated to a purpose larger than itself is empty and incapable of providing standards of good life. Needs theorists conveniently target or ignore this inconvenient but very important and harsh fact.

Gandhi's View of Man and Society

The preceding discussion suggests that the conception of person that sees man to be completely determined by nature, that is by biological, psychological and sociological conditions, is unable to provide an appropriate ground for moral evaluation and political action. Once man is reduced to history and culture, his fate hangs between the oppressive poles of reductionism and determinism. And yet various perspectives on man do have some notion of human freedom. To talk of human freedom is also to talk of suppressing some or other elements of nature and rising above it. Freedom may be worthwhile in its own right, however, its real worth lies in its instrumentality, its usefulness for seeking certain substantive end-perfection, self-development and so on. In this sense, the search for freedom is basically a quest for getting release from causal determination that constitutes an important characteristic of what is called nature. The quest for freedom is indicative of the fact that while man as a physical and living being is strictly subject to natural laws, he is more than this and by virtue of this, he is above causal determination. This is why, all attempts to express and ground human freedom in naturalistic terms come to naught. Man, therefore, has to be treated more than a biologically, psychologically and socially determined being; he has to be considered as an ethico-religious entity. The notion of person, therefore, has to do with man not only as an empirical phenomenon but also as a being that seeks perfectibility.

Man as an ethico-religious principle is simply a possibility. As Nagarjuna observes:

> "The sense of "I" is at cross-roads, it has a double reference. It shares at once two orders of being, the conditioned and the unconditioned; it is at once a universalizing as well as particularising tendency. It can work as much for liberation as for bondage, it can work non-clingingly as well as by clinging."[8]

If the sense of "I" traverses the path of particularising tendency, the empirical self becomes absolute bringing in its wake distinction of "I" and "Not - I" and treating them not as a relative distinctions but absolute ones. If, on the other hand, the sense of "I" inclines towards universalizing tendency, the empirical self is treated only as a centre of experience, a baseline from which one can begin the search for the conditioned and the quest for the real nature of one's being when the sense of self incorporates an ethico-religious dimension and emphasises the necessity of development, it then becomes necessary to transcend nature and chart out a pattern of development uniquely suitable for each person. Such a perspective recognises biological, psychological and sociological realities but refuses to be bound by them. In this sense, man is subject to the laws of nature but he possesses self-awareness and is capable of creating the form of his own existence independent of environing conditions. It recognises the importance of certain internal transformation impinging on the process of self development unique to man.

Gandhi refuses to accept the empirical self as true self and while recognising the brute in man, he calls for self-perfection. For him, while man is rooted in and springs from the animal world, he has the capacity to rise above it and can only if he so recognises and wills, set on a journey to give free play to his moral and spiritual propensity for self-development. In this view, the attributes of being uniquely human are neither fixed for all times nor immutable. He believes that goodness in man can be articulated, strengthened and perfected. Once the good of man is aroused, man can move on the path of self-realisation. He pegs this hope on the perfectibility of human nature.

For Gandhi, self-development is learning to be human, a learning that is characterised by a ceaseless process of inner illumination and self-transformation. It is basically an understanding of one's true being and letting that being unfold itself. For to know oneself is to perfect oneself. Recognising this as being the true orientation of personhood, it should be made clear that such a perspective recognises that it is transcendental but asserts the necessity of seeking the meaning of life in the world of here and now. This projects organismic vision which emphasizes the essential unity of existence since it sees the one reflected in all and all reflected in the one. This perception of essential unity dces not, however, preclude the recognition that while everything is the reflection of the one, one thing is distinct from the another. Since truth can be viewed and apprehended from various and not necessarily compatible positions, one has to recognise the "manysidedness" of reality.

The recognition of the manysidedness of reality within the framework of the essential unity of existence leads to the rejection of exclusivism. It recognises the essential uprightness of the many positions that can be taken to define reality. As such many paths, many ways can co-exist. The rejection of exclusivism also points to the fact that one must abstain from imposing one's way on others in order to preserve their integrity. Such an outlook leads necessarily to the adoption of *ahimsa* as the principle of social interaction.

It may be argued that the recognition of the manysidedness of reality may ultimately lead to differences among persons. Such differences, if they occur, are solvable because in the last analysis, the perception of the manysidedness of reality is located within the transcedental centre is the same in every being even though the path of its realisation may diverge from person to person. This is so because the perception of the manysidedness of reality is predicated upon a strong sense of shareability and commonality. The experience of self-development through self-transformation may be personal but it is not private precisely because such an experience resonates with the inner experience of others. Such a perspective emphasises shareability and commonality of outlook. It underlines equality, but not uniformity since it allows for different shapes of meaning as it is perceived and manifested in different persons and contexts.

Self-transformation is an inner experience and underlines inwardness. However, it is this principle of inwardness that externalises itself once the necessity of self-transformation in the world of here and now is accepted. In Maritainn's words:

> "Because of the very fact that I am a person and that I express myself to myself, I seek to communicate with that which is other with others, in the order of knowledge and love. It is essential to personality to ask for a dialogue and to a dialogue wherein I really give myself and wherein, I am really received."[9]

The necessity of harmonizing oneself with an ever-enlarging circle of relationship is only the other name of integration. Such an integration becomes possible only by extending the boundary of the self, not for absorption of everything else to oneself but for giving oneself to others. This extended self becomes the ground for sociality. Society then turns out to be a network of extended selves rather than a mechanical aggregate or an all-consuming totality. This perspective retains the primacy of the person but treats him as a drop in the ocean. This locates humanity in a highly complex web of interdependency.

Recognising the frailty of human nature and its attachments, such a perspective does emphasis the desirability of universalizing one's basic value commitments but insists on choosing a concrete path of making it possible the basic value commitments to be universally manifested. Such a concrete path offers itself in the principle of *Swadeshi,* that is, concern for immediate neighbourhood. This is, again, not an event of exclusiveness or narrow parochialism. Each individual or unit has to strike the universal concrete in terms of the milieu of its own cultural heritage. Only by proceeding from wherever we are, geographically, spiritually or emotionally, can we make the integral effort needed for the progress and peace of the whole humanity.

Without self-effort no amount of social reordering will yield any result. Gandhi says:

> "In the West, when they talk of the amelioration of the lot of masses, they talk of raising the standard of life .... how can an outsider raise the standard when the standard is within everyone of us. We can only strive to increase man's opportunities of realising and fulfilling his duties and getting nearer to God".[10]

To increase man's opportunities of realising and fulfilling his duties and getting near God will depend on how close the social order, the arena of man's making and doing, conforms to the basic value commitment delineated above. An appropriate social order must be based on *ahimsa,* harmony, service, duty, *Swadeshi,* self-restraint and self-sufficient autonomous local communities that emphasize non-possessiveness, equality, non-exploitation and decentralisation of decision making.

In the words of Gandhi again:

> "In his structure, composed of innumerable villages, there will be ever-widening never ascending circles. Life will not be a pyramid with the apex sustained by the bottom. But it will be an oceanic circle whose centre will be the individual always ready to perish for the villages, the latter ready to perish for the circle of villages, till at last becomes one life composed of individuals, never aggressive in their arrogance but ever humble, sharing the majesty of the oceanic circle of which they are integral units. Therefore, the outer most circumference will not wield power to crush the inner circle but will give strength to all within and derive its own strength from it. No one will be first and none the last".[11]

NOTES

1. Darid Hume, *A Treatise of Human Nature,* Book-1, Part-IV, Section-6.
2. Albert U. Hirschman (1978): *The Passions and the Interest*, Princeton University Press.
3. Ellen Meiksins Wood (1972): *Mind and Politics, An Approach to the Meaning of Liberal and Socialist Individualism,* Berkeley, University of California Press, p. 111.
4. John Dewey (1962): *Individualism: Old and New,* New York, Capricorn Books, p. 116.
5. Charles Taylor, *The Concept of Man,* B.N. Ganguli Memorial Lecture, C.S.D.S., Delhi, March 1981, pp. 4-5.
6. *Ibid.,* p. 9.
7. Erik H. Erikson (1977): *Childhood and Society,* Paladin, p. 244.
8. Venkata Ramanan (1978): *Nagarjuna's Philosophy,* Motilal Banarasi Dass, p. 100.
9. Tacques Maritainn (1966): *Challenges and Renewals—Selected Readings* (Ed), University of Notre Dame Press, p. 292.
10. C.W.M.G., Publication Division, Ministry of Information and Broadcasting, Govt. of India, Delhi, 1959, Vol. 35, p. 292.
11. Mahatma Gandhi, Quoted in Pyarelal, *Mahatma Gandhi—The Last Phase,* Ahmedabad, Navajivan Publishing House, 1956, Vol. II, pp. 580-81.

6

Gandhian Challenge to Acquisitive Society

The Gandhian doctrine of non-possession will primarily raise a question : Can it work in a modern society? or does it pose a challenge to modern society or a response? R.H. Tawney's model of modern society, The Acquisitive Society, can serve a frame of reference. In his own words : "Modern societies aim at protecting economic rights, while leaving economic functions, except in moments of abnormal emergency, to fulfil themselves. The motive which gives colour and quality to their public institutions, to their policy and political thought, is not the attempt to secure the fulfilment of tasks undertaken for the public service, but to increase the opportunities open to individual of attaining the objective which they conceive to be advantageous to themselves. Such societies, because of their whole tendency and interest and preoccupation, are to promote the acquisition of wealth."[1]

The motive force behind the "acquisitive society" is the propensity to accumulate wealth composed of goods for current consumption and goods for future consumption. On the positive side, this society has set impressive records in the expansion of productive capacity, advances in technology, exploitation of resources, affluence and abundance of goods and service. On the negative side, the same society has also generated severe strains and stresses on life and powerful tendencies towards the degradation of the total environment, social, economic, ecological, political, and last but not the least, moral. "And these consequences are not, as is often suggested, accidental maladjustment, but flow naturally from its dominant principle."[2]

That dominant principle is that "it assures men that there are no ends other than their ends, no law other than their desires, no limit other than that which they think advisable. Thus, it makes the individual the centre of the universe, and dissolves moral principles into a choice of expediencies for it relieves them of the necessity of discriminating between enterprise and avarice, energy and unscrupulous greed, property which is legitimate and property which is theft, the just enjoyment of the fruits of labour and idle parasitism of birth or fortune, because it treats all economic activities as standing upon the same level."[3]

Mahatma Gandhi shared this incisive insight into the inherent nature of modern acquisitive societies bent upon accumulation of goods and multiplication of wants as a never-ending process. He had serious doubts about the ability of modern societies to survive on its present course. He was fearful of the high probability of the reconstruction of societies through an eruption of violence. As an alternative to this path of violence, he offered a set of doctrines for social reconstruction consistent with his fundamental principle of nonviolence. In this set, the doctrine of non-possession holds a pivotal role. In this regard, this doctrine is both a challenge because it proposes a radical transformation of society through the transformation of individual. It is a response because it suggests a way to fill one of the most serious gaps in modern society, the moral gap—the widening gap between moral progress and technological and other material measures of progress.

Gandhian doctrine offers a philosophical response to the task of social reconstruction. Gandhian formulation must, however, be regarded as an idea to re-orient our thinking, not as a policy that can be readily implemented without a great deal of additional work. Such work, of necessity, must address the issues of precise definition of non-possession, its quantitative measurement, and institutional arrangements for the collection and disposal of surplus wealth.

Gandhi formulated the doctrine of non-possession as one of the key philosophical principles underlying the well-known political movement, known as the *Satyagarh* movement. Politically, it was nonviolent civil disobedience or civil resistance movement. Philosophically, it was a movement led by a force which is born out of an intense desire to follow the path of truth. In his own words : "Satyagrah is literally holding on to truth and it means, therefore, truth force. Truth is soul or spirit. It is, therefore, known as soul force."[4]

Gandhi viewed the *Satyagrah* movement, essentially, as a process of reformation and purification of the individual who was the key to his social order. Among other things, a *Satyagrahi*, a follower of truth, has to pursue the principle of non-hoarding or non-possession. In observing the vow of non-hoarding, wrote Gandhi, "the main thing to be borne in mind is not to store up anything which we do not require.

For agriculture, we keep bullocks, if we use them, and the equipment required for them. Where there is recurring famine, we shall, no doubt, store foodgrains. But we shall ask ourselves whether bullocks and foodgrains are, in fact, needed."[5]

In another context, he wrote : "This principle is really a part of non-stealing. Just as one must not deceive, so must one not possess anything which one does not really need. It would be a breach of this principle to possess unnecessary food-stuffs, clothing or furniture. For instance, one must not keep a chair, if one can do without it. In observing this principle, one is led to a progressive simplifications of one's life."[6]

It is clear that the Gandhian doctrine of non-possession is offered as an indictment of one of the most powerful drives in modern economic society. The drive for multiplication of wants is fuelled by an insatiable propensity for surperfluous or conspicuous consumption. One may justify such consumption as an essential prerequisite for economic growth and stability in an affluent society. This argument is, of course, based purely on economic grounds. To Gandhi, it was an economic issue as well as moral issue. To him, ethics and economics were inseparable. He believed that possession of goods, beyond the limit of need, distinguished from want or demand, is a form of theft and, therefore, immoral.

He realised that the perfect ideal of non-possession is unattainable because it demand total renunciation. His pragmatic mind would accept something short of the perfect realisation of the ideal, namely a movement towards it through the process of gradual reduction of wants and minimisation of consumption. In this regard, minimising behaviour rather than maximising behaviour emerges as one of the cardinal principles of the Gandhian vision of welfare economics.[7]

The doctrine of non-possession, if it implied only voluntary reduction of wants, could be construed as a totally negative doctrine. But Gandhi expounded it as a positive doctrine. According to him, the doctrine of non-possession would teach that everyone should limit his own possession to what is needed by him and spend the rest for the welfare of others. He considered this as a desirable nonviolent method of reducing inequality of income distribution and maldistribution of wealth. He was aware of the other means of dealing with these problems but he discounted this because of his fear that other methods would violate either the principle of non-stealing or the principle of nonviolence through the coercive powers of the state.

Gandhi would put utmost reliance on the individual and his moral awakening to bring about radical changes in the distribution of income and wealth in society.

Gandhian doctrine of non-possession has another important implication for economy of his ideal state. If this doctrine is widely adopted, this would change orientation of production from demands to needs. Unlike demands, needs do not have to be created they are already there. In every society, rich and poor, there are massive amounts of unmet social needs. If production was indeed geared to the satisfaction of economic needs of the masses, in all likelihood, it would have a favourable effect on growth and employment. As one Gandhian economist put it: "Gandhi's call for cutting down demands and his principle of non-possession *(aparigraha)* were designed both to create a quick rate of growth and full employment less on the basis of individual profit incentives and more on the basis of joint efforts and community advantage."[8]

It should, however, be pointed out that the suggested growth and employment effects of the doctrine of non-possession are not likely to materialise in the absence of structural changes in the national economy that Gandhi advocated. The principal structural change that he stressed was decentralisation of economic decision making and restructuring the small, village economy as essentially self-sufficient and self-governing economic unit. Gandhian principles of economics can work only in a Gandhian economic system; these cannot be superimposed on any othe economic system with radically different operating characteristics.

The essence of doctrine of non-possession is philosophical, not economic. As such, it is deeply rooted in the ancient Indian philosophical traditions with which Gandhi was thoroughly familiar. It should be pointed out that in the same philosophical tradition. *Artha*, meaning material possession, was regarded as one of the four fundamental goals of life.[9] It was clearly recognised that material possessions were essential prerequisites in daily life for the upkeep of a household, raising of a family and discharge of various social and religious duties and obligations. Implicit in this doctrine of *artha* is a concept of multi-order utility, if he feeds his family he derives a higher order of utility, if he feeds the hungry outside the family, he derives an even higher order of utility. This is a qualitative ordering of utility which is to be distinguished from the concept of ordinal utility which is still quantitative as used in conventional economics.

This notion of multi-order utility eliminates any possible conflict between the doctrine of *artha* and the doctrine of non-possession. There is no sanction against accumulation of possession and against attachment to possession beyond the quantities necessary for certain low-order but essential utility needs. To possess or not to possess that is not the question. The real question relates to how much to possess, what are the limits of possession for one's own use and how to make meaningful use of excess possession. Viewed in this manner, the doctrine of non-possession emerges as a highly positive doctrine. It is negative only in form, not in substance. The doctrine is an excellent example of how Indian philosophy reconciles the economic principle of accumulation of wealth with the philosophical principle of non-attachment to material wealth. As stated in one of the principal *Upanishads,* "one should accept only those things necessary for himself, which are set aside as his quota, and one must not accept other things, knowing well to whom they belong.[10] In the same context beyond the enjoyment of wealth for one's sake, a higher form of enjoyment is suggested : "Enjoy it with renunciation; do not covet any man's wealth."[11]

The same idea is articulated far more forcefully in the *Srimad-Bhagavatam.* Men are entitled to regard as their own just what would suffice to satisfy their hunger. Whoever would appropriate more to himself is a thief, and should be punished as such.[12] Many centuries later, a similar idea was vigorously putforth by Proudhon in his celebrated book *What is Property*?[13]

Beyond doubt, Gandhi derived the philosophical principle underlying his doctrine of non-possession from the inexhaustible sources of Indian philosophy. To me, he wrote, "The *Gita* became an infallible guide of conduct, words like *aparigraha* and *sambhava* (equality) gripped me. I understood more clearly in the light of *Gita* teaching the implication of word 'trustee'. I understood the *Gita* teaching of non-possession to mean that those who desired salvation should act like a trustee who, having control over great possessions, regards not an iota of them as his own.[14]

Gandhian socialism is a befitting challenge to acquisitive society. Gandhi accepted socialism as a part of his programme to do away with the social and economic inequalities. He strived to wash away tears from every eye and helplessness, fear and frustration from every heart. It is significant to note here that Gandhi did not derive his concept of socialism from his studies of Marx and Western socialist thought but it evolved out of his deeply religious outlook. Though he called himself as the foremost socialist and communist.[15] But he had his strong reservations about the practicability of the undiluted type of socialism in Indian condition.[16]

Gandhi claimed that he was a foremost socialist. Expressing his views on socialism he maintained, socialism is a beautiful word and so far as I am aware in socialism all the members of the society are equal, none low, none high. In the individual body, the head is not high because it is the top of the body nor are the soles low because they touch the earth. Even as limbs of the individual body are equal so are the members of the society. This is socialism. In it, the prince and the peasant, the wealthy and the poor, the employer and the employees are all on the same level. It is all unity. Looking at society, all the world over there is nothing but duality or plurality. Unity is conspicuous by its absence. In order to reach the state of unity, he may not look on things philosophically and say that we need not make a move until all are converted to socialism. Therefore, only truthful, nonviolent and pure hearted socialists will be able to establish a socialist society in India and the world.[17]

Gandhi believed and declared, "if we retained possession only of what we needed, no one would be in want and all would live in contentment.[18] Proudhon regarded property as theft in possession. Only that property is just which is shared by all not collectively but impersonally—directly and individual.[19] The property which, as a matter of fact, belongs to the society as a whole, if possessed by some persons or groups without the sanction of the society, the occupier is considered to have committed the theft. "Socialism in the real sense", says Gandhi, "has been handed down to us by our ancestors who taught, all lands belong to Gopal". It means Lord Krishna. In the modern language, it means state.[20] He believed that the sublime socialist goals of equality, liberty and fraternity could only spring out of love for humanity at large and not from violence, hatred, intrigues and vengeance. Hence, "truth and non-violence must incarnate in socialism.[21]

An equitable dispensation of nation's wealth is the key note of socialism. Gandhi believes that so long as the horrible distinction between the rich and the poor continues the attainment of socialism will be a far cry, an impossibility.[22] However economic equality, to

Gandhi, does not mean that everyone should literally possess the same amount. It simply signifies that everybody should have enough for his or her needs.[23] Economic equality, he holds, "must never be supposed to mean possession of an equal amount of worldly goods by everyone. It does mean, however, that everyone will have a proper house, sufficient and balanced food to eat, sufficient khadi with which to cover himself. It also means that the cruel inequality that obtains today will be removed by purely nonviolent means.[24] The real implication of equal distribution is that man shall have the required goods and services to fulfil all his natural needs and no more.

The Marxists and the communists in order to bring about this state of society would generate and accentuate hatred and when they get control over the state they will enforce equality.[25] Under Gandhi's scheme, the state no doubt will be there, but it would be there to carry out the will of the people rather than to force them to do its will.[26] If today all the owners are forcibly dispossessed of all their possessions the possessive instinct would still remain. It is this which is the root cause of conflicts and it is this which Gandhi wants to put an end to. Instead of dispossessing the rich, he would like the rich man to be a trustee of the society for the wealth he possesses. The rich man will be left in possession of his wealth, of which he will use what he reasonably requires for his personal needs and will act as trustee for the remainder to be used for the society. He asks the rich men to come forward and take initiative in the dispossession with a view to a universal diffusion of the spirit of contentment.

The theory of trusteeship comes very close to the ancient Hindu ideal. According to traditional Hindu view, "property is a mandate held by possessors for the common use and benefit of common men. Anyone if desires more without needing it commits theft and deserves punishment.[27] There is no justification that few should roll in luxury while too many starve. Following are the important characteristics of the principle of trusteeship:

(1) It makes no distinction between the private and non-private property.
(2) All property should be held in trust.
(3) It applies not only to tangible but also to intangible property.
(4) The ownership of property rests with God.

(5) The entire creation is the beneficiary.

Gandhi believes in the goodness of human nature. To him, none is beyond redemption.[28] Trusteeship, he regards, is the surest method to evolve a new social order of life of universal benefit in place of the present one where each gives for himself without regard to what happens to his neighbour. Thus realisation of the spirit of trusteeship would ensure the disappearance of the distinction of rich and poor and a real socialism free from all fear and hatred would evolve. Trusteeship is a means for the attainment of collective ownership. However, he realised that absolute non-possession is an abstraction. It is unattainable in its entirety.

Gandhi while agrees that the concentration of capital in the present set up is the fruit of exploitation to very large extent but if there is a choice between the individual and the state violence, he would prefer the violence of individual to that of the state as the lesser of the two evils.[29] He further holds, "while a number of instances could be cited where people adopted trusteeship, there was none where the state has really lived for the people.[30] But in case it is unavoidable, he would support a minimum of state ownership as a concession to human frailty.

Salient Features of Trusteeship

1. Trusteeship provides a means of transforming the present capitalist order of society which is an egalitarian one. It gives no quarter to capitalism, but gives the present owning class a chance of reforming itself. It is based on the faith that human nature is never beyond redemption.
2. It does not recognise any right of private ownership of property except so far as it may be permitted by society for its own welfare.
3. It does not exclude legislative regulations of the ownership and use of wealth.
4. It does not permit the individual to hold or use his wealth for the selfish satisfaction or in disregard of the interest of society.
5. It proposes to fix a limit for maximum income that could be allowed to any person in society. The difference between the maximum and minimum incomes should be reasonable and

equitable and variable from time to time so much so that the tendency would be towards obliteration of the difference.

6. The character of production will be determined by the social necessity and not by personal whim or greed.[31]

Six basic elements of Gandhian economics are well-known. They are complementary to each other and form the foundation of Gandhian economic order. As a matter of fact, these elements–*swadeshi,* bread-labour, *aparigraha,* trusteeship, non-exploitation and equality–provide the challenges and response to acquisitive society. In Gandhian economics, the distinction between 'basic' and 'non-basic' goods is fundamental. Gandhian economics will accept the hierarchy of 'needs' defined by Maslow. In these hierarchies, there is necessary consumption that satisfies physiological and security needs, on the one hand, and 'sel-actualisation,' on the other. The former groups of needs are socially determined, while later group is necessary for creative needs of an individual. Along with material goods to satisfy these needs must come the possibility to satisfy love, respect, and a sense of belonging.

Basic goods can be defined as all those goods that satisfy the needs, that is basic needs, self-actualisation needs, love, respect and a sense of belonging. The consumption of basic goods provides utility in the sense of uplift and creativity of the society and individual. By and large, the relationship between utility and consumption of non-basic goods is not well defined. A part of the consumption of such goods is positively harmful. The principles of consumption, production and distribution are different in Gandhian economics.

Consumption

Neo-Classical Basic Propositions	*Gandhian*
1. Resources are limited and wants insatiable.	Resources are abundant enough to satisfy needs of all in a comfortable way.
2. Consumer's goal is to maximize utility.	Consumer's goal is to satisfy needs.
3. Consumption is budget determined.	Consumption is need determined.
4. More is better and desirable for its own sake.	More is desirable and better only to a point of freedom from drudgery, discomfort, and arduous labour.

(Contd.)

	Neo-Classical Basic Propositions	*Gandhian*
5.	Multiplicity of material wants becomes the aim of life.	Restraint on material wants is the aim of life.
6.	Utility function of multiple wants has no upper bound.	Utility function of multiple wants has an upper bound defined by "necessary comforts" exclusive of luxuries.
7.	Individual utility functions are independent of each other.	Individual utility functions are inter-dependent.
8.	Socialist utility function is maximised through maximization of individual utility functions.	Socialist utility function is maximized through maximization of the number of economically satisfied individuals.
9.	Want-oriented society creates waste of economic resource, pre-occupation with earning for consumption deters the growth of an average individual in other aspects of life.	Need satisfying society requires only bread labour. Relatively independent and self-sufficient economy allows an average individual enough time for self-fulfilment.

Source : Romesh Diwan and Sushila Gidwani, *Elements in Gandhian Economics.*

In the capitalistic industrialised societies, production of both "basic" goods and "non-basic" goods forms a larger part. This is because the income elasticity of non-basic goods is far greater than that of basic goods. Since production is defined by profit or growth motives, it is more profitable to produce non-basic goods. However, a very large percentage of total production is made up of basic goods. The motivation for this emphasis comes both from sheer need as well as from moral and ethical considerations of love, humanism and respect. The motivation of the production of non-basic goods is basically creativity, self-expression and societal preservation.

In the Gandhian system, the production modes cannot be exploitative by their very nature. The technology must satisfy the following conditions :

(1) Technology must increase the productivity of the workers.
(2) Technology must not replace workers.
(3) The workers must have complete control over technology. The appropriate technological movements all over the world are attempts in this direction.

Production

	Neo-Classical	*Gandhian*
Goal of the economic activity:	Multiplicity and quantity or material goods.	To provide work for body and to satisfy economic needs of the society so that its members can fulfil themselves within a harmonious society. In other words, the goal is the moral progress. The progress of the permanent element in us. The material progress is contained in the moral progress but the reverse is not true.
Measure of success :	GNP and ever-rising standards of living.	Absence of starvation among masses.
Incentives:	Production for the sake of profits.	Produce just enough to satisfy one's needs in order to keep one's mind trained and educated for a harmonious growth.
What to produce?	Products which would fetch the highest rate of return. Utility is directly related to the price.	Goods which would satisfy the basic needs. Since consumption and production are localized, the value of the products is determined by the labour value rather than exchange value, the profits are absent.
For whom to produce?	Those who can pay.	For self
How much to produce?	Restricted only by the production capacity.	Constrained by the individual's needs and a socially desirable level which would not hinder individual's total growth.
Industrialisation:	A boon.	A curse.
Capital:	Essential	Only if it aids human beings.
Technology:	Essential	Only if it is simple and usable by the masses.
Labour:	A commodity of production to be exploited.	A source of human power which must be utilized for

(Contd..)

	Neo-Classical	*Gandhian*
		the benefit of its owner. It is the fundamental law of our being, viz. that we must work for our bread, that we eat, by the sweat of our brow; it is voluntary, not exploitable.
Labour Value:	All labour has exchange value which is derived from the interplay of the laws of supply and demand in the products as well as in the resource markets.	Only bread labour has value which is derived from the individual's need to maintain healthy body, mind and soul. The intellectual labour is self-satisfying, hence it has no exchange value. Since individual's satisfaction is incomplete without its social utility, it should be rendered freely to the society.
Employment:	MRC=MRP	Full employment regardless of cost, Since most of the labour is self-employed, the question of labour cost largely becomes irrelevant.
Occupations requiring:	All occupations.	Only those requiring bread labour, agriculture, printing, carpentry, shoe-making, gardening, house-making, handicrafts, weaving, spinning. The manufacture of everything needed to satisfy human wants and labour in all essential occupations count as bread labour. Also pursuit of education and training related to any occupation requiring labour is productive and intelligent labour.

Source : Romesh Diwan and Sushila Gidwani, *Elements of Gandhian Economics.*

Distribution Theory

	Neo-Classical	*Gandhian*
1.	There is a market for factors of production.	There is no market for factors of production.
2.	Entrepreneur corporation brings the factors together for of production by buying.	Trustees bring together agents and factors production by example and cooperation.
3.	The relationship is of employer-employee.	The relationship is one of trustees and cooperative workers.
4.	Workers are paid a wage.	There is no wage labour.
5.	Wages are paid on the basis of marginal productivity.	There are no wages. Everyone shares in the total output equally.
6.	There is income from the employment of capital. This is appropriated by the capital-owners.	There are no incomes accruing to capital. Capital, once installed, is maintained without generating incomes.
7.	Capital is owned by the capitalists.	Capital is owned by the community.
8.	Capitalists substitute capital for labour in order to maximize profits to the capitalist. In the ideal situation capital-labour substitution is infinite or its elasticity is one.	There is no substitution between capital and worker as long as it leads to displacement of workers. The function of capital is to enhance productivity without replacing worker and diminishing the humaneness of the work. The capital-labour substitution, thus, is zero.
9.	Risks of production are taken by the capitalists out of income from capital and for future profits.	Risks are taken by the community as a whole.
10.	Investments are made by the capitalists out of income from capital and for future profits,	Investment is made by the community as a joint decision to improve the quality of life in the community.
11.	Investments from profits are residuals after other costs are paid.	Investment decisions are made from total output and the remunerations to workers and trustees are from the residuals.
12.	There are various prices short-runs, long-runs, etc. These differ from each other.	There is only one price implicit in the long-run.
13.	Short-term prices are determined by demand.	Short-term allocations are determined by need and equality.
14.	Long-term prices are determined by average costs defined by the capitalists.	Long-term prices are determined by average costs. The costs, however, are defined by the community.
15.	Distribution is unequal.	Distribution is the essence of the system.

(Contd..)

Neo-Classical	*Gandhian*
16. Production and distribution are channelled by economic incentives.	Economic incentives are opposed diametrically by trusteeship.

Source : Romesh Diwan and Sushila Gidwani, *Elements of Gandhian Economics.*

Thus the basic principles of Gandhian economics differ from traditional economic thinking. Gandhian departure is of far reaching consequence. Acquisitive social order has created problems for the mankind in terms of unrestrained consumerism, rat race and multiplication of wants. It is the cardinal principle of economics that resources are limited while wants are unlimited. Hence, apparently they are irreconcilable. Finite cannot match the infinite. The economic rationality is based on rationality which tries to bring about equilibrium between these two facts. Various studies and attempts have been made to throw light on these issues. Gandhi's contribution is very noteworthy. This problem has been highlighted by study conducted by "Club of Rome" which portrayed the real picture of the situation.

Fred Hirsch's social limit to growth is also a poineer work, while J.K. Mehta's philosophy of wantlessness is brilliant. All these ideas confirm Gandhi's concept of minimisation of wants, non-possession and trusteeship. They are the effective and viable alternative of acquisitive social order. This is a solution to the problems created by acquisitive social order.

Gandhian response to the challenges to acquisitive social order is also shared by J.K. Galbraith who talked about private affluence and public poverty as the central crisis of the developed capitalist system. Gandhian doctrine tried its best to diffuse this central crisis so that new economic and social order may be established on peaceful and sustainable basis.

NOTES

1. R.H. Tawney (1921): *The Acquisitive Society,* New York, Harcourt Brace and Company, p. 29.
2. *Ibid.,* p. 33.
3. *Ibid.,* pp. 30-31.
4. Gandhi, *Young India,* 23 March, 1921, p. 90.
5. S. Narayan (1968) (Ed): *The Selected Work of Mahatma Gandhi,* Vol. 5, p. 28.

6. M.K. Gandhi (1959): *Ashram Observances in Action,* Ahmedabad, Navjivan Publishing House, p. 113.
7. A.M. Huq (1977): Welfare Criteria in Gandhian Economics, *Gandhi Marg*, January, pp. 576-584.
8. J.D. Sethi (1978): *Gandhi Today*, Durham, North Carolina University Press, p. 105.
9. Henrich Zimme (1951): *Philosophy of India*, Princeton University Press, p. 35.
10. Swami Prabhupada (1966): *Sri Isopanisad*, Los Angeles, Iskon Books, p.14.
11. Swami Rama (1972): *The Book of Wisdom, Isopanisad,* Illinois, North West Yoga Centre, p. 25.
12. N. Raghunathan (1946): *Srimad Bhagvatam*, Vighneshwara Publishing House, Madras, Vol.1.
13. P.G. Proudhon (1840): *What is Property?* London, Reeves.
14. M.K. Gandhi (1966): *The Story of My Experiment with Truth*, Navajivan Publishing House, Ahmedabad, p. 198.
15. *Harijan*, 13.03.1946.
16. C.B. Shukla, *Gandhi's Views of Life*, p.118.
17. *Harijan*, 30.07.1947.
18. From Yarvada Mandir, p. 24.
19. Ashok Mehta, *Studies in Asian Socialism*, p. 66.
20. *Harijan*, 2.01.1937.
21. *Young India*, 11.08.1920.
22. Pattabhi Sitaramaya, *Gandhi and Gandhism*, p. 53.
23. *Harijan*, 31.01.1946.
24. *Harijan*, 18.08.1940.
25. *Harijan*, 31.03.1946.
26. *Ibid.*
27. *Bhagwat Puran*, Chap. 14, Skand 7, Verse 728.
28. *Young India*, 8.08.1929.
29. *Young India*, 26.11.1931.
30. *Modern Review*, October 1935, p. 412.
31. Pyare Lal, *Towards New Horizons*, pp. 93-94.

7

Gandhian Criteria of Welfare Economics

Modern welfare economics has correlated a set of welfare criteria in terms of certain marginal or optimality conditions. If all these conditions are met theoretically, one can say, social welfare is maximised. Specifically, to maximise social welfare, it is required to achieve simultaneously a subjective optimum and a physical optimum, goods must be distributed among consumers in such a way that no one can improve his position except at the expense of some one else, and products as well as factors of production must be allocated in such a way that no greater output can be produced with same factors.

First, the definitions of welfare are not exactly the same. Conventional welfare economics uses a purely materialistic utilitarian or ethical neutral definition of welfare. Gandhi measures welfare in moral terms, although he does not exclude material well-being. Unlike modern welfare economics here the welfare criterion applies to all, not just the majority of society.

Second, some of the underlying assumptions in welfare economics such as given wants, given distribution of income, wealth and prosperity, are in conflict with the Gandhian model based on wantlessness. With regard to the distribution of income and wealth, Gandhian economics abandoned the position of ethical neutrality. Economic equality emerges as a dominant criterion of welfare.

In Gandhian economics, the social optimum lies in complete equality of all individuals. This would bring about the equilibrium conditions of society, both materially and morally. Redistribution of income and wealth, therefore, must be considered a major welfare criterion in Gandhian economics.

Third, the concept of social equilibrium does not mean the same thing in Gandhian and modern welfare economics. The marginal conditions in later are basically a set of static equilibrium conditions in the production, consumption and distribution sectors of the economy.

Here the emphasis on efficiency in the allocation of scarce resources, on the maximisation of production and material gains—in short maximising behaviour of the economic man. In Gandhian economics, social equilibrium is an optimum combination of material and moral progress through progressive movement towards a non-violent society founded on non-exploitative, humanistic and egalitarian society.

Our main concern of micro-economic theory is the optimum allocation of resources at individual level, i.e. how individual consumers and firms maximise their objective functions—consumers their utility function and firms their profit function. From the analysis of these aspects of economic theory, it may appear that if all individual firms optimise their resource allocation with a view to maximising their profit functions, the total output of goods and services available to the society will be maximum. And when all the individual consumers optimise their resource allocation to maximise their utility functions, the total utility enjoyed by the society as a whole will be maximum. In other words, if both firms and consumers maximise their respective objective functions, the total economic welfare of the society will be maximum.

This may, however, not be true because private and public interests can and do conflict. Therefore, optimisation of resource allocation from and individual point of view may not conform to the tests of optimum allocation of resources from the view point of society's well-being. The positive micro-economic theory leaves unanswered many pressing problems concerning the criteria of maximum social welfare and appropriate policy measures that can maximise the economic well-being of the society as a whole. The branch of economic analysis, which is concerned with these problems, is called welfare economics.

The term welfare has been defined in many diverse ways, perhaps, because it is extremely difficult to give it precise meaning. The difficulty arises from the fact that welfare of an individual or a group of individuals depends on diverse and immeasurable factors including social, political, economic and philosophical attitudes of the people towards life and society.

The concept of economic welfare used in economic literature is synonymous to utility or happiness.[1] The economic welfare of an individual, thus, equals the total utility he derives from the goods and services that he consumes, the leisure that he enjoys, and deeds he performs, but not all of these. The economic welfare of an individual equals the total utility derived from only those goods and services, leisure and deeds which can be exchanged for money or can be brought under the measuring rod of money.

On the basis of this concept of individual welfare, Bentham defined social welfare as the "sum total of the happiness or welfare of all the individuals in society". This is based on the cardinally measurable utilities of individual members of society.

It is met with certain serious objections. Utility cannot be cardinally measured, hence cannot be added to obtain the aggregate welfare. Since cardinal measurement of utilities is not possible, interpersonal comparison of utility is not possible in an objective and scientific way. Owing to these problems, Benthamite and Pigovian concept of social welfare had become inoperational as it could not be used objectively in any policy formulation. Therefore, cardinal utilitarian thesis of welfare had to be abandoned.

It was Vilfered Pareto, an Italian economist, who broke away from the cardinal utility tradition and gave a new orientation to welfare economics. He rejected cardinal utility concept and additive utility function on the ground of their limitations. Pareto introduced a new concept, i.e. the concept of social optimum. It is not possible to add up utilities of individuals to arrive at the total social welfare, it is possible to determine whether social welfare is optimum. Conceptually, social welfare is said to be optimum when nobody can be made better off without making somebody worse-off. In the words of Boulding, "a social optimum is defined as a situation in which nobody can move to a position which is less prefered". The test of increase in social welfare is that at least one person should be made better off without making anybody else worse off.

However, it is difficult to conceive economic policies which can improve the welfare of an individual without injuring the others. To overcome this problem, Kaldor, Hicks and Scitovsky have evolved the compensation principle. This principle states that the person, who benefits from an economic policy, must be able to compensate the person who becomes worse off due to this policy and yet remain better off, the compensation should, however, not exceed his benefit. (A) Classical welfare criteria, (B) Neo-classical welfare economics, (C) Paretian welfare economics, and (D) Post-Paretian contribution to welfare economics.

(a) Adam Smith—allocative efficiency-output, consumption satisfaction—level of satisfaction of a society is proportional to the level of its total physical output mixture of classical economics and those of marginal utility school.

(b) *Neo-classical welfare economists* are like Sidgewick, Marshall, Pigou etc. Sidgewick asserted distinction between production and distribution, while he accepted the classical view point that increase in production of wealth increases total happiness, he favoured the view that "a more equal distribution of wealth tends prima facie to increase happiness or welfare".

Marshall—Introduction of the concept of consumer's surplus did generate high hopes for being used as an instrument of social betterment. He also talked of material well-being.

Pigou—His enquiry is limited to that part of social welfare which could be brought directly or indirectly into relation with the measuring rod of money. Economic welfare is limited to the extent to which individual's wants are satisfied.

(c) *Paretian Welfare Economics:*
   (i) The concept of Pareto optimality,
   (ii) Marginal conditions of Pareto optimality.

According to Pareto criterion, any change that makes at least one person better off without making someone else worse off definitely causes an improvement in social welfare. Conversely, any change that makes at least one person worse off and no one better-off causes decrease in social welfare.

(d) *Compensation Criteria*

It is, however, difficult to imagine an economic change or implementation of a policy measure that does not affect any individual adversely. In reality, most economic changes make some people better off at the cost of some others. Pareto criterion does not evaluate such economic changes. Kaldor, Hicks and Scitovsky, have, however, devised compensation criteria that attempt to overcome the limitations of Paretian criteria of maximum social welfare. This is called new welfare economics. It is a culmination of a great tradition. It is a reconstruction of old welfare economics without assuming its two bugbears, namely, measurable utility and interpersonal comparability of utility. It had developed largely as a result of the invention of the indifference curve analysis. New

> welfare economics began an attempt to separate ethics from science and separate allocative efficiency from particular modes of social organisation. It has two major goals : (i) to set forth the conditions that must exist to maximise welfare and (ii) to separate out positive and normative issues-efficiency in equity aspect. According to Boulding, new welfare economics formulates propositions by which we may rank on the scale of better or worse alternative economic situations open to society.

The cardinal principle of new welfare economics is that indirect prescriptions are avoided. The declared purpose of new welfare economics to provide guidance for policy as is consistent with general standard of objectivity. New welfare economics provides criteria of general or even universal validity on the basis of which one could decide whether a course of action was desirable or undesirable from the economists' point of view, equity remaining the same. In other words, new welfare economics is a science which finds out what is the best thing to do in various situations.

Another cardinal feature of new welfare economics is that it finds the end of economic life within economics, not like old welfare economics which drew them from philosophy or political science making them fiduciary value judgement. New welfare economics is mainly concerned with the comparison of the efficiencies of alternative economic situations, with the allocative effects of change in economic policy. The basic postulate of new welfare economics is that the individual is the best judge of his own well-being so that the state of an economy is to be judged good or bad in terms of choices of the participants rather than by some externally imposed moral standard. In new welfare economics, utility, like other psychological entities, possesses only an ordinal magnitude, which cannot be used as a cardinal number.

A utilitarian, Bentham pictured man as essentially a pleasure seeking animal. Man seeks to maximise his happiness and minimise his pain. Utility is a power in object which will normally create satisfaction. Every commodity is quantum, cardinally measurable. For any given individual, the utility of any commodity is cardinally measurable variable. The pleasures and pains of each individual are measurable quantities being added into a compact or malleable quantity called the individual's happiness or welfare. To Bentham, the happiness of society is equivalent to the sum total of the happiness of all individuals in society. The individual happinesses are summed up into a social total, all of them being weighted equally.

In Marshall, an optimum allocation of resources is achieved only when the distribution of income is perfectly equal. To him, the allocation of resources is one which maximises social welfare in the sense of equalisation of income in society.

The purpose of this enquiry is to formulate a set of welfare criteria implicit in Gandhian economics. These criteria will be examined in parallel with the set of welfare criteria defined in modern welfare economics. One set of criteria cannot be recast into the mould of the other set as it will be counter-productive because of the fundamental differences between Gandhian economics and modern economics. There are differences in scope, structure, and philosophy. It will be more useful as well as fruitful to demonstrate the contrast between the two systems, each within its own frame of reference. This does not necessarily mean that the two systems are totally and mutually exclusive.

Mahatma Gandhi was one of those rarely gifted individuals in whom the economist, the political scientist, the sociologist and the philosopher were rolled into one. The product of his genius is a vast system of thought. This makes it difficult to look at any of the sub-systems, economics for instance in isolation. The entire system is based on two fundamental, interrelated principles : Non-violence and Truth. One cannot understand any of the structural components of this Gandhian system, economics in particular, without understanding the philosophical foundations of the super-structure. To use analogy, the total system of Gandhian thought was like a vast reservoir from which many streams flowed out each with individual characteristics, conditioned by the peculiarities of the terrain but all preserving a consistency with the essential qualities of the resources at the source. His economics, especially his welfare economics, clearly reflects this constituency.[2]

Mahatma Gandhi formulated his economic ideas and principles in the context of his design of an ideal social order which is a non-violent, non-exploitative, humanistic and egalitarian society. This social order embodied the fundamental philosophy of his life. He approached all facts of this social order, its economics, its politics and its sociology from philosophical premises—truth and non-violence, that governed his entire life. Therefore, it was impossible for him to produce an economics that would be ethically neutral. In his own words : "Economics is untrue which disregards moral values. This extention of the law of non-violence in the domain of economics means nothing less than the introduction of moral values.[3] With the disappearance of ethical neutrality in Gandhian economics, we also witness the demise of the economic man. That, at once, sets him apart from the mainstream of modern economics.

Although Gandhi was not an economist in the ordinary sense of the term, it is not difficult to credit him as being an economic model-builder. In his own way, he constructed a model which he claimed to be practical and operational in a given environment. He sketched out, in considerable detail, its basic goals, its structure, its components, its modus operandi, its data and variables. Viewed as an economic system, it has its own management scheme, and its own techno-structure. In a certain way, it is not a static but a dynamic model, embodying Gandhian theory of growth. He wrote : "The end to be sought is human happiness combined with full mental and moral growth. I use the objective moral as synonymous with spiritual.'[4] He did not overlook the purely material goals of an economic system. Any viable system, he insisted, must have the production capability to meet social demand for the basic necessities of life—food, clothing, shelter and other essential pre-requisites for survival. But he de-emphasised the pursuit of economic abundance for its own sake at all costs.

Moreover, he was fully aware of the possible demoralising effects of such abundance, dictated by the multiplicity of seemingly insatiable wants in an acquisitive society. He was unconvinced that abundance measured by physical volume of goods and services is either a necessary or sufficient condition for maximum individual or social welfare. On the contrary, an incessant drive for economic abundance, through accumulation, competition, and technological innovation, he felt, would promote economic aggression, exploitation and violence in society.[5] The production goal of a Gandhian economic system can be stated as maximisation of socially necessary goods and services, and the minimisation of luxuries and superfluous goods, constrained not only by the availability of scarce resources but also by an overriding moral purpose. The production and consumption of luxuries to stimulate effective demand was repugnant to Gandhian economic philosophy.[6] He was opposed to conspicuous consumption on moral and economic grounds.

In defining the goals of his ideal economic system, Gandhi raised an important issue of the possibility of a conflict between a goal to maximise output and a goal to maximise employment. This issue is generally glossed over in modern macroeconomics. It is implicitly assumed that output and employment move in the same direction. This is why, in a typical macroeconomic model such as the Keynesian model these two are treated interchangeable, dependent variables. It should be noted that movements of output and employment in the same direction do not rule out differential rates of change. Any variance between rates of change in output and employment with its substantial amount of disguised and open unemployment, this issue is by no means trivial.

Given Gandhi's social and moral philosophy and the peculiarities of socio-economic environment in India, his economic model would lean towards employment rather than output in defining an objective function to be maximised. One of his deepest concerns was the massive poverty, especially rural poverty in India. At the same time, he had a better perception of the nature of massive rural unemployment in India than he is given credit for. That type of unemployment is structural, seasonal, and technological, rather than cyclical. Deficiency of aggregate demand has very little to do with that type of unemployment. In the large scale diffusion of supplementary employment through appropriate low-capital-intensive technology and corresponding restructuring of the economy along the lines of decentralisation and small-scale industrialisation, he saw the only real, feasible and meaningful approach to the seemingly insoluble problem of Indian poverty.

Apart from economic feasibility, Gandhi's rationale rested on a moral and metaphysical notion of human labour. To him, labour is not just a commodity for sale in the market in exchange for wages to compensate for the disutility of labour, He was reluctant to measure the opportunity cost of work in terms of sacrifice of leisure. In his system, labour had a dignity and a moral substance which was not for sale. He was specially influenced by the following passage:

> Work is more excellent than leisure;
> The body's life proceeds not, lacking work
> .... If one eats
> The fruits of toil, that thief steals from his world,
> He that abstains

> To help the rolling wheels of this great world,
> Glutting his idle sense,
> Lives a lost life, shameful and vain.[7]

This moral and metaphysical notion of work greatly influenced Gandhi's economic thinking, the reconstruction of his economic model, and the specification of its techno-structure. The primary unit in his model is the individual man or household, and the primary organisational unit is the village. It is essentially a decentralised system where the fundamental economic decisions are to be made by the micro-units of the total system, the village communities. Though it seems that there is a hierarchy but Gandhian model is, in essence, non-hierarchical. In this structure, he wrote in a famous passage,

> "Composed of innumerable villages, there will be ever-widening, never ascending circles. Life will not be pyramid with the apex sustained by the bottom. But it will be an oceanic circle whose centre will be the individual, always ready to perish for the village, the latter ready to perish for the circle of villages, till at last the whole becomes one composed of individuals, never aggressive in their arrogance, but ever humble, sharing the majesty of the oceanic circle of which they are integral units. Therefore, the outermost circumference will not yield power to crush the inner circle but will give strength from it."[8]

It is apparent that although Gandhi was an individualist, his individualism has to be sharply differentiated from the individualism of the economic man, associated with classical and neo-classical political economy. Nor is the Gandhian model a throw-back to medieval feudalism. The feudalistic economic society was essentially pyramidal in design and exploitative in character, hardly compatible with the Gandhian principles of non-violence and decentralisation.

One may be tempted to characterise the Gandhian model as a closed system because of his emphasis on non-sufficiency. A self-sufficient economy will rule out any kind of international economic activity associated with foreign trade and investment. A student of international economics, armed with the theory of comparative advantage, the logic of mutually gainful trade, and the welfare criteria implicit in international division of labour, will reject self-sufficiency in favour of mutual dependency among nations. Gandhi was a pragmatist as well as an idealist. As a pragmatist, his astute mind saw behind the mask of theoretical sophistry, the ugly face of economic reality. Instead of mutual and equally gainful international exchange of commodities and capital, he saw a deleterious form of economic interdependence among inequal economic partners which really meant economic dependence of some nations on others. In such dependence, he saw an instrument of exploitation and possible violence—a serious threat to nations true independence and ultimate well-being. Being a pragmatist, he knew that absolute self-sufficiency is an unrealistic goal. He was willing to compromise, provided that international trade can be adapted to the needs, resources and welfare of non-violent and non-exploitative societies.

The Gandhian model is often criticised on ground that it has an anti-industrial and anti-advanced technology bias. To some, his model appears as a replica of the feudal model which is essentially a tradition-oriented, static and agrarian model. To serious students of Gandhian economics such criticism is both unfair and superficial. Gandhi never expressed unqualified opposition to industrialisation and modern technology. He was opposed to developing the Indian economy industrially along the same lines as those of Western industrial economies. Such industrialisation, he feared, would spell disaster, moral, economic, social and political. In fact, this is one of his most pungent indictments of Western civilization. Interestingly, his perception of the risks and failures of modern industrial societies is shared by many Western scholars.

Gandhi, however, favoured limited, selective and socially controlled industrialisation : Large scale, heavy, capital-intensive industries, centralised but strictly under public control, and decentralised, small-scale industries to diversify the village economic base. Such a mixed pattern of industrialisation he considered to be responsive to the needs and welfare of a non-violent society, dedicated to moral and material progress.

Likewise, he was not opposed to technological innovations *per se.* He recognised that technology has its place and, it wisely used, it can make a significant contribution to social welfare. But he was strongly opposed to indiscriminate use of technology which might lead to monopolistic exploitation and displacement of labour. These views can hardly be brushed aside as the prejudiced outpourings of an untrained economist. Many strands of thought from the works of

Schumacher, Joan Robinson and Marx can be identified with Gandhi's thoughts on modern technology. Again, althrough his strictures on technology, his humanism shines through "The supreme consideration," he wrote, "is man the machine should not tend to make atrophied the limb of man".[9] He was equally disturbed over the effect of machines on human mind. Like Marx, he saw in modern machine technology a powerful dehumanising force that alienates man from his product, from his community and most insidious of all, from himself. Yet the technostructure of the Gandhian model of the village economy would not rule out limited use of modern technology. He was receptive to the positive role machines can play in reducing the burden of human drudgery and increasing labour productivity without degrading human mind. Of necessity, such machine technology has to be highly selective, controlled and subservient to needs higher than the simple economic need for efficiency.

Now we have to see how Gandhian concept of welfare conforms or differs from the criteria laid down by the modern economics. Modern welfare economics has formalised a set of welfare criteria in terms of certain marginal or optimality conditions. These conditions apply to the consumption as well as production sectors. If all the conditions are met, theoretically, one can say, social welfare is maximised. Essentially, it amounts to specifying certain conditions under which resources of the community are most efficiently utilised to satisfy given wants within the framework of a given distribution of income. Specifically, to maximise social welfare, it is required to achieve simultaneously subjective optimum and a physical optimum: goods to be distributed among consumers in such a way that no one can improve his position except at the expense of someone else, and products as well as factors of production must be allocated in such a way that no greater output can be obtained with the same factor input. This is an overly simplified statement of welfare criteria in modern welfare economics but it will serve the purpose of composing Gandhian principles of welfare criteria.[10]

In some respects, it can be argued that Gandhian economics and modern welfare economics are not mutually exclusive. For instance, the optimality condition applicable to the consumption sector is perfectly compatible with the Gandhian principle of non-violence. Distribution of goods among consumers in such a way that no one can better his economic position except at the expense of someone else, in no way conflicts with the goals of a non-violent society. Beyond this, fundamental differences—conceptual and philosophical—arise between the two systems.

First, the definitions of welfare are not exactly the same. Conventional welfare economics uses a purely materialistic, utilitarian and ethically neutral definition of welfare. In Gandhian economics, welfare is defined essentially in moral terms, although it does not exclude material well-being. Maximisation of moral and, to the extent necessary, material welfare may be stated as the principal welfare criteria in Gandhian economics. Unlike modern welfare economics, in Gandhian economics, the welfare criteria applies to all, not just the majority of society. The Gandhian term *Sarvodaya* is significant in this respect. His welfare model, therefore, does not require the compensation principles.

Second, some of the underlying assumptions in welfare economics, such as given wants, given distribution of income wealth and prosperity are in conflict with the Gandhian model. 'Minimisation of wants' rather than given 'wants' may be construed as a Gandhian criterion of individual and social welfare. His materialistic optimum is restricted to the irreducible minimun of material goods and services, within the context of a given society, not unlimited abundance. Beyond that, the acquisition of material goods be considered unnecessary for the real welfare of non-violent society. With regard to the distribution of income and wealth, Gandhian economics abandoned the position of 'ethical neutrality'. Economic equality emerges as a dominant criterion of welfare. In the words of T.K.N. Unnithan, in Gandhian economics, "the social optimum lies in complete equality of all individuals. This would bring about the equilibrium condition of society, both materially and morally."[11]

This concept of social optimality in Gandhian economics sets it apart from the notion of optimality in modern welfare economics. The latter assumes away the problems of inequality in the distribution of income and wealth. To Gandhi, maximum social welfare with economic inequality is a fundamental contradiction. Economic equality to him meant "the levelling down of the few rich in whose hands is concentrated the bulk of nation's wealth, on the one hand, and a levelling up of the semistarved naked millions, on the other."[12]

Redistribution of income and wealth, therefore, must be considered a major welfare criterion in Gandhian economics. To bring about such a redistribution without violating the principle of non-violence, Gandhi formulated his controversial doctrine of trusteeship. The same could be attained by other more effective means. But he did not let the end justify the means if violence in any form was associated with the proposed means. "A violent and blood revolution," he wrote, "is a certainty one day unless there is a voluntary abdication of riches and the power that riches give and sharing them for the common good."[13] This is Gandhi's refined criterion of redistribution for the non-violent transformation of society into a welfare state.

Implicit in the Gandhian doctrine of trusteeship is a doctrine of social harmony. Gandhi did not accept the theory of inevitable conflict between labour and capital. If property and wealth are held as a trust to be used for public good, such conflicts need not arise. Gandhi asserted, "A true and non-violent combination of labour would act like a magnet attracting to it all needed capital and capitalist would then exist only as trustee."[14] Gandhi called this doctrine a form of non-violent socialism. Curiously enough, a similar doctrine of social harmony was preached by Adam Smith, the great exponent of individualism.

Third, the concept of social or general equilibrium does not mean the same thing to Gandhian and modern welfare economics. The marginal conditions in the latter are basically a set of static equilibrium conditions in the production, consumption and distribution sectors of the economy. Here, the emphasis is on efficiency in the allocation of scarce resources, on the maximisation of production and material gains, in short, on the maximising behaviour of economic man.[15] In the Gandhian economics, the notion of equilibrium is lifted to a much higher plane of thought. He defined social equilibrium as an optimum combination of material and moral progress through a progressive movement towards a non-violent society founded on economic equality and non-exploitation. This is Gandhian version of the magnificent dynamics of welfare state. In this model, we can identify elements of welfare criteria in the old and new welfare economies, and traces of welfare criteria in socialist economy. Yet, we find something distinctive, without a parallel in any known version of modern welfare theory.

In her critique of modern welfare economics, Professor I. H. Rima once wrote : "We have become increasingly aware in many aspects of contemporary life that welfare has more dimensions than those simply involved in the physical quantities of goods. The improvement of human life is more and more frequently a matter of optimising than it is a matter of maximising. Maximising is essentially an efficiency problem which is analytically possible to separate from the question concerning the desirability of using resources in one alternative rather than another. Value judgements are not involved in solving problems of the first type, but they are an integral part of the solution of the optimising problem".[16]

Even if we recognise the importance of the optimising problem, the definition of optimum, as understood by the modern welfare economics, leaves something to be desired. It is referred to as "Pareto Optimality", which essentially relates to "an optimum allocation of resources". "A Paretian Optimum", wrote one critic, "has come to occupy such an exaggerated position in the economists' thinking that after the phrase an optimum allocation of resources is used when what is implied is only a Paretian optimum—an optimum which may be far removed from what is feasible social optimum according to some morally impelling social welfare function."[17]

Gandhian economics, one can claim, produced just that, a set of welfare criteria for the attainment of a feasible social optimum according to some morally impelling welfare function.

NOTES

1. I.M.D. Little, *A Critique of Welfare Economics.*
2. A.M. Huq (1985): Welfare Criteria in Gandhian Economics in Romesh Diwan & Mark Lutz (Ed), *Essays in Gandhian Economics*, Gandhi Peace Foundation, Delhi, pp. 66-67.
3. Nirmal Kumar Bose (1948): *Selections from Gandhi,* Navajivan Publishing House, Ahmedabad, p. 41.
4. *Ibid.,* p. 73.
5. G.R. Madan (1966): *Economic Thinking in India*, S. Chand & Co.
6. B.N. Ganguli (1973): *Gandhi's Social Philosophy*, Vikas Publishing House, New Delhi, p. 73.
7. Edwin Arnold, *The Song Celestial* (The English Translation of the Bhagvadgita quoted by Gandhi, in his notes in *Young India*, 20 October, 1921.)
8. M.K. Gandhi (1947): *India of My Dream,* Edited by R.K. Prabhu, Bombay.
9. M.K. Gandhi (1958): *All Men are Brothers*, New York, Columbia University Press.
10. P.A. Samuelson (1947): *Foundation of Economic Analysis,* Harward University Press.
11. T.K.N. Unnithan (1956): *Gandhi and Free India*, Groningen, Holland, p. 85.
12. Nirmal Kumar Bose (1948): *Selection From Gandhi*, Navajivan Publishing House, Ahmedabad, p. 77.

13. *Ibid.*, p. 78.
14. M.K. Gandhi (1947): Towards a Non-Violent Socialism, *Harijan,* September 1947.
15. A. Bergson (1954): On the Concept of Social Welfare, *Quarterly Journal of Economics.*
16. I.H. Rima (1972): *Development of Economic Analysis*, Chicago : Richard D. Irwin Inc.
17. S.K. Nath (1964): "Are Formal Criteria Required", *Economic Journal,* September.

8

Sarvodaya and Gandhi

Sarvodaya may well be regarded as India's distinctive contribution to social philosophy. Its roots go back to almost 3000 years when Buddha and Mahabir went about preaching love or non-violence, and to those ancient seers who through the centuries taught and practised austerity and self-control, and sought to inculcate them in individual through social institution such as joint family system, caste and village organisation. In the family, caste and village community life, individual learnt to curb his own desires for the sake of his group to share his produce with others, to cooperate with them to feel loyalty to the group and to accept its discipline. He enjoyed economic security as his work and minimum requirements were assured to him by the group. There was a feeling of kinship and equality between him and other members of his group as in a family. It was a village communism without communism's violence.

It was from these sources that Gandhiji drew his inspiration for *Sarvodaya* or the ideal social order, although immediately it was from a reading of Ruskin's *Unto This Last*, Gandhiji was convinced that if individual and social lives were not thus based on love and high moral and spiritual principles, no amount of preaching establishing world organisations for peace, and resisting war will prevail, for peace is the end result of our daily living. Consequently, he was at great pains to show, even as our ancestors had done in the past, how the individual and society were to be transformed if we were to progress towards the great social order..

A small brochure entitled *"Sarvodaya,* its Principles and Programme" was issued in 1951 by the Navajivan Publishing House at short notice in response to pressing demand. Its chief aim was to give few pages information regarding the principles and programme of the *Sarvodaya Samaj* which was a fellowship started in Wardha, India, by Gandhiji's followers after his passing away. *Sarvodaya,* as the welfare of all, represents the ideal social order according to Gandhiji. Its basis is all embracing love. So, it has room in it for all without exception—prince and peasant, Hindu and Muslim, touchable and untouchable, white and black, sinner and saint. No individual or group is to be suppressed, exploited or liquidated. All are to be equal members of this social order all sharing in the produce of their labour, the strong protecting the weak and functioning as trustees for the weak, and each promoting of all.

As one of the essential qualities of love is self-giving or emptying oneself or dying for the loved one, self-control and self-suffering form one of the prime requisites realising *Sarvodaya.* India with her centuries of renunciation and austere self-control provides thus the best soil for it. In marked contrast is the Western craze for comfort, for multiplication of wants and self-indulgence. Gandhiji set himself in strong opposition to this trend in Western civilization precisely because he knew that it could not lead to *Sarvodaya* or justice, but only to greed, conflict and suppression of the weak by the strong, whether under capitalism or communism.

A philosophy such as this, of all embracing, self-suffering love, presupposes deep spiritual foundation. It implies a living faith in the one that pervades all. It requires also great self-discipline and training, and development of soul force. In its essentially spiritual basis it is the very anti-thesis of communism which is avowedly materialistic, although in regard to its goal *Sarvodaya* is similar to communism. Its basis being spiritual, the means for achieving *Sarvodaya* is also spiritual. Communism holds out the hope that the ideal social order can be realised only when the exploiter is done away with the physical force. For this, it builds on the class hatred and resorts to periodical purges and war. To Gandhiji, on the other hand, such a method seemed entirely futile, for hatred and violence were bound, sooner or latter, to recoil on their perpetrator, and to produce more hatred and violence in their wake. For ending oppression he evolved the technique of *Sarvodaya* or clinging to truth and even non-violence at the cost of untold suffering to oneself and even death was one of his distinctive contributions, and very central to his teaching.

Gandhiji was deeply influenced by *Unto This Last* and he translated it later into Gujarati, entitled '*Sarvodaya,* the welfare of all' :

(i) That the good of the individual is contained in the good of all.

(ii) That the lawyer's work has the same value as the barber's in as much as all have the same right of earning their livelihood from their work.

(iii) That a life of labour, i.e. the life of the tiller of the soil and the handicrafts man is the life worth living. The first of these I knew. The second I had dimly realised. The third had never occurred to me. *Unto This Last* made it as clear as daylight for me that the second and the third were contained in the first. I arose with the dawn ready to reduce these principles to practice.[1]

A votary of *Ahimsa* cannot subscribe to the utilitarian formula of the greatest good of the greatest number. He will strive for the greatest good for all and die in the attempt to realise the idea. He will, therefore, be ready to die, so that the others may live. The greatest good of all inevitably includes the good of the greatest number, and therefore, he and the utilitarian will converge in many points in their career. But there does not come a time when they must part company and even work in opposite direction. The absolutist will even sacrifice himself.[2]

If we see our dream of *Sarvodaya* i.e. true development realised we would regard the humblest and lowest Indian as being equally the ruler of India with the tallest of the land. This presupposes that all are pure or will become pure if they are not. And purity must go hand-in-hand with wisdom. No one would then harbour any distinction between community and community, caste and outcaste. Everybody would regard all as equal with oneself and hold them together in the silken net of love. Everybody would know how to earn an honest living by the sweat of one's brow and make no distinction between intellectual and physical labour.[3]

Spiritual Basis

In its spiritual basis means are all important. The progress towards the goal will be in exact proportion to the purity of means. This method may appear to be long, perhaps too long, but I am convinced that it is the shortest.[4] Similarly, rights and duties are inter-linked and interdependent. If all simply insist on rights and no duties, there will be utter confusion and chaos. If instead of insisting on rights every one does his duty, there will immediately be the rule of order established among mankind. One individual's duty is the right of other and *vice versa.* These things cannot be separated and society is founded and survives on the complementarity of the two. When one is conscious of his rights, he should be aware of his duties as well.

People in the West generally hold that the whole duty of man is to promote the happiness of the majority of mankind, and happiness is supposed to mean only physical happiness and economic prosperity. Even if the laws of morality are broken in the quest of happiness, it does not matter very much. This exclusive search for physical and economic well-being prosecuted in disregard of morality is contrary to divine law, as some wise men in the West have shown. One of these was John Ruskin who contends in *Unto This Last* that men can be happy only if they obey the moral law. Morality is an essential ingredient in all the faiths of the world, but apart from religion, our commonsense indicates the necessity of observing the moral law. Only by observing it can we hope to be happy.

Truth and non-violence are cardinal points in Gandhian concept of Sarvodaya. Truth should be very breath of life. When once this stage in the pilgrim's process is reached, all other rules of correct living will come without effort, and obedience to them will be instinctive or rules of life. But without truth it is impossible to observe any principles or rules in life. Truth is the right designation of God. *Ahimsa* is not the crude thing it has been made to appear. Not to hurt any thing is no doubt a part of *Ahimsa.* But it is the least expression. The principle of *Ahimsa* is violated by evil thought, by undue haste, by lying, by hatred, by wishing ill to anybody. It is also violated by holding on to what the world needs. Without *Ahimsa* it is not possible to seek and find truth. *Ahimsa* and truth are so intertwined that it is practically impossible to disentangle and separate them. They are like two sides of the coin. *Ahimsa* is means and truth is the end. If we take care of means, we are bound to reach the end, sooner or later. When non-violence is accepted as the law of life, it must pervade the whole being and not to be applied to isolated acts. It is profound error to suppose that whilst the law is good enough for individual it is not for masses of mankind.[5]

Fearlessness is indespensible for the growth of other noble qualities. How can one seek truth or cherish love, without fearlessness? As Pritam says, "The path of Hari (The Lord) is the path of brave, not the cowards". Here Hari means truth, and the brave are those armed with fearlessness.[6]

Non-stealing and non-possession are the essential attributes of *Sarvodaya.* Non-possession is allied to non-stealing. A thing not originally stolen must nevertheless be classified as stolen property, if we possess it without needing it. Possession implies provision for the future. A seeker after truth, a follower of law of love cannot hold anything against tomorrow. God never stores for tomorrow. The rich have a superfluous store of things which he does not need, and which are, therefore, neglected and wasted, while millions are starved to death for want of sustenance. If each retained possession only of what he needed, no one would be in want, and all would live in contentment. From the stand-point of pure truth the body too is a possession. We thus arrive at ideal of total renunciation and learn to use the body for the purposes of service so long as it exists, so much so that service and not bread, becomes with us the stuff of life. We eat and drink, sleep and wake, for service alone. Such an attitude of mind brings us real happiness.[7]

Renunciation does not mean abandoning the world and retiring into the forest. The spirit of renunciation should rule all the activities of life. A householder does cease to be one, if he regards life as a duty rather than as an indulgence. A life of sacrifice is the pennacle of art, and is full of true joy. One who would serve will not waste a thought upon his own confort. His service, like virtue, is its own reward, and he will rest content with it. Voluntary service of others demands the best of which one is capable, and must take precedence over service of self. In fact, the pure devotee concentrates himself to the service of humanity without any reservation whatever.

Bread-Labour

The law, that to live man must work, first came home to Gandhiji upon reading Tolstoy's writing on bread-labour. But even before he had began to pay homage to it after reading Ruskin's *Unto This Last.* The divine law, that man must earn his bread by labouring with his own hands, was first stressed by Russian writer T. M. Bondaref. Tolstoy advertised it and gave it wider publicity. The same principle has been set forth in the third chapter of *Geeta* where we are told that he who eats without offering sacrifice eats stolen food. Sacrifice here can only mean bread-labour. Reason too tells us to an identical conclusion. How can a man, who does not do body labour, have the right to eat? In the sweat of thy brow shalt thou eat thy bread; says the Bible. Here is a world-wide conflict between capital and labour, and the poor envy the rich. If all worked for their bread, distinction of rank would be obliterated; the rich would still be there, but they would deem themselves only trustees of their property, and would use it mainly in the public interest.

Bread-labour is a veritable blessing to one who would observe non-violence, worship truth and make observance of *Brahmacharya* a natural act. This labour can truly be related to agriculture alone, but at present at any rate, everybody is not in a position to take to it. If this is impossible, each family should see to its own scavenging. Evacuation is as necessary as eating, and the best thing would be for everyone to dispose of his own waste. Sacrifice may be of many types. One of them may be bread-labour. If all laboured for their bread and no more then there would be enough food and enough leisure for all. Such labour will be the highest form of sacrifice. Men will, no doubt, do many other things either through their bodies or through their minds, but all this will be labour of love for the common good. There will then be no rich and no poor, no high and no low, no touchable and no untouchable. This may be an unattainable ideal. But we need not, therefore, cease to strive for it. Even if without fulfilling the whole law of sacrifice, that is, the law of our being, we performed physical labour enough for our daily bread we should go long way towards ideal. If we did so, our wants would be minimised, our food would be simple. We should then eat to live, not live to eat. Let anyone who doubts the accuracy of this proposition try to sweat for his bread, he will derive the greatest relish from the productions of his labour, improve his health and discover that many things he took were superfluities.

May not men earn their bread by intellectual labour? No. The needs of the body must be supplied by the body. Mere mental, i.e. intellectual labour is for the soul and its own satisfaction. In the ideal state, doctors, lawyers and the like will work solely for the benefit of the society, not for self. Obedience to law of bread labour will bring about a silent revolution in the structure of society. Men's triumph will consist in substituting the struggle for existence by the struggle of mutual service. The law of the brute will be replaced by the law of man. Compulsory obedience to a master is a state of slavery, willing obedience to one's father is the glory of sonship. Similarly, compulsory obedience to the law of bread labour breeds poverty, disease and discontent. It is a state of slavery. Willing obedience to it must bring contentment and health. Intellectual work is important and has an undoubted place in the scheme of life. No man, I claim, ought to be free from that obligation. It will serve to improve even the quality of his intellectual output.[8]

Swadeshi

The votary of *Swadeshi* will, as a first duty, dedicate himself to the service of his immediate neighbours. This involves exclusion or even sacrifice of the interests of the rest, but exclusion or the sacrifice would be only in appearance. Pure service of our neighbours can never, from its very nature, results in disservice to those who are far away but rather the contrary. It is only when the doctrine of *Swadeshi* is wrongly understood, that mischief results. For instance, it would be travesty of the doctrine of *Swadeshi,* if to coddle my family, I set about grabing money by all means, fair or foul. The law of *Swadeshi* requires no more of me than to discharge my legitimate obligations towards my family by just means and the attempt to do so will reveal to me the universal code of conduct. The practice of *Swadeshi* can never do harm to anyone, and if it does, it is not *swadharma* but egotism that moves me. There may be occasions, when a votary of *Swadeshi* may be called upon to sacrifice his family at the alter of universal service. In *Swadeshi*, there is no room for selfishness; or if there is selfishness in it, it is of the highest type, which is not different from the highest altruism. *Swadeshi* in its purest form is the acme of universal service.

It was by following this line of argument, that I hit upon khadi as the necessary and the most important corollary of the principle of *Swadeshi* in its application to society. What is the kind of service I asked myself, what the teeming millions of India most need at the present time, that can be easily understood and appreciated by all that is easy to perform and will at the same time enable the crores of our semi-starved countrymen to live? And the reply came, that it is the universalising of khadi or spinning wheel alone, that can fulfil these conditions.[9]

Let no one suppose that the practice of *Swadeshi* through khadi would harm the foreign or Indian mill owners. A thief who is weaned from vice, or is made to return the property that he has stolen, is not harmed thereby. On the contrary, he is the gainer, consciously in the one case, unconsciously in the other. Similarly, if all the opium addicts or drunkards in the world were to shake themselves from their vice, the canteen keeper or the opium-venders, who would be deprived of their customers, could not be said to be losers. They would be the gainers in the truest sense of the term. The elimination of the wages of sin is never a loss either to individual concerned or to society, it is pure gain.

It is the greatest delusion to suppose that the duty of *Swadeshi* begins and ends with merely spinning some yarn anyhow and wearing khadi made from it. *Khadi* is the first indispensable step towards the discharge of *Swadeshi Dharma* to society. But one often meets men, who wear khadi, while in other things they indulge their taste for foreign manufactures. Such men cannot be said to be practising *Swadeshi.* A votary of *Swadeshi* will carefully study his environment, and try to help his neighbours wherever possible by giving preference to local manufactures even if they are of an inferior grade or dearer in price than things manufactured elsewhere. A true votary of Swadeshi will never harbour ill towards the foreigner, he will not be actuated by antagonism towards anybody on earth.

Swadeshism is not a cult of hatred. It is a doctrine of selfless service, that has its roots in the purest *Ahimsa* or love.

The broad definition of *Swadeshi* is the use of all home-made things to the exclusion of foreign things, in as far as such use is necessary for the protection of home industry, more especially those industries without which India will become pauperised. In my opinion, therefore, *Swadeshi* which excludes the use of everything foreign no matter how beneficent it may be.[10] Respect for all religions and anti-untouchability are ingredients of true *Sarvodaya.* Religions are the different roads converging to the same point. What does it matter that we take different roads so long as we reach the same goal? In reality, there are as many religions as there are individuals.[11]

There is one rule, however, which should always be kept in mind while studying all great religions and that is that one should study them only through the writings of known votaries of the respective religions. Religion is very personal matter. We should, by living the life according to our rights, share the best with one another, thus adding to the sum total of human efforts to reach God. None can born untouchable, as all are sparks of one and the same fire. It is wrong to treat certain human beings as untouchables from birth. This observance is not fulfilled merely by making friends with untouchables; but by loving all life as our ownselves. Removal of untouchability means love for, and service of the whole world, and this merges into *Ahimsa.*

Removal of untouchability spells the breaking down of barriers between man and man, and between the various orders of Being. We find such barriers erected everywhere in the world.[12]

Economic Order

Economic order of *Sarvodaya Samaj* consists of various elements. Basis of this economic order is non-violence. Under the new outlook, one can cease to think of getting what one can but shall decline to receive what all cannot get. It ought not to be difficult to make a successful appeal to the masses in terms of economics and a fairly successful working of such an experiment must lead to immense and unconscious spiritual results. Spiritual law does not work on a field of its own. On the contrary, it expresses itself only through the ordinary activities of life. It thus effects the economic, social and political fields.[13]

Human element is essential for economic efficiency. Man is an engine whose motive power is the soul. The largest quantity of work will be done when the motive force, the will or spirit of the creature is brought to its greatest strength. The universal law of the matter is that, assuming any given quantity of energy and sense in master and servant, the greatest material result obtainable by them will be not through antagonism to each other but through affection of each other. Unselfish treatment will produce the most effective return.

What is really desired, under the name of riches, is essentially power over men in its simplest sense, the power of obtaining for our own advantage the labour of servant, tradesman and artist so that the art of becoming rich in the common sense is not only the art of accumulating much money for ourselves but also contriving that our neighbour shall have less. In accurate terms, it is the art of establishing the maximum inequality in our own favour. Men are wealth, not gold and silver. That country is the richest which nourishes the greatest number of the noble and happy human beings; that man is the richest who having perfected the functions of his own life to the utmost, has also the widest helpful influence, both personal and by means of his professions, over the lives of others.[14]

If I pay due wages to my men, I shall not be able to amass unnecessary riches to waste money on luxuries and to add to the mass of poverty in the world. The workman who gets due wages from the employer will act justly to his subordinates. Thus the stream of justice will not dry up, but gather strength as it flows onward and the nation with such a sense of justice will be happy and prosperous. True economics is the economics of justice. People will be happy in so far as they learn to do justice and be righteous. All else is not only vain but leads straight to destruction. To teach the people to get rich by hook or by crook is to do them an immense disservice.[15] An economics that inculcates Mammon worship and enables the strong to amass wealth at the expense of the weak is a false and dismal science. It spells death. True economics, on the other hand, stands for social justice, it promotes the good of all equally including the weakest, and is indispensable for decent life.[16]

Everybody is born equal, meaning that we have a right to equal opportunity, all have not the same capacity. People with talents will have more and they will utilise their talents for this purpose. If they utilise their talent kindly, they will be performing the work of the state. Such people are the trustees. Such people will be allowed to work more but the bulk of his greater earnings must be used for the good of the state, just as the income of all earning sons of a father go to the common family fund.[17]

The real implication of equal distribution is that each man shall have the wherewithal to supply all his natural wants and no more. To bring this ideal into being the entire social order has got to be reconstructed. A society, based on non-violence, cannot nurture any other ideal. To the same extent as we progress towards our goal we shall find contentment and happiness and to that extent too, we shall have contributed towards bringing into being of non-violent society.[18]

The *Swaraj* of my dream is the poor man's *Swaraj.* The necessaries of life should be enjoyed by you in common with those enjoyed by the princes and the moneyed men. This is not necessary for happiness. I have not the slightest doubt that *Swaraj* is not *Purna Swaraj* until these amenities are guaranteed to you under it.[19]

In answer to a question, Gandhiji replied that if India was to live an exemplary life of independence which would be envy of the world, all *bhangis,* doctors, lawyers, teachers, merchants and others would get the same wages for an honest day's work. Indian society may never reach the goal but it was the duty of every Indian to set his sail towards that goal and no other if India was to be a happy land.[20]

Gandhiji suggests that if India is to evolve among non-violent lines, it will have to decentralise many things. Centralisation cannot be sustained and defended without adequate force. Simple homes from which there is nothing to take away require no policing, the palaces of the rich must have strong guards to protect them against dacoity. Rurally organised India will run less risk of foreign invasion than urbanised India, well equipped with military, naval and air forces. You cannot build non-violence on a factory civilization, but it can be built on self-contained villages—rural economy eschews exploitation altogether and exploitation is the essence of violence. Centralisation as a system is inconsistent with non-violent structure of society.[21]

Sarvodaya spirit is ingrained in India's past. To observe morality is to attain mastery over our mind and our passions. We notice that the mind is restless bird, the more it gets the more it wants, and still remains unsatisfied. The more we indulge our passions the more unbridled they become. Our ancestors, therefore, set a limit to our indulgences. They saw that happiness was largely a mental condition. Even psychology explains that happiness is a function of attitude. A man is not necessarily happy because he is rich, or unhappy because he is poor. The rich are often seen to be unhappy and the poor to be happy. Millions will remain poor and observing this, our ancestors dissuaded us from luxuries and pleasures. We have no life-corroding competition. Each followed his own occupation and trade and charged a reasonable wage. Justice was tolerably fair. The ordinary practice was to avoid courts. There were no touts to lure people into them, the common people lived independently and followed their agricultural occupation.[22]

Gandhiji held the view that industrialism was to be curse for mankind. Industrialism depends entirely on your capacity to exploit, on foreign market being open to you and on the absence of competition. The present distress is undoubtedly insufferable. Pauperism must go. But industrialism is no remedy.

Machinery has its place, it has come to stay. But it must not be allowed to displace necessary human labour. An improved plough is a good thing. But if by some chance one man could plough up by some mechanical invention of his the whole of the land of India, and control all the agricultural produce and if millions had no other occupation, they would starve, and being idle, they would become dunces as many already become.

I would welcome every improvement in the cottage machine but I know that it is criminal to displace hand labour by the introduction of power-driven spindles unless one is at the same time ready to give millions of farmers some other occupations in their homes.[23] Are you against all machinery? My answer is emphatically no. But I am against its indiscriminate multiplication. I am uncompromisingly against all destructive machinery. But simple tools and instruments such as machinery as saves individual labour and lightens the burden of the millions of cottages, I should welcome.[24]

What I object to is the craze for machinery, not machinery as such. The craze is for what they call labour-saving machinery. Men go on saving labour till thousands are without work and thrown on the open streets to die of starvation. The impetus behind it all is not the philanthropy to save but greed. It is against this system of things that I am fighting with all my might. One thing should be clear that our supreme consideration is man. The machine should not tend to make atrophied the limbs of man. For instance, take the case of the Singer Sewing Machine. It is one of the few useful things ever invented and there is a romance about the device itself. This is rare service to mankind which help them without displacing anybody.

Gandhiji advocated the industrialisation of the villages in a different way which he called rural industrialisation. The revival of the village is possible only when it is no more exploited. Industrialisation on a mass scale will necessarily lead to passive or active exploitation of the villagers as the problem of competition and marketing come in. Therefore, we have to concentrate on the village being self-contained, manufacturing mainly for use. Provided this character of the village industry is maintained there would be no objection to villagers using even the modern machines and tools that they can make and can afford to use. Only they should not be used as a means of exploitation of others.[25]

When production and consumption both become localised, the temptation for speed up production indefinitely and at any price disappears. All the endless difficulties and problems that the present day economic system presents, too, would then come to an end. There could be no unnatural accumulation or hoards in the pockets of few and want in the midst of plenty in regard to the rest.

Then you do not envisage mass-production as an ideal future for India? Oh yes, mass-production, certainly, but not based on force. After all, message of spinning wheel is that. It is mass-production, but mass-production in people's own homes. If you multiply individual production to millions of times, would it not give you mass-production on a tremendous scale? I oppose machinery only because and when it concentrates production and distribution in the hands of the few. I hate privilege and monopoly. Whatever cannot be shared with masses is taboo to me—that is all.[26]

Relation between capital and labour under this ideal situation will be different from what is thought to be in the existing context. When we come to believe that capital is all in all on earth. But a moment's thought would show that labour has at its disposal capital which the capitalist will never possess. Ruskin taught that labour had unrivalled opportunities. Sir Daniel Hamilton, an economist and himself a capitalist, came to the conclusion through his research and experiment that it was wrong to think that a piece of metal constituted capital. He says it is wrong even to think that so much produce is capital, but he adds that if we go to the very source, it is labour that is capital and that living capital is inexhaustible.[27]

Trusteeship

Gandhiji opines: I am for the establishment of right relations between capital and labour. I do not wish supremacy of one over the other. I do not think there is any natural antagonism between them.[28]

Trusteeship is the cornerstone of *Sarvodaya.* Gandhiji held the position that everything belonged to God and was from God. Therefore, it was for His people as a whole, not for a particular individual. When an individual had more than his proportionate portion he became a trustee of that portion for God's people. If this truth is imbibed by the people generally, it would become legalised and trusteeship would become a legalised institution. He wished it became a gift from India to the world. There would be no exploitation and no reserves. My theory of trusteeship is no make-shift, certainly no camouflage. I am confident that it will survive all other theories. It has the sanction of philosophy and religion behind it. That possessors of wealth have not acted up to the theory does not prove its falsity. It proves the weakness of the wealthy. No other theory is compatible with non-violence.[29]

The Draft on Trusteeship was finalised by Gandhiji which consists of six essential elements :

(i) Trusteeship provides a means of transformimg the present capitalist order of society into an egalitarian one. It gives no quarter for capitalism, but gives the present owning class a chance of reforming itself. It is based on faith that human nature is never beyond redemption.

(ii) It does not recognise any right of private ownership of property except inasmuch as it may be permitted by society for its own welfare.

(iii) It does not exclude legislative regulation of ownership and use of wealth.

(iv) Thus under the state regulated trusteeship, an individual will not be free to hold his wealth for selfish satisfaction or in disregard of the interest of society.

(v) Just as it is proposed to fix a decent minimum living wage, even so a limit should be fixed for the maximum income that could be allowed to any person in society. The difference between such minimum and maximum incomes should be reasonable and equitable and variable from time to time so much so that the tendency would be towards obliteration of the difference.

(vi) Under the Gandhian economic order, the character of production will be determined by social necessity and not by personal whim or greed.[30]

Gandhiji told the *zamindars* in a very clear tone. All your fears and misgivings, permit me to tell you, are those of guilty conscience. Wipe out justices you may have been consciously or unconsciously guilty of. The ryots themselves have no greater ambition than to live in peace and freedom and they will never grudge your possession of property provided you use it for them.[31]

As regards the ownership of land, real socialism has been handed down to us by our ancestors who taught : All land belongs to Gopal, where then is the boundary line. Man is the maker of that line and he can, therefore, unmake it. Here Gopal means God and in modern language it means the state, i.e. the people. That the land today does not belong to the people is too true. But the fault is not in the teaching. It is in us who have lived up to it. Gandhi said in answer to a question that notion of cooperation was that the land would be held in cooperation by the owners and tilled and cultivated also in cooperation. This would cause a saving of labour, capital, tools, etc. The owners would work in cooperation and own capital, tools, animals, seeds, etc. in cooperation. Cooperative farming of his conception would change the face of land and banish poverty and idleness from their midst. All this was only possible if people became friends of one another and as one family.[32]

Social Order

Gandhiji also visualised a social order compatible with conception of Sarvodaya Samaj. Gandhi holds that non-violence is not merely a personal virtue, it is also a social virtue to be cultivated like other virtues. Surely, society is largely regulated by the expression of non-violence in its mutual dealings. What is desired is an extension of it on a larger national and international scale. The individual and society are interdependent. To quote Gandhi :

> I value individual freedom but must not forget that man is essentially a social being. He has risen to his present status by learning to adjust his individualism to the requirements of social progress. Unrestricted individualism is the law of the beast of jungle. We have to learn to strike the mean between individual freedom and social restraints. Willing submission to social restraint for the sake of well-being of the whole society enriches both the individual and the society of which one is a member.[33]

Gandhiji ruled out any scope for untouchability in his ideal social order and supported *Varnashrama Dharma* which is the mission of man on this earth. He also discussed caste *vs.* varna. Historically speaking, caste may be regarded as man's experiment or social adjustment in the laboratory of Indian society. Law of Varna establishes certain sphere of action for certain people with certain tendencies which avoided all unworthy competition. But my conviction is that an ideal social order will only be evolved when the implications of this law are fully understood and given effect to.[34]

He appreciated the institution of marriage. The wife is not the husband's bond slave, but his companion and his helpmate, and an equal partner in all his joys and sorrows—as free as the husband to choose her own path.[35] Marriage is a natural thing in life, and to consider it derogatory in any sense is wholly wrong. The ideal is to look upon marriage as a sacrament and therefore to lead a life of self-restraint and the marital relation.[36]

He further asserts that voluntary widowhood consciously adopted by a woman who has felt affection of a partner adds grace and dignity to life, sanctify the home and uplifts religion itself. Widowhood imposed by religion or custom is an unbearable yoke and defiles the home by secret vice and degrades religion. Marriage confirms the right of union between two partners to the exclusion of all others but it confers no right upon one partner to demand obedience of the other to one's wish for union. What should be done when one partner on moral or other grounds cannot conform to the wishes of other is a separate question. Personally, if divorce was the only alternative, I should not hesitate to accept it, rather than interrupt my moral progress assuming that I want to restrain myself on purely moral grounds.[37]

Political Order

Gandhiji also described the political order of the *Sarvodaya* state. Character would be the basis of *Sarvodaya* state. *Swaraj* means self-control. Only he is capable of self-control who observes the rules of morality, does not cheat or give up truth, and does his duties to his parents, wife and children, servants and neighbours. Such a man is in enjoyment of *Swaraj,* no matter where he lives. A state enjoys *Swaraj* if it can boast of a large number of such good citizens. India must indeed have *Swaraj* but she must have it by righteous methods. Our *Swaraj* must be real *Swaraj* which cannot be attained by either violence or industrialisation. India was once a golden land, because Indians then had a heart of gold. The land is still the same but is a desert because we are corrupt. It can become a land of gold again only if the base metal of our present national character is transmuted into gold. If every Indian sticks to truth, *Swaraj* will come to us of its own accord. True democracy or *Swaraj* of the masses can never come through untruthful and violent means, for the simple reason that the natural corollary to their use would be to remove all opposition through the suppression or extermination of the antagonists. That does not make for individual freedom. Individual freedom can have the fullest play only under a regime of unadulterated *Ahimsa.*[38]

Sarvodaya Democracy

In this structure composed of innumerable villages, there will be ever widening, never ascending circles. Life will not be a pyramid with the apex sustained by the bottom. But it will be an oceanic circle whose centre will be the individual always ready to perish for the village, the latter ready to perish for the circle of villages, till at last the whole becomes one life composed of individuals, never aggressive in their arrogance but ever humble, sharing the majesty of the oceanic circle of which they are integral units. Therefore, the outermost circumference will not wield power to crush the inner circle but will give strength to all within and derive its own strength from it. Let India live for this picture, though never realizable in its completeness. True democracy cannot be worked by twenty men sitting at the centre. It has to be worked from below by the people of every village.[39]

If we want Swaraj to be built on non-violence, we will have to give the villages their proper place. Under the Swaraj based on non-violence nobody is anybody's enemy, everybody contributes his or her due quota to the common goal, all can read and write, and their knowledge keeps growing from day to day basis. No one is a pauper and labour can always find employment. There is no place under such a government for gambling, drinking and immorality or for class hatred. The rich will use his riches wisely and usefully, and not squander them in increasing their pomp and worldly pleasures. Hindu-Muslim differences, untouchability, vertical differences between high and low, these must not be.[40]

Political Power

To me political power is not an end but one of the means of enabling people to better their condition in every department of life. Political power means capacity to regulate national life through national representatives. If national life becomes so perfect as to become self-regulated, no representation becomes necessary. There is then a state of enlightened anarchy. In such a state, everyone is his own ruler. He rules himself in such a manner that he is never a hindrance to his neighbour. In the ideal state, therefore, there is no political power because there is no state. But the ideal is never fully realised in life. Hence a classical statement of Thoreau that government is the best which governs the least.[41]

Gandhiji looks upon an increase in the power of state with the greatest fear, because, although while apparently doing good by minimising exploitation, it does the greatest harm to mankind by destroying individuality which lies at the root of all progress. The state represents violence in a concentrated and organised form. The individual has a soul, but as the state is a soulless machine, it can never be weaned from violence to which it owes its very existence. It is my firm conviction that if the state suppressed capitalism by violence, it will be caught in the coils of violence itself and fail to develop non-violence at any time.

What I would personally prefer, would be, not a concentration of power in the hands of the state but an extension of the sense of trusteeship; as in my opinion, the violence of private ownership is less injurious than the violence of the state. However, if it is unavoidable, I would support a minimum of state ownership. What I disapprove of is an organisation based on force which a state is, voluntary organisation there must be.[42] In the democracy which I have envisaged, a democracy established by non-violence, there will be equal freedom for all. Everybody will be his own master.

Self-Government

As every country is fit to eat, to drink and to breathe, even so is every nation fit to manage its own affairs, no matter how badly.[43] Self-government means continuous efforts to be independent of government control whether it is foreign government or whether it is national. Swaraj government will be a sorry affair if people look up to it for the regulation of every detail of life.

By *Swaraj* I mean the government of India by the consent of the people as ascertained by the largest number of the adult population, male or female, native born or domiciled, who have contributed by manual labour to the service of state and who have taken the trouble of having registered their names as voters. I hope to demonstrate that real *Swaraj* will come not by acquisition of power by a few but by acquisition of the capacity by all to resist authority when abused. In other words, *Swaraj* is to be attained by educating the masses to a sense of their capacity to regulate and control authority.[44]

By political independence I do not mean an imitation of the British House of Common or the Soviet rule or Fascist rule of Italy or the Nazi rule of Germany. They have systems suited to their genius. We must have ours suited to ours. I have described it as *Ramraj,* i.e. sovereignty of the people based on pure moral authority.[45]

The rule of majority has a narrow application, i.e. one should yield to the majority in matters of detail. But it is slavery to be amenable to the majority, no matter what its decisions are. Democracy is not a state in which people are like sheep. Under democracy individual liberty of opinion and action is zealously guarded. I therefore believe that the minority has a perfect right to act differently from the majority as long as it does not act in the name of the Congress.[46] In matter of conscience the law of majority has no place.[47]

Gandhiji swore by the franchise of all adults, male and female, above the age of twenty-one or even eighteen. He would bar old men like himself. They were of no use as voters. India and the rest of the world did not belong to those who were on the point of dying. To them belonged death, life to the young. Thus he would have bar against persons beyond certain age, say fifty, as he would against youngster below eighteen. Side by side with adult franchise, or even before that, he pleaded for universal education, not necessarily literacy except as perhaps an aid. He would give them sufficient knowledge in the rich languages of which any country would be proud of.[48] Gandhiji held that the people of all provinces belonged to India and India belonged to all. The only condition was that no one could go and settle in another province to exploit it or rule it or to injure its interest in any way. All were servants of India and they lived only in the spirit of service. In regard to people from outside settling in a province, Gandhiji observed: Naturally, they should not form a separate colony as if they were foreigners. Live in Rome as the Romans do, is a sound common sense maxim so long as it does not apply to Roman vices. The process of progressive blending must be one of rejecting the bad and absorbing the good. The bane of our life is our exclusive provincialism, whereas my province must be co-extensive with the Indian boundary so that ultimately it extends to the boundary of the earth. Else it perishes.[49]

State should undoubtedly be secular. Everyone living in it should be entitled to profess his religion without let or hindrance, so long as the citizen obeyed the common law of land. He supported the partnership with Britain on equal terms. The partnership must mean that exploitation shall cease, and if Great Britain should not desist from it, India should sever the connection. Regarding relations to other nations, Gandhi observes; it is calculated not only to hurt other nations but to benefit all in the true sense of the word. India's freedom as conceived by me can never be a menace to the world.[50]

My notion of *Purna Swaraj* is not isolated independence but healthy and dignified interdependence. Through *Swaraj,* we would serve, the whole world. There is no limit to extending our services to our neighbours across state-made frontiers. God never made those frontiers.[51]

There will be an international league only when all the nations, big or small, comprising it are fully independent. The nature of that independence will correspond to the extent of non-violence assimilated by the nations concerned. One thing is certain. In a society, based on non-violence, the smallest nation will feel as tall as the tallest. The idea of superiority and inferiority will be wholly obliterated.[52]

Resistance to Evil

Non-violence is not a resignation from all real fighting against wickedness. On the contrary, the non-violence of my conception is a more active and real fight against wickedness than retaliation whose very nature is to increase wickedness. I contemplate a mental and therefore a moral opposition to immoralities. I seek entirely to blunt the edge of the tyrant's sword, but by putting up against it a sharper edged weapon, but by disappointing his expectation that I would be offering physical resistance. The resistance of the soul that I should offer would elude him. It would at first dazzle him and at last compel recognition from him, which recognition would not humiliate him but would uplift him.[53]

Satyagrah

In *Satyagraha*, there is not the remotest idea of injuring the opponent. *Satyagrah* postulates the conquest of the adversary by suffering in one's own person. The hardest heart and the grossest ignorance must disappear before the rising sun of suffering without anger and without malicea.[54]

Non-violence in its dynamic condition means conscious suffering. It does not mean meek submission to the will of the evil-doer, but it means the putting of one's whole soul against the will of the tyrant. Working under this law of our being, it is possible for a single individual to defy the whole might of an unjust empire to save his honour, his religion, his soul and lay the foundation for that empire's fall or its regeneration.[55]

The Satyagrahi's course is plain. He must stand unmoved in the midst of all cross-currents. He may not be impatient with blind orthodoxy, nor be irritated over the unbelief of the suppressed people. He must know that his suffering will melt the stoniest heart of the stoniest fanatics. He must know that relief will come when there is least hope for it. For such is the way of the cruelly-kind Deity who insists upon testing His devotee through a fiery furnace and delights in humbling him to the dust.[56]

There is no room for cowardice in Satyagrah philosophy. My creed of non-violence is an extremely active force. There is hope for a violent man to be some day non-violent, but there is none for a coward. I have therefore said more than once that if we do not know how to defend ourselves, our women and our places of worship by the force of suffering, i.e. non-violence, we must, if we are men, be at least able to defend all these by fighting.[57]

There are two ways of defence. The best and the most effective is not to defend at all but to remain at one's post-risking every danger. The next best but equally honourable method is to strike bravely in self-defence and put one's life in the most dangerous positions. Non-violence and cowardice go ill together. I can imagine a fully armed man to be at heart a coward. Possession of arms implies an element of fear, if not cowardice. But true non-violence is an impossibility without the possession of unadulterated fearlessness.[58]

I do believe that where there is only a choice between cowardice and violence, I would advise violence. I would rather have India resort to arms in order to defend her honour than that she should, in a cowardly manner, become or remain a helpless witness to her own dishonour. But I believe that non-violence is infinitely superior to violence, forgiveness is more manly than punishment. Forgiveness adorns the soldier. But abstinence is forgiveness only when there is the power to punish; it is meaningless when it pretends to proceed from a helpless creature. But I do not believe India be helpless. I do not believe to be a helpless creature. Strength does not come from physical capacity, it comes from an indomitable will.[59]

It is never the intention of a *Satyagrahi* to embarrass the wrong doer. The appeal is never to his fear; it must be, always to his heart. The *Satyagrahi's* object is to convert, not to coerce, the wrong doer. He should avoid artificiality in all his doings. He acts naturally and from inward conviction. This required a detached state of mind and it is a state very difficult to reach. Nevertheless, for a *Satyagrahi* it is absolutely essential. Three-fourths of the miseries and misunderstandings of the world will disappear, if we step into the shoes of our adversaries and understand their standpoint. I have found that mere appeal to the reason does not answer where prejudices are age long and based on supposed religious authority. Reasons must be strengthened by suffering and suffering opens the eyes of understanding. Our motto must ever be conversion by gentle persuasion and a constant appeal to the head and the heart.[60]

A *Satyagrahi* bids goodbye to fear. He is, therefore, never afraid of trusting the opponent. Even if the opponent plays him false twenty times, the Satyagrahi is ready to trust him the twenty first time, for an implicit trust in human nature is the very essence of his creed.

Certain rules have been, prescribed for *Satyagrahi* by Gandhiji :

(1) There must be common honesty among *Satyagrahis.*

(2) They must render heart discipline to their commander. There should be no mental reservation.

(3) They must be prepared to lose all, not merely their personal liberty, not merely their possessions, land, cash, etc. but also liberty, possessions of their families, and they must be ready cheerfully to face bullets, bayonets or even slow death by torture.

(4) They must not be violent in thought, word or deed towards the enemy or among themselves.[61]

A non-cooperator is nothing if he is not humble. He who offers a little sacrifice from a lowly and religious spirit quickly realises the littleness of it. Once on the path of sacrifice we find out the measure of our selfishness and must continually wish to give more and not be satisfied till there is a complete self-surrender. Thus, humility is the basic quality of non-cooperator.[62]

Fasting unto death is an integral part of *Satyagrah* and it is the greatest and most effective weapon in its armoury under given circumstances. Not everyone is qualified for undertaking it without a proper course of training. Fast is the last weapon in the armoury of the votary of *Ahimsa.* When human ingenuity fails, the votary fasts. This fasting quickens the spirit of prayer. Fasting is spiritual act and, therefore, addressed to God. Such a fast is undertaken in obedience to the dictate of the inner voice and, therefore, prevents haste.[63]

Gandhiji was against 'Sitting Dharna'. He called it barbarity, for it is a crude way of using coercion. It is also cowardly because one who sits *Dharna* knows that he is not going to be trampled over. It is difficult to call the practice violent but it is certainly worse. If we fight our opponent we at least enable him to return the blow. I know that the overzelous students who sat *Dharna* never thought the barbarity of the deed. Let non-cooperationists therefore beware of everything they do. There must be no impatience, no barbarity, no insolence, no undue pressure.[64]

Our tyranny, if we impose our will on others, will be infinitely worse than that of the handful of Englishmen who form the bureaucracy. Theirs is a terrorism imposed by a minority struggling to exist in the midst of opposition. Ours will be a terrorism imposed by a majority and therefore worse and really more godless than the first. We must therefore eliminate compulsion in any shape from our struggle. The indispensable condition of success is that we encourage the greatest freedom of opinion we may not in the very act of fighting the restraint on opinion be guilty ourselves of imposing it on others.[65]

It is essence of *Satyagrah* that those who are suffering should alone offer it. Cases can be conceived when what may be termed sympathetic *Satyagrah* may be legitimately applied.

The idea underlying *Satyagrah* is to convert the wrong doer, to awaken the sense of justice in him, to show him also that without the cooperation, direct or indirect, of the wronged the wrong doer cannot do the wrong intended by him. If the people in either case are not ready to suffer for their causes, no outside help in the shape of *Satyagrah* can possibly bring true deliverance.[66]

In a *Satyagrah* campaign the mode of fight and the choice of tactics, whether to advance or retreat, offer civil resistance or organise non-violent struggle through constructive work and purely selfless humanitarian services, are determined according to the exigencies of the situation. Discipline has a unique place in non-violent strategy, but much more is required. In a *Satyagrah* army, everybody is a soldier and a servant. Mere discipline cannot make for leadership. The latter calls for faith and vision.[67] In every great cause, it is not the number of fighters that counts but it is the quality of which they are made that becomes the deciding factor. The greatest men of the world have always stood alone. *Satyagrah* is one of the most powerful methods of direct action, a *Satyagrahi* exhausts all other means before he resorts to *Satyagrah.* He will, therefore, constantly and continually approach the constituted authority, he will appeal to public opinion, educate public opinion, state his case calmly and coolly before everybody, who wants to listen to him and only after he has exhausted all these avenues will he resort to *Satyagrah.*

At the root of the doctrine of equal distribution must be that of the trusteeship of the wealthy for superfluous wealth possessed by them. For according to the doctrine they may not possess a rupee more than their neighbours. This can be done either by violent means or by resorting to peaceful and non-violent measures. Decidedly, latter is superior to the former. The violent action will not suit the society. Therefore, non-violent way is evidently superior. The rich man will be left in possession of his wealth, of which he will use what he reasonably requires for his own personal needs and will act as a trustee for the remainder to be used for the society. In this case, honesty on the part of the trustee is assumed. If rich fails to pay heed to this doctrine, then non-violent, non-cooperation and civil disobedience as the right and infallible means can be resorted to. No rich man can accumulate wealth without the cooperation of the poor in society. If this awareness were to penetrate and to spread amongst the poor, they would become strong and would learn how to free themselves by the means of non-violence from the crushing inequalities which brought them to the verge of starvation.

Class war is foreign to the genius of India. Socialism and communism of the West are based on conceptions which are fundamentally different from ours. Their belief is in the essential selfishness of human nature. Gandhiji disagrees for he holds that the essential difference between man and the brute is that former can respond to the call of the spirit in him, can rise superior to the passions that he owns in common with the brute and, therefore, superior to selfishness and violence which belong to the brute nature and not to the immortal spirit of man. This is the fundamental conception of Hinduism. Our socialism or communism should, therefore, be based on non-violence and harmonious cooperation of labour and capital, landlord and tenant.[68]

The idea of class war is not convincing hence does not appeal to me. Gandhi holds that in India a class war is not only inevitable, but it is avoidable if we have understood the message of non-violence. Those who talk about class war as being inevitable, have not understood the implications of non-violence or have understood them only skin-deep. It is equally wrong to presume that Western socialism or communism is the last word on the question of mass poverty.

Now the question of state action comes in. I am afraid that for years to come India would be engaged in passing legislation in order to raise the downtrodden, the fallen, from the mire into which they have been sunk by the capitalists, by the landlords, by the so-called higher classes, and then, subsequently and scientifically by the British rulers. If we are to lift these people from the mire, then it would be the bounden duty of the National Government of India, in order to set its house in order continually to give preference to those people and even free them from the burdens under which they are being crushed.

For combating social menace and communal disturbances, Gandhi suggested formation of Peace Brigade and prescribed qualifications for members of the Brigade. At the same time, he laid down conditions for the volunteers of the Peace Brigade:

(1) A volunteer may not carry any weapon.
(2) The members of the corps should be easily recognisable.
(3) Every volunteer must carry bandages, scissors, needle and thread, surgical knife, etc. for rendering first aid.
(4) He should know how to carry and remove the wounded.
(5) He should know how to put out fires and know how to manage rescue work.
(6) He should be well acquinted with the residents of the locality.
(7) He should recite Ramanama ceaselessly in his heart and persuade others to believe to do likewise. He also suggested to meet social evils like theft, assault on women and other infirmities which afflicted a civil society but he believed in moral persuasion and not physical force and coercion to deal with the situation.

Work and Work Programme

For establishing *Sarvodava Samaj,* the qualifications have been prescribed by Gandhiji for *Satyagrahi.* These qualifications are regarded essential for *Sarvodaya* worker:

(1) He must have living faith in God.
(2) He must believe in truth and non-violence.
(3) He must be leading a chaste life and be ready to give up his life and property for the sake of his cause.
(4) He must be habitual khadi-weaver and spinner.
(5) He must be a teetotaller and free from intoxicants.
(6) He must carry out with willing heart all the rules of discipline as may be laid down from time to time.[69]

Details of the constructive programme were given by Gandhiji in his pamphlet entitled : "Constructive Programme, Its Meaning and Place". The items listed in the pamphlet are : 1. Communal unity, 2. Removal of untouchability, 3. Prohibition, 4. Khadi, 5. Other village industries, 6. Village sanitation, 7. Basic education, 8. Adult education,

9. Women, 10. Education in health and hygiene, 11. Provincial languages, 12. National language, 13. Economic equality, 14. Kisans, 15. Labour, 16. Adivasis, 17. Lepers, 18. Students and 19. Improvement of cattle.

These are illustrative of the items of constructive programme but they are not exhaustive. It is obvious that Gandhiji had a holistic view of man and society and he spurned compartmentalisation. *Sarvodaya Samaj* means reconstruction of new social order based on peace, prosperity, happiness and welfare of all based on non-violence which is enduring and sustainable for mankind in the long run.

Many other distinguished disciples of Gandhiji have also expressed their opinions based on empirical experiences and insight developed through interaction with the masses. People want a revolutionary programme and think that a revolution cannot be wrought without bloodshed. Vinoba refused to accept this contention. He holds that those who think that a revolution cannot be wrought without bloodshed are not revolutionists at all. The object before them is not revolution but bring about an exchange of places of the present unhappy and happy one. A revolution must signify universal happiness without exception. A *Sarvodayist* wants to try for universal happiness and nothing less than universal happiness. While the Western mind is trained to think in terms of the greatest good of the greatest number, the Indian mind, from its very childhood, is taught to think in terms of the good of all. There was a time when a microscopic minority enjoyed at the cost of a great majority. Today the majority wants to be happy at the cost of the minority. But in India, quite contrary to this, we are taught to do unto others as we would like to be done unto ourselves. So long as people insisted on imposing their ideas on others without any regard to whether these others had understood or accepted them, the seed of violence, imperialism and world wars would not be rooted out. Lord Krishna tendered his best advice to Arjuna but at the end he asked him to do as he liked *Yathechhasi Tatha Kuru*. That should be their ideal, opines Vinoba.[70]

About economic equality, Vinoba compares it with five fingers of the hand. The moral of this analogy is that even if there cannot be absolute equality, there should also not be disproportionate inequality, but there should be equity, even though there is inequality.

J.C. Kumarappa, another votary of Gandhian philosophy, has also highlighted the problem of equitable wage. In capitalistic economics, labour is dealt with as a commodity to be bought and sold so wages appear as a price for this human considerations. Where we desire to deal with man as a human being, the consideration should be based on social values. Vinoba here talks in terms of discriminating equality. He holds that equality does not mean that every one should have five acres of land and the same kind of house or equal yardage of cloth. We only want that the things, which are necessary for life, such as air, water and land should be equally accessible to all. None will grudge the surplus which may be left over with some after all had enough of these things. We want equality tempered with discrimination we aim at spiritual equality based on discrimination.[71]

According to K.G. Mashruwala, khadi is the symbol of self-sufficient labour. The need of the hour is production with this new ideal. It has been repeatedly emphasised that if we utilise to the fullest extent our hands with the barest and simplest of instrument at our command our needs will be more than satisfied. Non-exploitation, decentralised society, simplicity, beauty of life and economic equality will be necessarily achieved if we learn to look at manual labour from this new point of view.[72]

K.G. Mashruwala lays down the fundamental principles of *Sarvodaya* approach to the problem of India's development :

(1) Respect for life is the first principle of *Sarvodaya.*
(2) Resources of nature being an essential means for this purpose. But between life and nature, the development of life should be the end and that of nature the means for it.
(3) Hence, the first concern of every society, as well as the state, should be to provide employment for every person within it according to his capacity, with such work as means as are immediately available to it.
(4) Standard of life should be distinguished from standard of living, it is the former that is fundamental and not the latter. A rise in the standard of living might even lower the standard of life by reducing man's physical, moral, intellectual and spiritual standards, power and potentialities.
(5) Planning must proceed with two objects : removal of natural or man-made impediments in the road to development of man, and provision of means, training and guidance for it.
(6) The obstacles in the way of his development are:
    (a) too much centralisation of the government and the production of wealth;

(b) the ownership and control by a few people or by big corporations;

(c) money dominated economy creating a large body of parasite;

(d) the institution of slavery in its modern forms;

(e) institution of interest along with rights of proprietorship over large units of wealth;

(f) on the one hand, the absolute neglect of the common man's health and training, implements, seeds, raw materials by the state; on the other, enforcement of rights and traditions, inculcation of customs, habits, vices, fashions and luxuries and provision of temptation, all bound to lead to his progressive deterioration from generation to generation; and

(g) the institution of political, economic and social order, in which he can play practically no part, take no initiative, but finds himself thoroughly tied down on all sides.

(7) Unless there are other nations available for unrestrained exploitation, no amount of the development of natural resources without the removal of these hindrances will bring about the welfare of even a majority, not to say even one particularly in fully populated countries. The problems of unemployment and high prices and hence sub-human conditions of living, disease, poverty, hunger, slavery of the masses, unsafe and disgraceful conditions for women, dacoities, robberies and corruption in administration and trade are bound to remain and may even increase. There might be plenty of goods and plenty of food, and yet there will be all the evils of insufficiency, unsatisfied needs and want of scope for the play of one's abilities.

(8) Even if the government planned nothing beyond the removal of these obstacles as rapidly as possible, the people would prosper, if not rapidly, at least slowly. If the plan seeks to go further to provide positive aids to the people, the immediate objective should be : (i) to be thoroughly self-sufficient; (ii) the food should not only be abundant, but should be normally available to every one; (iii) it should also be normally available to every able-bodied person in an honourable manner, and not by way of charity, doles, etc. Provision of

> employment of everyone should be joints item with production of food on a self-sufficiency basis; (iv) training of the people on the basis of Nai Talim of which Basic Education is a part; (v) agricultural implements should be available without creating indebtedness; (vi) public utility services whether managed by government or private agencies should not be administered for profit; (vii) temptation for intoxicants and luxurious habits should not be encouraged and licensed for revenues.

These are a few objectives of *Sarvodaya* planning. All planning, short-term or long-term, must be directed towards the achievement of these ends.[73]

According to K.G. Mashruwala, it appears that Vinobaji and other leaders of constructive work have placed a five-fold programme of work before the nation. Nation has tersely summed up in one half of his verse as follows :

> Internal purity, external cleanliness, labour, peace and dedication.

सर्वे भवन्तु सुखिनः,
सर्वे सन्तु निरामयः,
सर्वे भद्रानि पश्यन्तु,
मा कश्चित दुःख भाग भवेत।

NOTES

1. Gandhiji (1943): *Autobiography,* Pt. IV Chap. XVIII.
2. *Young India*, 09.12.1926.
3. *Harijan*, 18.01.1948.
4. *Amrit Bazar Patrika*, 17.09.1933.
5. *Harijan*, 05.09.1936.
6. From Yervada Mandir, 1945, p. 27.
7. Ibid.
8. *Harijan*, 23.02.1947.
9. M.K. Gandhi (1954): *Sarvodaya* (The Welfare of All), Navajivan Publishing House, Ahmedabad, p. 23.
10. *Young India*, 17.06.1926.
11. *Hind Swaraj*, 1946, pp. 35-36.
12. From Yervada Mandir, 1945, pp. 31-34.
13. *Young India*, 03.09.1925.

14. Gandhiji's Paraphrase of *Unto This Last,* 1951, p. 57.
15. *Ibid.,* pp. 50-53.
16. *Harijan*, 09.10.1937.
17. *Young India*, 26.11.1931.
18. *Harijan*, 25.08.1940
19. *Young India*, 26.03.1931.
20. *Harijan*, 16.03.1947.
21. *Harijan*, 18.01.1942.
22. *Hind Swaraj*, 1908, Ch. XIII.
23. *Young India*, 05.11.1926.
24. *Young India*, 17.06.1926.
25. *Harijan*, 29.08.1936.
26. *Harijan*, 02.11.1934.
27. India's Case for Swaraj, 1932, p. 393.
28. *Young India*, 08.01.1925.
29. *Harijan*, 16.12.1939.
30. *Harijan*, 25.10.1952.
31. *Amrit Bazar Patrika*, 02.08.1934.
32. *Harijan*, 09.03.1947.
33. *Harijan*, 27.05.1939.
34. *The Modern Review*, October, 1935, p. 413.
35. *Autobiography*, 1948, p. 38.
36. *Harijan*, 22.03.1942.
37. *Young India*, 08.10.1925.
38. *Harijan*, 25.05.1939.
39. *Harijan*, 18.01.1948.
40. *Harijan*, 25.03.1939.
41. *Young India*, 02.07.1931.
42. *The Modern Review*, 1935, p. 412.
43. *Young India*, 15.10.1931.
44. *Young India*, 29.01.1925.
45. *Harijan*, 02.01.1937.
46. *Young India*, 02.03.1922.
47. *Young India*, 04.08.1920.
48. *Harijan*, 02.03.1947.
49. *Harijan*, 21.09.1947.
50. *Young India*, 03.04.1924.
51. *Young India*, 31.12.1931.
52. *Harijan,* 11.02.1939.
53. *Young India*, 08.10.1925.
54. *Young India*, 19.02.1925.
55. *Young India*, 11.08.1920.
56. *Young India*, 04.06.1925.
57. *Young India*, 16.06.1927.
58. *Harijan*, 15.07.1939.
59. *Young India*, 11.08.1920.
60. *Young India*, 29.09.1921.
61. *Harijan*, 22.10.1938.

62. *Young India*, 29.09.1921.
63. *Harijan*, 21.12.1947.
64. *Young India*, 02.02.1921.
65. *Young India*, 27.10.1921.
66. *Harijan*, 10.12.1938.
67. *Harijan*, 28.07.1940.
67.(a) *Harijan*, 25.08.1940.
68. *Amrit Bazar Patrika*, 02.08.1934.
69. *Harijan*, 25.03.1939.
70. *Harijan*, 07.07.1951.
71. *Harijan*, 20.12.1952.
72. *Harijan*, 28.04.1951.
73. *Harijan*, 27.10.1951.

9

Total Revolution and Gandhi

Many people think that Gandhi's greatest concern was the achievement of Indian independence and that all his energy was directed towards that end. But it is necessary to realise that the political emancipation of a people was, to Gandhi, only the means for the fulfilment of a large mission. For Gandhi's purpose, global in its sweep, was much more than liberation of a single colony.

It was indeed to help a whole people to see the central truth, the foremost societal reality of our times, which had to, as Gandhi saw it, from the pattern of institutional growth for years to come. To help India, as the first among others, to perceive that goal of a new society was then the purpose. Ambitious Gandhi had, however, a three-fold task before him.

First of all, he had to fight a colonial power, as India's slavery stood in the way of realization of the global reality—his truth. He was then to lay down the conceptual foundations of the new society as well as to find appropriate methods for its realisation. The tasks were all the more difficult as Gandhi did not believe in building models and in imposing any frame on a community. After that he was then striving for a new society which had to grow from amongst the existing one.

For fulfilment of this social scheme, Gandhi wanted to determine the goal, structure and rationale for the new society and lay it before the people. To find the institutional framework suited for its maintenance and fruition as well as to discover the psychological stimulus for individual and community behaviour which will progressively lead towards those goals, were some of his endeavours. Last but not the least, in importance was his efforts to discover the means, not very different from the ends necessary to reach that goal. What he desired to accomplish in this context was to devise a specific structure of social action one that would develop and sustain political processes in the new society. That society of Gandhi's seeking was, however, to be radically different from the existing reality and, therefore, needed nothing less than a revolution for its fulfilment.

Gandhism is an inarticulate and mostly unwritten philosophy but nevertheless it presents a definite pattern of beliefs and attitudes towards the problem of life and the world capable of generating very active force towards, 'social change' or 'social revolution'. The essence of revolution is 'change', of course, it is a kind of change which is distinguished by its scope and speed. The term revolution, outside the natural sciences, cannotes a sweeping and sudden change in the entire power structure of the whole society. It is a major break in the continuity of development in the old and existing order. Changes occur and reoccur in human society. It seems that change is the eternal and immutable law of nature. But changes take place either consciously or unconsciously, suddenly or gradually, thoroughly or partially. In the former case alone, it is called revolution, otherwise it may be evolution or a reform as the case may be.

The essence of revolution is the sudden and thoroughgoing changes, not a violent upheaval which frequently accompanies it. On the other hand, we can show that the genuine revolution as a social phenomenon starts well in advance of the violent manifestation and has been practically accomplished before the manifestation takes place. This is a fact of history. The ground work for the great revolutions, like the English, the American, the French, and even Bolshevik and Chinese revolutions prepared much ahead in the minds of the people. Revolution is often preceded by cultural crisis.[1] Hence, Victor Hugo calls revolution as the larva of civilization.[2]

Great revolutions are work of principles than of bayonets. The revolution begins first in the best heads and then run down to the populace. That revolution is synonymous with violence, is the result of wrong study of history. However, in the 19th century politics the term revolution when used was meant to refer to political revolution. It is for their reason that the idea of revolution and violence appears so closely connected. For no political system is so flexible as to be susceptible to fundamental change by legal means, and illegality implies resort to force. But this simplistic identification is superficial and misplaced today, recasting of the social order is far more important characteristics of revolution than a mere change of government by the use of violence and force. This aspect of revolution distinguishes also from coup de etal, rebellion and insurrection.[3] Hence, strictly speaking, there was hardly any instance of total revolution in the past, which ushered a thorough going and extensive change in the socio-economic and political order of society. Hence, we can call them 'revolts' instead of revolution.[4]

For instance, in ancient Greece or Rome, many times the rule of the kings were changed into an aristocrat 'Republic and Republic into Empire'. During the middle ages, we hear about many a wars against feudal or Church tyranny. The English revolution during Charles I was a protest against arbitrary taxes, the American revolution too began on the question of 'no taxation without representation' and French revolution began with an effort to limit the power of kings and so on. However, none of them had a picture of total revolution.[5] What they had in mind were theoretical formulations. There was a wide gulf between theory and practice. For example, the battle cry of liberty, equality, etc. never meant socialisation of industry, abolition of private property or power at the working base.

But before we could establish the idea that violence is not a necessary element of revolution, we must examine the Marxian theory of revolution, which is indeed the first attempt at a planned and well-designed doctrine of revolution. Marxian theory of revolution is based on two fundamental beliefs: (i) doctrine of class struggle, and (ii) theory of relative morality.

According to Marx, "the history of hitherto existing societies is the history of class struggle which is inevitable and even automatic".[6] The 'forces of production' and 'production relations' create contradictions which lead to class conflict. With this class-struggle arises a violent crisis, we have a revolution in terms of establishment of the dictatorship of proletariat after overthrowing the bourgeoisie. This doctrine of class struggle very much resembles the Darvinian theory of struggle for survival. Even according to Hegel, the reality is constituted by the conflict of thesis and anti-thesis. To quote Marx, "Force is the midwife of every old society pregnant with how one" ... between equal rights force decides.[7] According to Engels, revolution is the forcible overthrow of the existing social order by the proletariat. Lenin supporting this view, says that "a violent revolution is inevitable against bourgeoisie government".[8] Thus, concludingly, it may be said that Marxism believes in the doctrine of inevitability of violence in revolution.

This view is not tenable. A genuine revolution cannot be legitimately identified with violence otherwise every act of murder, or every bloody war, however unjust they might be, will be called revolution. But we know that a real revolution always means a fundamental change in our ideas and ideologies, ethos and values of life. And it is foolish to say that we can change anybody's ideas or ideologies through some external physical force. Coercion may create some pattern of conformity but cannot change the heart and mind of the people.[9] However, Marxism holds that dynamics of change rests with the society and, therefore, if we change the society the individuals will be changed. But man is not merely a Pavlovian dog fit to be conditioned or reconditioned in accordance with the scheme of some self-made master having supreme political power. True, man is a social creature but he is also psychological being. He must listen to demands of human psychology which is against all force. It is human nature to react to force and to give to love and confidence. In fact, ideas create revolutions. There is more dynamite in an idea. But we cannot change anybody's mind through force. Hence, we can conclude that the more of violence, the less of real revolution. Hence bloody revolution is not a fact of revolution, it is a delusion.[10]

Bloodshed creates upheavals but not revolution.[11] Similarly, confiscation of property may be called rebellion but not revolution. Real revolution takes place when we change, our values change. All cultural change is a record of opinion change. However, the fundamental precondition of an everlasting revolution is that it should appeal to head and inspire the heart. Taken both the rational and irrational parts of man, let us accept that our opinion and attitudes are derived both rationally and irrationally. Those who think that our attitudes and opinions can never change betray an awful ignorance of human psychology. Nobody will doubt the enormous malleability of man and plasticity of human nature. One continues to change till his death. Similarly, our social structure is subject to incessant change. Society influences man but also creates history. He does not merely interpret the world but also alters it. The dynamics of change involves the idea of triple transformation of heart, head and social situations.[12] In fact, social change involves a double change—change in the individual and change in the social situation. Any change in the social situations depend upon a change in the heart of man. However, what occurs first is a change of opinion and then change of heart, consequent upon which there is complete change in the philosophy of life. Then only there is change in society because society consists of individuals. This is the science of revolution.[13] Even Marxists cannot honestly refute this doctrine of change of heart and change of ideas, though at times, they ridicule it like anything. The human heart functions in its own way, be he an atheist or a communist. It has its own throbbings and institutions. One who has feeling and intelligence is bound to respond to new ideas.[14]

Violent revolutions are the results of hopes unrealised and aspirations ruthlessly suppressed. The atmosphere of the whole society is surcharged with hate, fear and desire to revenge. Hence, violent revolutions, naturally, lead to unending spiral of counter-revolutions and civil wars, in which all human considerations of love, sympathy and fellow-feelings are forgotten. But the worst is that violence cannot establish a new social order based on higher and nobler values of life. Whatever will be established by violence can be destroyed by counter-violence. Thus the violent revolution carried the seed of its own destruction. It extirpates the vanquished, and divides the survivors, into two classes—bullies and cowards. It is an all round ruination of society. Its short-term glamour of success ends in disillusionment.[15] For thinking minds to blossom, for arts and science to flourish the first condition is a settled society where peace and harmony must prevail. Values and dignity of individual are accepted and respected.

The first and perhaps the worst casualty of a violent revolution is that of individual freedom and democracy. For example, during the French Revolution, a mild and weak monarch like Louis XVI was replaced by the mighty Nepolean; in England, the gentle Charles I was replaced by Cromwell; in Russia, Czar was replaced by a greater Czar, i.e. Stalin and Stalinism, and such examples can be exhaustive in the world history to prove this contention. These examples prove that violent revolutions have led to expansion of individual liberty, on the other hand, it had led to curtailment and suppression of individual freedom and abrogation of democracy and its values. When there is no regard for dignity of man and morality is reduced to a matter of convenience, there is no consideration of democracy. The political power is usurped by the political thugs, pindaris, and other unscrupulous power loving politicians, who ultimately drive out the reformers and idealists and entrench themselves into the authority for ever. Asoka Mehta opines that Grasham's law applies to Indian politics where bad politicians drive out good and conscientious politicians out of active politics through operation of manipulative strategies. Gandhi, on the other hand, believed that "True democracy can only be an outcome of non-violence".[16] Power never comes to the people at work and instead it goes either to a single powerful politician, like Hitler in Germany, Mussolini in Italy, Stalin in Russia or a self-perpetuating Junta of powerful politicians as in modern Russia or China. Thus in either case, the people at their working places do not and cannot share the fruits of revolution. So, the more of violence, the less of individual freedom.

A revolutionary ideology cannot for long remain isolated from practical life. It must arouse the masses to the pitch of enthusiasms. But in violent revolution, even the legitimate participation of the people is not possible. The powers of the modern state has greatly increased in this technological stage and any mass action against the authority of the state, to be successful, is bound to be non-violent. The world is sick of armed rebellions. The masses will not respond. In a movement in which masses have no active participation can do no good.[17] In the non-violent revolution, even the weakest can participate without becoming weaker. It means construction of a mass movement hence a quickening of the collective and community life. Therefore, the method of non-violent revolution is the swiftest the world has seen for it is the surest.[18] It is needless to say that it is the nobler way since it teaches the people to suffer voluntarily in the cause of truth and justice. Here we educate ourselves as well as our opponents in unselfishness from the beginning, so it blesses him who uses it, as well as him against whom it is used. Lastly, if we depend upon external violence for the vindication of our cause, then one who can yield greater violence may claim that justice lies in his side.[19]

Marx's adherence to the doctrine of economic interpretation of history led him to formulate the theory of material basis of revolution. But empirically, it has been proved that the social and political change in history have been caused and conditioned by changed ideas and values than by material causes. Our basic ideas evolve out of common social atmosphere, beliefs, emotions and needs. Each social change is brought about by corresponding change in its basic categories, which guide social thought, judgement, emotions and actions. Social revolutions try to show the weaknesses, inadequacy and contradiction of existing categories, and provide rational and emotional basis for the new philosophy. Hence, it is a misconception to think of material basis of revolution. It may be one of the components of revolution and not the exclusive one. It is neither supported by history, nor by scientific study. In America, there was nothing very wrong economically during the period of American revolution. Even in

France, there is no evidence to show that material conditions were worse during Louis XVI than Louis XIV or Nepolean. It was also true in medieval Europe and ancient Greece and Rome, people may have suffered from poverty and other ills without rising in revolt. In fact, revolutions in England, France or even Russia were inspired more by new ideas in religion and political governance than by economic and material considerations. There are many causes of revolutions, such as social discontent, continued political oppression, spiritual disquiet, growth of scientific inventions, revival and spread of knowledge, geographical discoveries, movements of people, imperial expansion, psychological causes like Odipus complex, influence of foreign education and culture, economic exploitation, class-struggle influence of a particular philosophy of life, internal dissentions among rulers, political corruptions, weakening and loss of credibility of the authority of the state, etc. Then it is wrong to think that the material and economic causes alone can create revolutions.

We have now considered, in details, the conditions in which a revolution becomes imperative and also why the revolution must be non-violent. However, it mast be clear that "a non-violent revolution is not just a violent revolution without violence".[20]

All the evidences we have from psychology, from history and philosophy, we are constrained to believe that for a new revolutionary vision, we must spell out into cogent and concise terms about relationship of means to ends and about innate nature of man. If man is bad by nature, nothing good can come out of him. In that case, we must give up all our efforts of education or lessons in socialism, democracy and internationalism etc. However, if he is good and only accidentally bad, we can hope to awaken and develop his goodness. But this can happen only by love, sympathy and faithful behaviour. Crowther rightly said, "You can bring the horse to the pond but you cannot make it drink. You can enact laws not to kill or steal but you cannot compel to be benevolent and sacrificing." So every action of regeneration of man must be moral because every effort enobles and elevates. Hence, there can be no room for bad means in pursuits of a good end. Even Marxist of today like Prof. A. Shishkin of Soviet Academy of Science speaks like Ruskin and Gandhi, "the means which are demoralising man and are cultivating cruelty, baseness, etc. cannot serve the noble end of the liberation of the people. We adopt the means that are strengthening the moral consciousness of man".[21] He further adds, "that is why, when one says that for Marxist the morality is a matter of convenience, one reveals serious misunderstanding of Marxism".[22] This speaks like *Mahabharata* and *Manusmriti*. By unrighteousness, man prospers, gains what appears desirable, conquers enemies, but perishes at the root."[23] What these ideas point to, is a form of strategy that is simultaneously revolutionary and supportive of life. With it we shall not fall into traps of either irrelevance or counter-revolution. This will be the revolution of man and for the mankind. Gandhian concept of revolution is all pervasive and all embracing. Gandhi was firmly entrenched in India's traditional spiritual wisdom and the very fact that he made effective application of it in all the different spheres of social, economic and political activities, is an unimpeachable evidence of his view which he shared with India's philosophers and religious reformers that there can be no efficient and effective organisation of our social inter-relationships without their deep roots in the understanding of human nature itself. We know how in spite of great material affluence that mankind might not have ever seen before, the problems with which mankind is faced have far outnumbered those with which men of ancient times struggled. It is familiar knowledge these days that social problems in such a prosperous and economically affluent country like America are agitating the minds of the thinking people there. Father Sheen reports that 'crime' in the United States has reached alarming proportions and in support of his contention he has cited statistics pertaining to various crimes which have increased many-fold. Alan Richartson has this to say about the state of affairs in the United Kingdom. It is hardly necessary to list the symptoms of the moral degeneration of Western civilization for these are obvious to all. The absence of sense of responsibility in the industrial order the insatiable demands of almost all sections of the community for more money for less work, the boredom of aimlessness, particularly among the youths, the mounting crime statistics, drug-addiction, suicides, broken homes, illegitimacy, venereal diseases, gambling and so on.[24]

Can we say that is a picture here in India is different from that which has been just depicted about the Western culture? Are not these social problems of a great catastrophic and dangerous character? and can we in the face of what we observe in India say that there is anything in consonance with our past traditions. This situation is posing serious challenges to social scientists today. We must ask if these social scientists who have so much fuss and jargons about the methods, data and so many other techniques which they bring to bear upon social evils of today, which unfortunately are increasing the more our government spends money over the many schemes for their eradication. There is no doubt that the methods which sociologists make use of in their study of human behaviour are quite barren and ineffective inasmuch as positivistic in their whole approach as they are, they can never come forward with any universal panacea for the evils to which our social life is subject.

It is just here that we are reminded of the place of Indian social thought and contribution of Gandhi made to it so far its revival and renewal for the elimination of our social evils are concerned. Preoccupied with empirical methods which are quite useful so far as the investigation of things in space and time are concerned, they extend their application even to the enquiry relating to human behaviour which doubtless is governed and controlled by human choice, desire and will, a sense of valuation, the consideration of means and ends. In fact, it is man that is at work in society rather than it is society solely that influences the man. Indeed, society without man is an abstraction and empty word and the kind of society that we have is determined by the kind of man that we are.

Some of the noted writers have agreed that there is no such thing as group mind. Gustave Le Bon maintained that the individual mind is superior to the group mind and that it is by concentration on the discipline of heart and mind of the individual that we can dream of a better society.[25] Quite in keeping with the best aspiration and ideals of Hindu thought and culture that Gandhiji firmly believed that religion alone can take care of all our ills on the individual and collective levels. Religion without perfection of human character is ineffective. It is the discipline of our whole personality that religion takes under its charge and it is the individual trained and disciplined in the light of true religion that alone can be the exemplar of society. Indian social thought is in this respect characteristically distinct from the Western social thought which derived its origin from Plato and Aristotle whose ideas also were shaped by the society in which they lived and whose constructive insights could not extend beyond the worship and adoration of the state. Patriotism was the highest virtue and religion had been adopted merely as a means for furthering social interests.

Gandhi was a man with firm convictions about the social significance of the Hindu religion and by what he taught, spoke and practised he demonstrated the truth of the fact that the temporal powers of the earth cannot vanquish the eternal flame of the spirit and that it is by the application of the spiritual laws to our social, economic and political problems that peace, prosperity and happiness can be ensured. Gandhi said, "To see the universal and all-pervading spirit of truth face to face, one must be able to love the meanest of creation as oneself. And a man who aspires after cannot afford to keep out of any field of life. That is why, my devotion to truth has drawn me into the field of politics; and I can say without the slightest hesitation and yet in all humility, that those who say that religion has nothing to do with politics do not know what religion means". The aphorism defining the nature of *Dharma* clearly and categorically hammers the truth that in India religion has never been meant to be something quite cut off from the worldly concern; rather it has been taken to be the very basis of human activity in all the undertakings in the different spheres of social, economic and political life. The vertical communications and horizontal relationships are related to each other as causes and effects and both are mutually implicative. It is religion alone that can be said to be the truly human preoccupation because nothing else can claim any title to integrative function that it possesses and it sundered from theology, politics, economics, psychology and sociology have been allowed to enjoy autonomy, we have, in effect, shaped human relations of their very vitality, their very life blood by which alone can they be sustained.

Gandhi's idea of peace is not a negative one, nor is non-violence negative in connotation. Both indicate a positive psychological attitude. Peace is not only a temporary suspension of armed conflict. Hobbes told us long ago that "war consists not in battle only nor in the act of fighting". It is the effect of perversion of the human will. It consists in the attitude of hostility between nations. War is war whether it is hot or cold and if it is to be averted and peace attained then the world needs the psychology that Gandhi, in line with the Indian social thought, wanted to be implanted in the minds and wills of every human being in the world. The socialistic pattern of society, which too has one of Gandhi's dreams that had its origin in Indian social thought. The insistence on *Asteya,* non-stealing and *Aparigrah,* a non-acceptance, which are common cardinal virtues necessary for the attainment of *Moksha,* have social implications. If all men realised the obligation of service, they would regard it as a sin to amass wealth, and then there would be, no inequalities of wealth and consequently no famine or starvation.[26] Bertrand Russel in his book, *Political Ideals,* tells us that there are in man two impulses, the possessive and the creative and that best life is the one in which the creative impulses play the largest part and the possessive impulses the smallest. He tells us further that the temptation to misuse of power is lessened by increasing the opportunities for the creative impulses, and by shaping education so as to strengthen these impulses and secondly, by diminishing the outlets for the possessive instinct. The diffusion of power, both in the political and economic spheres, would greatly diminish the opportunities for acquiring the habits of command, out of which the desire for exercising tyranny is apt to spring".[27]

Before analysing the concept of Total Revolution as conceived by Gandhi and finally popularised by Jayprakash Narayan, it would be in the fitness of the thing to discuss the concept of cultural revolution in China and its impacts on the Chinese society as a whole. Mao's final effort to regain control over the progress of revolution came in the form of power struggle against Liushaoqui and his supporters. Ever since Liu assumed power as head of state, Mao had continued to challenge his politics. Mao was not only angered by Liu's economic policies, but chairman and many of his supporters believed that revolutionary development of all aspects of Chinese society had stagnated. For them, China was still mired in enervating traditional cultural conventions, customs and habits that were millennia old. If Chinese society was to evolve from socialism to communism in accordance with Marxist theory then drastic change was necessary what was needed, according to Mao, was nothing less than a thorough revamping of Chinese culture. All aspects of culture had to be changed so that working class values replaced traditional bourgeois customs because, according to Marxist, cultural consciousness reflects economic values of the prevailing class. Mao Tse-tung explained to fellow revolutionaries:

> "In the world today, all culture, all literature and art belong to definite classes and are geared to define political lines. There is in fact no such thing as art for arts sake, art that stands above classes or art that is detached from or independent of politics".[28]

When the society is in its feudal or capitalist stage, culture is identified with the values of the wealthy. Education, literature and the arts all have their roots implanted deeply in this past and, more importantly, are often available only to the privileged. A problem for

Marxists is that the existence of elite is not necessarily challenged by a socialist revolution. Although specific groups, such as the land owners and wealthy bourgeoisie, may be annihilated during the revolution, they are merely replaced by another elite, namely party leaders and whose talents are needed in new social order. Actual makers of revolution had not forsaken attitudes from the past, since cultural values respected for centuries tend to pass into the new social order. The universities also produced a new privileged class. Mao feared that this situation would perpetuate a schism within society based on the privilege and deference accorded to those who possessed knowledge rather than those who did manual labour. Such attitudes were deeply ingrained in Chinese society with its Confucian heritage, a tradition which revered the Mandarin Scholar, with his long finger nails, a symbol of life without physical labour. As a result, the status of the new intellectual class, many of whom were sons and daughters of the revolution, was challenged by the Maoists in order to produce a new Chinese culture—a proletarian culture. Mao also believed in the need of permanent "revolution" to keep revolutionary and proletarian values alive. The generation of students and young leaders coming of age during the 1960s was too young to have experienced the privation of civil war. They had tittle appreciation for the struggles undertaken by the older generations to produce new society. Mao wanted to entrust China's future to youths and not to those he charged with taking the capitalist road. Moreover, Mao sought out the youth of the working class to lead the cultural revolution, since his goal was to establish a proletarian culture, a culture defined by the masses. Such changes did not come easily. There were many within the CCP who did not agree with such ideas. These people not only presented serious obstacles to the Maoist strategy, but they were also the ones who held power during the mid-1960s.[29]

On April 30, 1965 premier Zhou En-lai outlined the goals of Cultural Revolution:

> "A socialist cultural revolution with a significant historical meaning is now rising in our country. This is a fierce long-term struggle in the ideological sphere between the proletariat and the bourgeoisie. We have vigorously to promote proletarian thoughts and smash bourgeois thought in all academic, education, journalistic, art, literacy and other cultural circles. This is a crucial problem concerning the

> country as a whole, a problem of development in the socialist revolution in the present stage. It is of the atmost importance, involving the fate and future of our party and our country."

The cultural revolution was an attempt to transform Chinese society in a more profound way than the reform programme of the 1950s. Chinese culture would undergo a genuine metamorphosis and everyone would be called on to play a role in the drama. Confucian tradition and residual bourgeois materialism and capitalism were to be completely erased. These goals were never realised, but the cultural revolution dramatically and often painfully changed many people's lives. Society was rearranged at all levels when Maoist consistently enforced the downward transfer officials, intellectuals, the upper crust who survived the violence were routinely sent to rural areas to labour and live among the peasants. By 1967, at least 400,000 "enemies of the people" were forced to leave cities for rural areas. Urban high school students worked in factories or on farm for two or more years before going on to college. Managers did labourers' job and labourers participated in decision making and management. Careers were postponed for years, many were ruined. The teenagers sent to factories and farms far from home and family were often a problem than a help for local management. Efficiency was sacrificed for the spirit of revolution. Moreover, the well-being of millions of young Chinese was abandoned for the revolution.

The cost of human suffering is hard for the mind to grasp. Hu Yaobang, general secretary of the Communist Party, estimated that between the Anti-Rightist Campaign of 1967, which prepared the ground for the cultural revolution, and the conclusion of the upheaval, 100 million people became victims of its violence. (This is roughly one-tenth of the China's population.)

The rapid economic and industrial development characteristic of the first half of the 1960s was also sacrificed mainly by the rampages of the Red Guards. One sector profoundly affected by cultural revolution was education. The closing of schools disrupted educational continuity. Entirely new groups of students entered the university. The cultural revolution admission committee allowed only those with correct backgrounds to study beyond high school levels. Along with education, the arts and literature also came under heavy fire during cultural revolution. The cultural revolution also affected China's status internationally and it wreaked terrifying havoc in China bringing wholesale destruction to lives and property throughout the late 1960s

Unfortunately, what was supposed to have been a cultural revolution became instead a revolution against culture. The era of cultural revolution came to an end with the fall of the 'Gang of Four'. The impact of cultural revolution on Chinese culture has not been erased and perhaps never will be. The Marxist notion that the values and beliefs of the state reflect the interest of economically determined classes was the stimulus behind Mao's goal to produce a proletarian culture. Although Maoists' plans were not completely successful, significant changes in the arts were made. China's post-Mao leadership embarked on a revision of Mao's philosophy to launch a new modernisation campaign, now known as China's Second Revolution. This is the minimum and inevitable price which the society is obliged to pay if it opts for violent and coercive measure or even if it is imposed on it as happened in Russia, China and other countries where Marxian doctrine of class struggle and annihilation of the so-called class enemy were in operation. These events are sufficient to corroborate the points raised and emphasised by Gandhi.

It has been pointed out that Jayaprakash Narayan popularised the concept of Total Revolution. While unfolding his plan of struggle on behalf of the students struggle committee of Bihar at a mammoth public meeting at Patna on 5th June 1974, JP declared that the struggle was not going to be limited to securing the demands of the students, including resignation of the Ministry and the dissolution of the Assembly in Bihar, but it will bring about a Total Revolution or *Sampoorna Kranti,* which alone could solve the urgent problems of the country and usher in a new society. Greeted by the thunderous applause, the term immediately caught the imagination of a large number of people in the country. JP himself referred to it in almost all his subsequent speeches, stressing that it meant in essence an all comprehensive social revolution. Gandhi had already stressed the various aspects of social revolution. Numerous articles appeared in the press both eulogizing and attacking the concept of total revolution and JP was repeatedly asked to explain what he exactly meant by it.

Almost all who either eulogized or attacked the concept of total revolution thought that JP had for the first time used the term. Many still continue to think and write in the same vein. Actually, it was Karl Marx who had first used this term more than a century and a quarter before JP popularised it. Writing the *Poverty of Philosophy* (1847), he remarks:

> "Meanwhile the antagonism between the proletariat and the bourgeoisie is a struggle against class, struggle which carried to its highest expression is a total revolution".[30]

In a different sense, i.e. signifying a radical transformation not merely of our material conditions but also of the moral character of the individuals. The idea of total revolution was implicit in many of Gandhi's writings and speeches.[31] Vinoba explained the idea further. As early as in 1951, he declared: "My aim is to bring about a three-fold revolution. First, I want a change in people's heart; secondly, I want to create a change in their lives; and thirdly, I want to change the social structure".[32] In the sixties, he spoke in this vein frequently enough to warrant the use of "Towards Total Revolution" as the title of a book containing his speeches and published in 1968.[33] At least once he also used the term total revolution.[34] It has been aptly observed in a recent study that JP's movement for total revolution was continuation of the preceding movements for non-violent revolution through *Bhoodan* and *Gramdan*.[35] JP was fully justified in remarking on occasion: "There is hardly any difference between *Sarvodaya* and total revolution. If there is any then *Sarvodaya* is the goal and total revolution is the means. Total revolution is basic change in all aspects of life. There cannot be *Sarvodaya* without this".

Without using the term 'total revolution', JP himself had been emphasising since the mid-forties, if not earlier, the need for a social revolution which would not merely bring about a change in the structure of society, but also an improvement in the character of the individuals comprising it.[36] After he joined the *Bhoodan* Movement in the fifties, he laid particular stress on it. In course of an article published in 1969, he also used the term "total revolution" to describe the objectives of *Sarvodaya* movement in India, referring to the Bhoodan and *Gramdan* programmes, he observed: "Gandhi's non-violence was not just plea for law and order, or a cover for the *status quo* but a revolutionary philosophy. It is indeed a philosophy of a total revolution, because it embraces personal and social ethics and values of life as much as economic, political and social institutions and processes.[37] It is, however, a fact that the term 'total revolution' became a recurrent theme of JP's speeches and writings only since 1974 and it is only since then that it has taken its place in Indian political discourse.

What led JP to give a call for total revolution? More than a quarter century of experience of public life in independent India, first as a Marxist turned socialist and later as a *Sarvodaya* leader, had convinced him that piecemeal reforms of socio-economic and political system operating in India since the achievement of independence would not be able to bring about any significant change in the lives of mass of the people and that what required was a radical transformation of the entire social system. He, of course, recognised that *zamindari* has been ended, land reform measures adopted by the various legislatures and untouchability abolished by law. But most of the Indian villages still continued under the grip of the big and medium landowners, generally belonging to upper castes. The majority of villages in almost all parts of India consisted of small and marginal farmers, and landless labourers comprising Harijans and others belonging to the backward castes. Their conditions continued to be miserable. Harijans were still burnt alive.

The condition of *Adivasis* was similar and they continued to be mercilessly cheated and exploited by the money lenders. From the point of view of social and economic development, the picture was frightful. Population has gone on rising, so had poverty. More than forty per cent of population live below the poverty line and denied even some of the barest necessities of life, such as drinking water, food and clothing, housing, education and medical care. The question was: could a radical change in their gloomy picture be brought about by merely a change of government or enactment of some laws? JP's emphatic answer was no. In Indian context, examples are galore that despite enactments and legislations in various fields, situations continue to be the same. This systemic change was to be brought about neither by legislation nor by force from above but through public education and non-violent struggle by the people from below. In those countries where revolutions had been attempted through violence or force, power has passed into the hands of a coterie and people at large had failed to secure control over government. JP repeatedly warned the Indian people against being tempted by the example of such revolutions. "My conclusion, after a study of violent revolution", he observed in 1969, "is that a violent revolution does bring about a revolution in the sense that it uproots the old social order and destroys it from foundation, but it fails in achieving the objectives for which the revolution is made".[38] During the same year, he again stressed that once the revolutionaries of the day seize power, the people are inescapably subjugated to the juggernaut of the party and the state. Explaining why this happens, he further added, "It is not that the violent revolutions deceive and betray, it is just the logic of violence working itself out. It cannot be otherwise".[39] In a successful violent revolution, there is a widespread unorganised revolutionary violence which succeeds in accomplishing the destruction and uprooting of the old order. After this accomplishment, however, it becomes necessary to organise a force to stop further violence and to protect and consolidate the gains of revolution. Whoever controls that force wields supreme power. It is thus power passes from the hands of the people to a small coterie, sometimes even to one individual who rules in the name of revolution and keeps the people out of power.[40] Such an outcome can be avoided if a revolution is brought about through non-violent method.

The most important characteristic of this method is that its means must be in harmony with its ends. If the end is a non-violent society, the means must also be non-violent; if human freedom is the end, coercive means are ruled out; if man is an end in himself he cannot be used as a means; if truth is to be the basis of new life, untruthful means are inadmissible; if the end is dispersal of power, the means cannot be centralised power.[41] While referring to total revolution in course of his speeches and writings in 1974-75, JP continued to lay stress on the fact that such a revolution had to be brought about through the non-violent method and care should be taken to see that the democratic structure of the state was maintained intact. Indeed, one of the objectives of total revolution was to strengthen democracy by ensuring direct participation by the people in the work of government as far as possible. As JP put it in his notes on 23 August 1975 while in prison, "Total revolution has to be peacefully brought about without impairing the democratic structure of society and affecting the democratic way of the people."[42] JP's thinking is, however, not wholly identical with Vinoba's. He, for instance, differs from the latter in assigning priority to systemic change over change in the thinking and behaviour pattern of the individual. JP had been consistently emphasising the importance of the latter since the mid-forties and this had been partially responsible for his shift from socialism to *Sarvodaya*. Thus, while accepting that a non-violent revolution is likely to require a longer span of time than a violent revolution to accomplish its social objectives, he observes: "The basic systemic changes would happen first and the individual and group adaptations, mostly psychological latter".[43] Vinoba had a different approach to revolution. Merely a big change, he observes, does not make for revolution. As long as there is no revolution inside, there cannot be revolution outside. Changing mental attitude is termed as revolution. According to him, changes in individuals come first and then these lead to systemic change. Social revolution is secondary to individual revolution and is the sum total of revolution.[44]

He also welcomed a struggle because in his opinion, during a period of struggle the masses of revolution would be widely scattered among the people and contributes significantly to their awakening. This acceptance of the need of struggle in certain situation on JP's part further distinguishes his concept of non-violent revolution from that of Vinoba. For Vinoba never appreciated the need for struggle against the government and thought that in conditions obtaining in India after achievement of independence a social revolution could be brought about by changing the consciousness of the people through the power of thought.[45] In December 1973, Vinoba observed: In Gandhi's days, there was no freedom of thought and expression. But in India today we enjoy the highest measure of freedom in the world. *Satyagrah* as practised by Gandhi has, therefore, become quite irrelevant in India.[46]

JP not merely realised that road to total revolution may, in certain conditions, lie through a non-violent struggle against the government of the day; he also, towards the end of his life, advocated what amounts to a non-violent class struggle. If and when a situation develops calling for a local, regional or national struggle either by way of protest against injustices and oppression or for ushering in a new social order, they (youths) are expected to play a leading role in it. I must make it clear that I do not see any prospect for total revolution without a long drawn out struggle and without masses participating in such a struggle.[47] Here it would be needless to add, while JP differs from Vinoba on the methods to be adopted for ushering in total revolution, that positions cannot be characterised as un-Gandhian. It was certainly not Gandhi's position that after the achievement of independence there could be no situation calling for a struggle against the government. Thus he observed in 1930: "My non-violence would not prevent me for fighting my countrymen on the many questions which must arise when India has become free." He further added: "I know that if I survive the struggle for freedom, I might have to give non-violent battle to my own countrymen which may be as stubborn as that in which I am now engaged:[48]

> Gandhi further wrote in the *Harijan* of 25 August 1940. If ...... in spite of the utmost effort, the rich do not become guardians of the poor in the true sense of the term and latter are more and more crushed and died of hunger, what is to be done? In trying to find out a solution to this riddle, I have lighted on non-violent non-cooperation and civil disobedience as the right and infallible means.[49]

Detailed discussion has been made regarding the concept and genesis of total revolution and very little about the real contents of the same. Marx, Gandhi and Vinoba used the term total revolution on different occasions but the term was not put to wider public discussion and scrutiny. Even Ram Manohar Lohia talked in terms of *Sapta Kranti* (Seven Revolutions) and he enumerated the term in the following way:

(i) Equality between man and woman;
(ii) Abolition of inequality based on race and colour;
(iii) Abolition of caste system and preferential treatment to backward sections of the society;
(iv) Against foreign subjugation and for establishment of Lok Raj;
(v) Opposition to private capital and for equality and planned production;
(vi) Against unjust interference in the personal life and for democratic polity; and
(vii) Against armament and for *Satyagrah*.[50]

Lohia was not only one of the founders of Congress-Socialist Party but also a leading light of socialist movement in India. Lohia was a rebel intellectual of Indian politics. He was a die hard supporter of Gandhi's *Satyagrah* and non-violence but he treated Gandhian philosophy as inadequate. He was a socialist but treated Marx as one-sided. He was a nationalist of the first water but advocated the concept of the world government. He was modern in true sense of the term but always and still a votary of peace and non-violence. Here it is legitimate to emphasise the point that Lohia was conscious of the total transformation of social, economic and political structure not only of India but the world community as a whole.

Here the concept of *Sapta Kranti* cannot be equated with total revolution but it is a precursor of the same philosophy. These issues resemble with the main issues raised and discussed by JP in total revolution. Some of the points raised by Lohia have got international dimension as peace is indivisible for the whole mankind.

Now let us come to the nature of change which total revolution is expected to bring about. As discussed earlier, such a revolution will be all-inclusive and will touch all aspects of life. According to JP, it will be "a combination of seven revolutions, social, economic, political, cultural, ideological or intellectual, educational and spiritual".[51] But there is nothing sacrosanct about this number and it can be reduced or increased through regrouping or change of words. What is important is a thorough going change in all aspects of life.

JP could not spell out these changes in detail, except to point out again and again that the problems facing India could not be solved nor a new society created merely through a change of rulers or even of a system of government, but only through a radical transformation touching all aspects of life. However, a picture of social order, he was aiming at, is available in some of the tracts he wrote in late fifties and early sixties, particularly *A Plea for Reconstruction of Indian Polity* (1959) and *Swaraj for the People* (1961). That he stuck to the picture drawn there even while talking about total revolution is confirmed by the fact that while containing a few points not touched upon earlier, the outline of his ideas on the nature of the new social order which he jotted down in his notes in prison in 1975, conforms to that picture in all its essentials.[52]

In *A Plea for Reconstruction of Indian Polity,* JP rejects the Western model of democracy on the ground that it does not give full scope to the people to participate in the management of their affairs and is based on an atomised view of society the state being in inorganic sum of individuals.

In its place, he pleads for a model of democracy based on integrated concept of society and providing the fullest possible scope to the individual to participate in the management of his affairs without the intermediation of political parties. The latter, according to JP, functions without any control over them by the people or even by their own members and are the source of many evils. It is not only the party system which lies at its back and which cannot work without it. In JP's ideal society, therefore, parliamentary democracy will be replaced by a new kind of polity which he describes as a communitarian or partyless democracy.

The problem of devising a new polity he emphasises is a part of the larger problem of social reconstruction. Modern industrialism has resulted in disintegration of the human society and made man an alien among his own fellowmen. The problem is how to remedy this situation and put man in touch with man, so that they may live together in meaningful, understandable and controllable relationships. In short, the problem is to recreate the human community. The essential attributes of a true community are sharing, participation and fellowship. The new socio-political system must be so devised as to provide a congenial environment for the fostering of these qualities.

The base of the new social organisation will be the local or primary communities, neither so small that a balanced development of community life and culture become difficult, nor so large that life in them become impersonalised. They will be neither rural nor urban, but agro-industrial based on a balance between agriculture and industry. Just as a number of families come together to build common life at the level of primary community, so the primary communities will come together and cooperate among themselves to tackle common problems and build the regional communities. A number of regional communities will in their turn join together to form the district community. The district communities will federate to form the provincial communities, and the latter will join hands to form the national community. As we proceed from the base upward, there will be less and less to do for the bigger community, it will deal only with such matters as defence, foreign relations, currency and inter-state coordination.

The political structure of the community must correspond to its social structure and rise storey by storey from the foundation, which will consist of self-governing, self-sufficient, agro-industrial, urban-rural, local communities. The existing villages and townships can be converted into such communities, if sincere efforts are made in this direction. The work must begin at all levels. The most important political institution of the local community should be the village assembly *gramsabha* with all the adults of the community as its members. The executive *panchayat* should be selected by general consensus of opinion in the *sabha,* without anybody standing for the election of any office. The *Sabha* and *Panchayat* should be given responsibility to manage things that really matter; for instance, it should be their duty to ensure that no one in the village goes without food, clothing and shelter, every child receives primary education and everyone receives primary medicare. The next level of political structure will be that of the regional community, with the *Gram Panchayats* of district will be integrated into District Council, the District Councils into State Assembly, and the State Assemblies into National Parliament. Thus, the political institutions at each level will be an integration of the institutions at the lower levels. There will be indirect instead of direct election. Here JP's elaboration of the political structure resembles in essence with the Gandhian concept of Village Republics. Lohia also profounded a theory of *Chaukhambha Raj,* i.e. Four Pillar State in which the basic and the top will be integrated and centripetal and centrifugal forces will converge at every point to impart cohesion and effectiveness of the state. Both will be complementary to each other and supportive as well.

Later on, JP changed his views regarding indirect election which might encourage parochialism and retard the growth of a national outlook among all citizens. Besides, such a system might be more liable to be corrupted by moneyed interest as number of electors would be small, except at the lowest level. He, therefore, formulated a method of election which would be direct, yet so organised as to give the institutions of *Panchayati Raj* at every level a definite role in it. The role of the political party should be restricted as far as possible and the people enabled to select their own candidates for election through popularly constituted Electoral Councils. For it is necessary for the fulfilment of democracy, no matter what kind. That its processes are as little divisive as possible or, to put it positively, as cohesive and unitive as possible.

The political structure sketched above will require for its base a new kind of economic structure. While the satisfaction of material needs of man will be its objective, it will not endeavour to satisfy the insatiable hunger for more and yet more which modern industrialism, capitalist, socialist and communist have created. JP strongly argues in favour of this view in *A Plea for Reconstruction of Indian Polity.* I believe, he observes, "that a man really to enjoy liberty and freedom and to practise self-government, it is necessary voluntarily to limit his wants, otherwise the greed for more and yet more will lead to mutual conflict, coercion, spoilation, war, and also to a system of production that will be so complex as to bind democracy hand and foot and deliver it to a bureaucratic oligarchy". If the present science of economics comes in the way of the development of a economy based on a voluntary limitation of wants, a new science of economics may have to be created together with new methods of planning and new techniques have been discussed in detail in *Swaraj* for the people.

What would be the essential features of decentralised economy in India? According to JP, in such an economy care being taken to constantly improve the efficiency and productivity of small machine without escalation to its cost. It must be regional surveying and planning so that the resources of a particular region might be utilised to the full to satisfy the needs of the regions, though, of course, surplus of one region can be exchanged for those others. A programme of rural industrialisation must be launched and finally the organisational pattern of decentralised industry should be such as to keep it free from bureaucratisation and exploitation. The institution of *Panchayati Raj* should be involved in the process of development of decentralised economy.

During agitation in 1974-77, he made only two or three important additions to the picture drawn above. In the first place, he again and again stressed that along with a change in the political and economic systems, there was need also for a radical transformation of the social customs and institutions. In particular, he pleaded for the abolition of the caste system and practice of dowry at the time of marriage. The other important point stressed by him was for a radical transformation of the educational system by including the mass of the people within its scope and relating it to the real needs of the people, particularly those living in the rural areas. He also stressed the need for a cultural revolution to bring about a change in the life style of the people. Mao also tried his best to change the attitude of the people and life style, and thought process by cultural revolution but he failed as it was imposed from above and enforced by threat, coercion and force. Naturally, it was not embraced willingly and assimilated voluntarily, hence after the fall of 'Gang of Four', everything was scattered to pieces and thrown to winds.

Finally, JP took pains to stress that the goals of total revolution, as also its form and programme, would go on changing with the change in times, certain tasks may appear urgent at a given time. But after they were accomplished, new tasks are likely to emerge and the votaries of total revolution will have to attend to them. As he put it in 1976; "Total revolution is permanent revolution. It will always go on and keep on changing both our personal and social lives. The revolution knows no respite, or halt, certainly not a complete halt".[53]

To sum up, the concept of total revolution has had both Marxist and Gandhian origins and indeed as old as the concept of a social revolution. However, it is a fact that it is JP's use of this term has made it a part of the Indian political terminology. JP developed his concept of total revolution on the basis of a synthesis not merely of Marxist and Gandhian concepts of social revolution but also of the principles of Western democracy. He was keen to see that struggle for total revolution should not, in any way, impair the working of democratic institutions in the country. But he realised that it was a distant goal and an abrupt transition to it was neither feasible nor desirable.

There is a good deal of the element of utopia in these goals. But that is true of the ideals placed before humanity by all great revolutionaries and path finders. If partyless democracy seems utopian, can anything different be said about the stateless society which was the ideal of both Marx and Gandhi. For in trying to reach that ideal humanity is likely to come nearer and nearer to it without ever completing the journey. The same may be said about JP's concept of total revolution. Behind all these exercises lies a search for a new social order based on freedom, equality and human fellowship. The concept of total revolution is also remarkable for its significant contribution to the methodology of a non-violent social revolution. Gandhi, who had first thought to such a revolution, had given equal emphasis to constructive work, organisation and struggle. Vinoba, who further developed this concept, developed new forms of constructive work in the shape of *Bhoodan* and *Gramdan.* He laid considerable stress on the needs to spread the fundamental principles of a just social order among the people. However, he completely turned his face against struggle and pinned his faith entirely in persuasion, which he described as positive *Satyagrah* in contrast to the former, which he called negative *Satyagrah.* JP, however, could not leave behind a model of struggle for total revolution. Although of great historical significance, particularly from the point of view of safeguarding democracy in our country, the struggle which he laid in 1974-77, describing it as a struggle for total revolution, because in reality, at any rate by the middle of 1975, quite distinguishable from struggle of various political parties and their leaders for power. Most of those leaders had no interest in either JP or his concept of total revolution and completely forgot both as soon as they succeeded in securing their objective, i.e. power. The experience of JP was neither accidental nor unusual and the result was natural and inevitable. This is equally true of all the revolutionaries all over the world. Allied to it is the issue whether a movement or struggle for total revolution can be successfully carried to its logical conclusion without the existence of a political party fully committed to the cause of total revolution and equipped to take over power and implement its programme if and when an opportunity for doing so presents itself. An organisation on the pattern of the Lok Sewak Sangh of Gandhi's conception, committed to influencing government from outside can also serve the cause of total revolution but then such an organisation will have to confine itself to the task of ideological preparation of the masses for such a revolution through dissemination of ideas, constructive work and participation in local struggle against injustice and be prepared to wait patiently for such preparation to bring results through a change in people's consciousness and its impact on those who hold or secure power in a given time.

The question now arises, what will be the form of that society in which it will be possible for the people to run their affairs directly and develop all those values of life that characterise the socialist society: cooperation, self-discipline, and sense of responsibility? This is a question which deserves top consideration but has been paid the least attention. Science has turned the whole world into a neighbourhood but man has created a civilization that has turned even neighbours into strangers. Gandhi abhors the structure where man is alienated from his own environment and surroundings. Further, man is a product both of nature and culture. So far his balanced growth, it is necessary that a harmonious blend between the two is effected. Acquisitive culture has got to be given up which has created rat race for mankind.

A harmonious blending of nature and culture is possible only in a comparatively smaller communities. Let us quote Huxley from his *Science, Liberty and Peace:*

> "Now it seems pretty obvious that man's psychological, to say nothing of his spiritual, needs cannot be fulfilled unless, first, he has a fair measure of personal independence and personal responsibility within and towards a self-governing group, unless, secondly, his work possesses a certain aesthetic value and human significance, and unless, in the third place, he is related to his natural environment in some organic root and symbiotic way".[54]

It was for these reasons that Gandhiji insisted that the Indian village and village self-government *(Gram Raj)* were the foundations for his picture of society, the society of equal and free human beings as brothers in peace. How, for instance, would these small self-reliant, self-governing communities be related together is a major question that immediately springs to mind.

There is, of course, Gandhi's grand conception before us :

> "In this structure, composed of innumerable villages, there will be ever widening, never ascending circles. Life will not be a pyramid with the apex sustained by the bottom. But it will be an oceanic circle whose centre will be the individual, always ready to perish for the village, the latter ready to perish for the circle of the villages, till at last the whole becomes one life composed of individuals, never aggressive in their arrogance, but ever humble, sharing the majesty of the oceanic circle of which they are integral part."

Thus the concept of revolution as conceived and explained by Gandhi is comprehensive, integrative and all embracing keeping in mind the holistic picture of man and society.

NOTES

1. D.M. Dutta, "Philosophical Basis of Social Revolution", *Proceedings of Indian Philosophical Congress,* p. 259.
2. Victor Hugo, *Dictionary of Thought,* p. 555.
3. Alfred Mansel, Revolution and Counter-Revolution, *Encyclopaedia of Social Science,* Vol. XIII, p. 367.
4. J.B. Kripalani, Philosophical Basis of Revolution, *Proceedings of Indian Philosophical Congress.*
5. *Ibid., Pre-Marxian Revolution,* pp.121-34.
6. Marx and Engels, *Communist Manifesto.*
7. K. Marx, *Capital,* p. 75.8.
8. V. I. Lenin, *Selected Works,* Vol. II, pp. 350-53.
9. Vinoba Bhave, *Bhoodan,* English Weekly, June, 8, 1956.
10. J.B. Kripalani, *op.cit.,* I.P.C., p. 143.
11. Thakur Das Bung, *Kranti Ki Pukar,* pp. 36-37.
12. Achut Patwardhan, Quoted in Bhagwan Das Kela, in *Rajya Vyavastha Sarvodaya Ki Dristise,* p. 91.
13. Bhoodan, 02.07.1954.
14. *Bhoodan* English Weekly, 19.03.1958.

15. D.M. Dutta, *op. cit.*, p., 113.
16. Gandhi's Correspondence with Government, p.175.
17. M.K. Gandhi, *Young India,* 12.02.1925.
18. *Ibid., Young India,* 30.04.1945.
19. N.K. Bose, *Studies in Gandhism.*
20. Manifesto of Non-Violent Revolution, *Peace News,* 11th September, 1969.
21. His Article on Contemporary Philosophy of Social Revolution, *Indian Philosophical Congress,* 1957, p.188.
22. *Ibid.*, p.188. ,
23. *Manusmriti,* IV. 174, *Mahabharat,* Santi Parva, 109.
24. Alan Richartson, *Religion in Contemporary Debate,* p. 42.
25. Sheen, *Philosophy of Religion,* p. 97.
26. *Amrit Bazar Patrika,* 2nd August, 1934.
27. Bertrand Russel, *Political Ideals,* pp.12-24.
28. Jine Grasso, Jay Corrin & Michael Kort (1997): *Modernisation and Revolution in China,* MF Sharpe, New York.
29. *Ibid.*
30. K. Marx, F. Engels and V.I. Lenin, *On Historical Materialism,* Moscow, p.83.
31. B.N. Ganguli (1973): *Gandhi's Social Philosophy,* Delhi, pp. 145-260.
32. Vishvanath Tandon, (Ed.) (1981): *Selection for Vinoba,* Varanasi, p. 91.
33. Suresh Ram (Ed.) (1968): *Towards Total Revolution,* Jhanjavur.
34. Jayaprakash Narayan (1978): *Towards Total Revolution,* Brakmanand (Ed.), Vol, IV, Bombay, p. 115.
35. Geoffrey Ostergaard (1985): *Non-Violent Revolution in India,* New Delhi, p. 207.
36. *Ibid.*, p.104.
37. *The London Times,* 13th October, 1968.
38. Bimal Prasad (Ed) (1980): A Revolutionary Quest, *Selected Writing of Jayprakash Narayan,* Delhi, p. 286.
39. *Ibid.*, p. 294.
40. *Ibid.*
41. *Ibid.*, p. 295.
42. Jayprakash Narayan (1977): *Prison Diary,* Bombay, p. 33.
43. Narayan, p.21 .
44. Ostergaard, p. 389.
45. Vishwanath Tandon, p. 95.
46. Ostergaard, p. 63.
47. Bimal Prasad, p. 338.
48. *The Collected Works of Mahatma Gandhi* XIII, New Delhi, p. 436.
49. Jayprakash Narayan, p. 87.
50. Onkar Sharad (1969): *Lohia Ke Vichar,* Lokbharati Prakashan, Allahabad, p. 11.
51. Narayan, p.87.
52. Narayan, *Prison Diary,* pp. 61-64.
53. Narayan, *Prison Diary,* p. 338.
54. Huxley, *Science, Liberty and Peace.*

10

Gandhi and the Socialistic Pattern of Society

Political destiny of independent India should be determined by Indians themselves and this has been put forward by Mahatma Gandhi as early as in 1922:

> "*Swaraj* will not be a free gift of the British Parliament; it will be a declaration of India's full self-expression. That it will be expressed through the Act of Parliament is fine but it will be merely a courteous ratification of the declared wish of the people of India even as it was in the case of the Union of South Africa."

The ideals of Mahatma Gandhi and resolve and pledge of the people were embodied in the Preamble to the Constitution of India, which, as amended in 1976, summarises the aims and objects of the Constitution:

> " We, the People of India, having solemnly resolved to constitute India into a Sovereign, Socialist, Secular, Democratic Republic and to secure to all its citizens: Justice, social, economic, and political, liberty of thought, expression, belief, faith, and worship; Equality of status and of opportunity; and to promote among them all: Fraternity assuring the dignity of the individual and unity and integrity of the Nation."

That this democratic republic stands for the good of all is embodied in the concept of welfare state, which inspires the Directive Principles of State Policy. The economic justice assured by the Preamble can hardly be achieved if democracy envisaged by the Constitution were combined to political democracy. In the words of Pandit Nehru:

> "Democracy has been spoken of chiefly in the past as political

democracy, roughly represented by every person having a vote. But a vote by itself does not represent very much to a person who is down and out to a person, let us say, who is starving or hungry. Political democracy, by itself is not enough except that it may be used to obtain gradually increasing measure of economic democracy, equality and the spread of good things of life to others and removal of gross inequality".[1]

Radhakrishnan has also put it:

"Poor people who wander about, find no work, no wages and starve, whose lives are a continual round of sore affliction and pinching poverty, cannot be proud of the constitution or, its law."[2]

In brief, the Constitution of India promises not only political but social democracy as explained by Ambedkar in his concluding speech in the Constituent Assembly:

> "Political democracy cannot last unless there lies at the base of it social democracy. What does social democracy mean? It means a way of life which recognises liberty, equality and fraternity which are not treated as separate items in a trinity. They form a union of trinity in the sense that to divorce one from the other is to defeat the very purpose of democracy. Liberty cannot be divorced from fraternity."

The realisation of so many objectives would certainly mean an extension of the functions of state. The goal envisaged by the constitution, therefore, is of a welfare state and establishment of a socialist state. At the Avadi Session in 1955, Congress explained this objective as a socialistic pattern of society by a resolution:

"In order to realise the object of Congress.....and to further the objectives stated in the Preamble and the Directive Principles of the State Policy of the Constitution of India, planning should take place with a view to the establishment of a socialistic pattern of society, where the principal means of production are under social ownership or control, production is progressively speeded up and there is equitable distribution of national wealth."

During the late sixties and seventies, the trend has been from a socialistic pattern towards a 'socialistic state', which is not only bringing industries and private enterprises under state ownership and management but also itself carrying on trade and business as a state function.

That the goal of the Indian policy is socialism has since been ensured by inserting the word 'socialist' in the Preamble, by the Constitution (42nd Amendment) Act, 1978. It is to be noted, however, that the 'socialism' envisaged by the Constitution of India is not the usual scheme of state socialism which involves nationalisation of all means of production, and abolition of private property. As the then Prime Minister Indira Gandhi explained :

> "We have always said that we have our own brand of socialism. We shall nationalise the sectors where we feel necessary. Just nationalisation is not our type of socialism."[3]

Constitution of India, therefore, does not seek to abolish private property altogether but seeks to put it under restraints so that it may be used in the interest of the nation, which includes the upliftment of the poor. Instead of a total nationalisation of all property and industry, it envisages a 'mixed-economy' but aims at offering equal opportunity to all, and abolition of vested interests.

Article-I of the Declaration of Human Rights (1948), adopted by the United Nations, says :

> "All human beings are born free, equal in dignity and rights. They are endowed with reason and conscience and should act towards one another in a spirit of brotherhood."

A fitting commentary on the foregoing contents of the Preamble, our Constitution can be best offered by quoting a few lines from Prof. Earnest Barker, one of the modern thinkers on democratic government :

> "There must be a capacity and passion for the enjoyment of liberty, there must be a sense of personality in each and of respect for personality in all, generally spread through the whole community —before the democratic state can be truly achieved. Perhaps it can be fairly demanded only in a community which can achieve a sufficient standard of material existence, and a sufficient degree

of national homogeneity to evote itself to an ideal of liberty which has to be worked out in each by the common effort of all. If the problems of material existence are still absorbing... the ideal of living a common life of freedom, in other words, of attaining a particular quality of life will seem an ideal dream. If again, the problems of national homogeneity are still insistent, and there is no common feeling of fellowship, if some sections of the community are regarded by others, whether on the ground of their inferior education, or on the ground of their inferior stock, or any other ground, as essentially alien and heterogeneous—the ideal of the common life of freedom will seem equally illusory."[4]

Combining the ideal of political, social and economic democracy with that of equality and fraternity, the Preamble seeks to establish what Mahatma Gandhi described as the "India of My Dream", namely :

"... an India in which the poorest shall feel that it is their country in whose making they have an effective voice... an India in which all communities shall live in perfect harmony. There can be no room in such an India for the curse of untouchability or the curse of intoxicating drinks and drugs. Women will enjoy the same rights as men."[5]

Historically speaking, socialist ideas were floated and discussed by the young socialists in Congress party. They lacked independent organisation for propagation and consolidation of socialist forces actively engaged in freedom movement. All socialists of the country gathered at Patna under the presidentship of Acharya Narendra Dev on 17th May 1934. The conference decided to form a regular and organised socialist party on the national level within the Congress. In this very conference, Lohia had presented an outline of the socialist movement. A proposal in regard to the aim of the party was presented, aim of the party is establishment of socialistic pattern of society. The formation of the Congress-Socialist Party was a very important event in the political history of India. The Communist Party of India had step-motherly feelings against that new party since its birth. The Communist Party welcomed that party by using objectives like 'Social Facist' and 'Hot Disguise of Capitalism'. During that period Jayaprakash Narayan was supporter and sympathiser of communists on all issues except on the issue of nationality.[6]

In 1942, Lohia told Gandhi about one more suggestion. The

suggestion was of inviting all the governments of the world with a scheme of making foundation for a new world which has four elements :

(i) If capital of a country is invested in another, it should be confiscated;
(ii) Everyone should have liberty to go or settle anywhere in the world;
(iii) Political freedom to all nations of the world; and
(iv) World citizenship.[7]

The task of organising democratic socialist forces in India has been in progress since 1934. During the period, the organisational framework as well as ideological foundations of the party of democratic socialism changed. But urge to evolve a democratic way of life and build an equalitarian society remained throughout the guiding spirit of the socialist movement. The organisational evolution of the party of socialism passing through the phases of Congress-Socialist Party, Socialist Party, Praja Socialist Party, Samyukta Socialist Party and ultimately Socialist Party was accompanied by corresponding evolution of socialist policies and perspective.

The socialist movement in India did not grow in isolation but it emerged as an integral part of the freedom struggle against imperialism. This was reflected in the birth of the Congress-Socialist Party in 1934. After the 1932 Civil Disobedience Movement, the Congress-Socialist Party was formed with the primary object of radicalising and spreading socialist thought in the country. The party strived to give socialist content to the objectives of the Congress.

At the very first conference of the Congress-Socialist Party held in Bombay in 1934, the party declared complete independence of India is our goal and by complete independence we mean, India's liberation from British imperialism and establishment of a socialist society. The blueprint of the economic reconstruction adopted at the conference pleaded for all power to the toiling masses, economic planning, nationalisation of key industries, government's control over foreign trade, abolition of feudalism and landlordism without compensation, redistribution of land and cooperative farming. From the formation of the Congress-Socialist Party upto the outbreak of the Second World War, Gandhiji exerted little impact on socialist thinking and actions. The intervening years of the Second World War and the post-war period represented a period of intense self-analysis by the socialists. During this period, Gandhiji's teachings were re-examined and re-evaluated in the light of the experiences of the socialist and communist movements the world over and in the context of the peculiar economic problems that confronted India. The present ideological foundations of the democratic socialist movement in our country now bear a distinct stamp of some of the most important contributions of Gandhiji.

For years 'scientific socialists' of different schools had professed their faith in the dictum 'ends justify the means'. Gandhiji on the basis of his moral philosophy asserted that the divorce of means from the ends would defeat the very noble aim one desires to accomplish. The substance of these ideas, not on the moral but on the political plane, received increasing support from socialists when horrifying results of divorce of means from the ends came to light from the experiences of Stalinist Russia. Jayaprakash Narayan accepted Gandhi's formulation and urged the Indian socialists in 1951 to adopt the correctives, Gandhiji's philosophy offered in this regard.

Ever since the Avadi Session of the Indian National Congress adopted the important resolution on the socialistic pattern of society. The resolution runs as follows :

> "In order to realise the object of the Congress as laid down in Article-1 of the Congress constitution and to further the objectives stated in the Preamble and Directive Principles of State Policy of the Constitution of India, planning should take place with a view to the establishment of a socialistic pattern of society, where the principal means of production are under social ownership or control, production is progressively speeded up and there is an equitable distribution of national wealth."

The object of the Congress mentions "the establishment in India, by peaceful and legitimate means of a cooperative commonwealth based on equality of opportunity and of political, economic and social rights. Preamble includes justice, social, economic and political, and equality of status and opportunity". The Directive Principles of State Policy point out that the state shall strive to promote the welfare of the people by securing and protecting, as effectively as it may, a social order in which justice, social, economic and political, shall inform all the institutions of national life.

Article 39 of the Constitution asks the state to direct its policy towards ensuring that all the citizens, men and women, equally shall have "the right to an adequate means of livelihood and that the ownership and control of material resources of the community are so distributed as best to subserve the common good".

On the economic front, this resolution calls for "a substantial advance on the economic and the social plane with the definite objective of increasing production greatly, raising standard of living and having progressively fuller employment so as to lead to full employment within a period of ten years". It further reiterates that "the national aim is a welfare state and a socialist economy". These are the laudable objectives of the ruling party which attracted people's attention for a better and brighter future, but alas, they were deceived and betrayed as these are the political slogans to garner votes and beat the leftists in the country. Lack of vision and commitments have been reflected in the subsequent policies and programmes, adopted by the same group now leading to globalisation, liberalisation and privatisation. How far they are compatible with welfare state and socialist economy needs elucidation.

Shreeman Narayan summarizes the contents of socialistic pattern of society in the following terms :

(a) The basic objective of a socialistic pattern of society would be the establishment of a social and economic order based on equality of opportunity and on social, economic and political justice;
(b) Such a society would do away with all distinctions of caste, creed, sex or social and political status and would ensure that the right to work and a living wage to all able bodied citizens. In other words, a socialistic pattern of society would create conditions for full employment;
(c) The state shall own or effectively control the principal means of production and material resources of the community in the best interest of the nation;
(d) The society shall organise the economic system in such a manner that it does not result in the concentration of wealth and means of production to the common detriments;
(e) Systematic attempts are made to increase and speed up the total production of wealth in the country;
(f) It is also necessary that there should be equitable distribution

of the national wealth and the existing economic disparities are reduced to the minimum;

(g) Such a transformation of the social and economic order must be brought about through peaceful and democratic methods; and

(h) A socialistic pattern of society would necessitate a bold decentralisation of economic and political power in the form of village panchayats and organisation of small scale and cottage industries on a very wide scale.[8]

Further, Shreeman Narayan enumerated the principles of socialistic pattern. There are seven basic principles underlying a socialistic society :

(i) Full employment and right to work;
(ii) Maximum production of national wealth;
(iii) Maximum national self-sufficiency;
(iv) Social and economic justice;
(v) Use of peaceful non-violent and democratic methods;
(vi) Decentralisation of economic and political power through the establishment of village panchayats and industrial cooperatives; and
(vii) Ideal of *Unto This Last.*[9]

He asserts that it is our sacred duty to try our best to follow these ideals to the best of our ability and judgement. Imitating the ideals of foreign countries, either in the sphere of capitalism or of socialism, would lead us astray. India is endowed with a very rich cultural heritage and it is on the basis of those human values that we desire to build up a truly socialistic society in this ancient land of ours.

The basic presumption about Gandhism in India has been that it is a panacea for all the social and economic ills of the country. Many think that it is a substitute for socialism. There is another school of thought which subscribes to the view that Gandhism is opposed to socialism and Gandhi stood against all that was socialist, modern and progressive. Some persons have gone to the extent of suggesting that Gandhi impeded the growth and speed of socialist movement in India and always tried to defend and champion the cause of rich and affluent. Unfortunately, Gandhi has been differently perceived by the people according to their convenience and class interest.

Gandhi's firm belief in the creative force of religion in human life never allowed him to think politics without reference to religion. There are no politics devoid of religion. To him, politics bereft of religion was a death trap because it killed the soul. Religion was bequeathed to him in legacy. He was greatly influenced by *Ramayana* and *Bhagvad Gita.* In subsequent years, other great religions of the world too had some impacts on Gandhi. Gandhi himself admitted that it was the 'New Testament' which really awakened me to the rightness and value of passive resistance; the *'Bhagvad Gita'* deepened the impression and Tolstoy's *The Kingdom of God is Within You* gave it a permanent form.[10]

This spirit of religion promoted Gandhi to enter into political, social and economic territories of the country. Essentially a religious man, he loved every creature, even the lowliest ones. It was due to this deep sympathy for his fellowmen, he entered into political arena and took active interest in the affairs of the country. Gandhi thus injected religion into politics which became mystified. Gandhi tried to bring religion to the masses rather than keeping it mysteriously hidden into the hills, caves and forests. He believed in all pervading God was Truth and Truth was God. He always advocated that God was. His religion, therefore, may roughly be identified with morality in reference to politics. The attempt to spiritualise politics was, therefore, a logical corollary to his deep-rooted faith in religion and morality."[11]

The chief contribution of Mahatma Gandhi to the realm of politics and political thought is the peculiar blending of ethics and politics. Machiavelli separated ethics from politics. To him, the interest of the state justified everything, i.e. the end justified the means. In other words, a complete divorce of ethics from politics was the bulwark behind which the legal and political theory of Machiavelli originated and developed. Gandhi repudiated Machiavellian theory and advocated a theory of lasting union of ethics and politics.

In Gandhian philosophy, means and ends are inseparable. Gandhi was firm in his belief that wrong means could never lead to the right end. To Gandhi, the means could be compared to a seed, the end to a tree and there was just the same inviolable connection between the means and the end as there was between the seed and the tree.[12] Gandhi seemed to have some impact of Aristotle, according to whom ethics was a part of politics or social science. His politics was ethical and his ethics political or social. Gandhi shared this view with John Stretchy and Aldous Huxley who emphasised the need of good means for good ends. John Stretchy said: If we have learnt anything in our epoch, it is that the means and methods profoundly condition the good. A socialism achieved by democratic means will inevitably be a basically different thing from a socialism achieved by dictatorial coercion.[13] Huxley was also of the opinion that "a state of greatest possible unification could be reached by essentially unifying, i.e. good means and not by divisive, i.e. bad means.[14]

Gandhi was an ethical absolutist and was never prepared to make any compromise with what he regarded as essential and fundamental moral principles. Gandhi emphasised the purification of human action through the implementation of the concept of purity of means emphasised by the religious prophets. Gandhian theory of moralization of social and political action highlighted the importance of love and justice and discarded the game of power politics. He was opposed to reducing politics to the game of cynical manipulation based on fraud, deceit, force and self-interest. In his opinion, politics was not an art of seizing power and prestige, but means to serve the mankind. He would like politics to be made a branch of ethics and thus become an art which should be used for social good and eventually as an instrument in the cosmic and spiritual awareness of man.[15]

The New Oxford Dictionary of English defines 'socialism' as a political and economic theory of social organisation which advocates that the means of production, distribution and exchange should be owned or regulated by the community as a whole. The term socialism has been used to describe positions as far apart as anarchism, Soviet state communism, and social democracy, however, it necessarily implies an opposition to the untrammelled working of the economic market. The socialist parties that have arisen in most European countries from the late 19th century have generally tended towards social democracy. Tremendous changes have taken place during the last century in the socio-economic and political configuration of the world, hence, it is difficult to define socialism in concrete terms and within given parameters. The phrase socialism is most intricate and complicated, many-sided and confused question that have plagued the mind of thinkers as well as practitioners of socialism. Prof. Joad has rightly observed that "Socialism is like a hat that has lost its shape because everybody wears it".[16] Socialism bears different meanings to different persons and the disputants use the one convenient to the point they immediately wish to make. As early as 1891, a newspaper of Paris had compiled some six hundred definitions of socialism. Norman Thomas rejected the previous definition and considered modern socialism in line with the declarations and political actions of democratic socialist parties during recent years. He has defined socialism as "a political and economic theory of social organisation, the essential feature of which is governmental control of economic activities to the end that competition shall give way to cooperation and that the opportunities of life and reward of labour shall be equitably proportioned"[17]

Socialism is, by no means, a synonym of collectivism or collective ownership. It has always been concerned for good life. Socialism aims at the establishment of a society fit to be described as a fellowship of freemen where each individual has fullest possible opportunity for development. The members of such a free society will use their resources and skills no longer for war but for the conquest of abject poverty and remedial diseases.

History of socialism traditionally begins with an account of collectivist doctrines from Plato to Thomas More which can be linked with movements in the western thought since the American and French revolutions. This approach has the advantage of establishing a perspective on which the ideal socialism, like democracy is rooted in sentiments as ancient and permanent as human society itself, the rise of socialism for the purpose of conceptual framework, can be traced back to 1789, the year of French Revolution since, "there is the point from which it is possible to trace not only a continuous development in the field of thought and movements seeking to give practical expression to it".[18] Even before socialism entered the scientific phase with the emergence of Karl Marx and Frederic Engels, the great utopians of the past century the Frenchmen Charles Fourier and Henry Saint Simon and the Englishman Robert Owel had criticised capitalism and made brilliant conjectures about the basic features of future socialist society. But their theories focused as they were on the consciousness of the bourgeoisie had never found practical application. "Utopian socialism", wrote Lenin, "could not explain the real nature of wage-slavery under capitalism; it could not reveal the laws of capitalist development, or show what social force is capable of becoming the creator of a new society."[19]

Whenever and wherever may be the roots of socialism, the dominant fact is that the classical theory of socialism propounded some two centuries back has undergone a basic change. Neither the utopian socialism nor the scientific socialism can claim full application in terms of practical operation on different soils of the world. Nothing is so remarkable as the progressive conquest of understanding of the physical world by human ingenuity. While there has been this conquest of external conditions, there is, at the same time, the strange spectacle of lack of moral fibre and of self-control in man as a whole. Science is advancing far beyond the comprehension of human race and posing problems which most of us are incapable of and understanding much less of solving. Technology was evolved to solve the problems of mankind but unfortunately it is dictating the society and deciding the future survival of mankind. Now new technologies are required to solve the problems created by the technology itself. Progress in science and technology has been accompanied by mental exhausion of civilization itself.

It would be a folly to treat socialism primarily as an economic doctrine. Socialism is basically an ethical revolt against the terrible dehumanising process involved in the institutional apparatus of capitalism. The moral case for socialism is that it is based on a philosophy of optimism about human nature. Socialism has taken various modes of expression at various levels and times. However, despite its varied versions, socialism exhibits a thread of unity. All the versions share a common sentiment of protest against the system of capitalism. In short, socialism stands for social control over the machinery and output of production.

Marxian communism aims at the overthrow of capitalist system through revolutionary means, and believes in the necessity of setting up a dictatorship of the proletariat until the remnants of capitalist ideology and habits of thought are liquidated. Evolutionary democratic socialism, on the other hand, adheres to the method of constitutional procedure all throughout it seeks power through ballot, rather than bullets and keep up the democratic tradition even when in power. The choice between Marxist revolutionary communism and evolutionary democratic socialism is like other vital choices not a matter of pure logic. Historical facts limit the range of discretion in social action. In India, democratic socialism seems to be natural solution of fundamental economic ills. In more precise terms, socialism stands for cooperative common wealth controlling all the means of production and regulating distribution according to some methods of joint control.

The moral case upon which socialism bases its claim rests on view of the nature of man that denies that economic motives, though they have their parts in the affairs, are the sole or primary force which should govern human society on that uncontrolled competition. The socialists believe that cooperation among nations can produce a better international society than can war, and so cooperation among individuals for the solution of their common social, political and economic problems can establish a better society where the personality of man can find wider opportunity for development.

Socialist movement in India is traceable during the 20th century. The concept of socialism, Asian resurgence and internationalism were constant themes in the speeches and writings of the Indian leaders in the twenties and thirties of the 20th century. At the end of 1906, Dadabhai Naoroji in his presidential speech at the Congress session at Calcutta held that the transfer of power from Britishers to the Indians was the only cure for the great and unavoidable economic malaise that expressed itself in the drain of country's riches and its impoverishment. The demand for *Swaraj* made at the Calcutta Session of the Congress in 1906 was the call around which the most progressive and radical-minded leaders rallied the people in the struggle against colonial oppression.

Russian Revolution of 1917 was a major international event of its time, which furthered the awakening of India. It awakened Asia by example of its heroic struggle against oppression and aroused in the Indian patriots a desire to follow that example. The socialist ideas began to spread rapidly among the radical youths after the events in the USSR. In 1925, Communist Party of India was established with very limited support from some trade unions and some groups of educated people and students in urban areas. Distinctively Western in origin, the communist movement in pre-independent India was a colonial adjunct of the Communist Party of Great Britain which in term was suborned to MOSCOW. The Sino-Soviet ideological conflict had repurcussions on the Indian communist movement and in the wake of this conflict the CPI split into two: CPI and CPI(M).

The emergence of the socialist group within the Congress party was a logical outcome of widening gap between the moderates and the radicals. Many young Congressmen, dissatisfied and disillusioned with the techniques of Gandhi, formed a socialist group in 1934. Though Nehru was not apparently associated with the socialist group, his sympathies for socialism were no secret. He visited Moscow and European countries and became supporter of socialism and internationalism. In his presidential address at the 49th Congress session at Lucknow, he said, "I am of firm belief that the solution of the problems of the world and particularly of India lies in socialism. I want the Congress to emerge as a socialist organisation and strengthen those forces of the world which are striving to build up new civilization. Though I am taking part in the programmes of village industries, my mental attitude differs from the attitude of those who are against industrialisation and socialism."[20] Jayaprakash Narayan was equally eloquent in declaring that there was only road to socialism, i.e. Marxism, and its success was illustrated by the achievements of the Soviet Union. To sum up, the socialist trend in the political thinking of a number of Indian leaders, though engrafted earlier, took concrete shape and manifestations only after 1920.

Gandhi's religious bent of mind did not allow him to entrench his faith in what is called socialistic or radical approach. Instead of a radical transformation of social structure as the solution of world's ills, he gave the recipe of the 'change of heart' theory as the panacea of all ills. Gandhi firmly believed that not only the social system should be changed but the human heart must experience a fundamental moral transformation. The gap between the thinking of Gandhi and that of a vast number of his political followers arose from the fact that they did not agree with his approach towards modern civilization. As early as 1908, Gandhi made clear his understanding of the difference between Indian and Western civilizations. The aim of the Indian civilization to elevate the moral being, that of the Western civilization is to propagate immorality. The latter is Godless, the former is based on a belief in God.[21] Gandhi's economic programmes, indigenous methods of production and cottage industries did not favour the reorganisation of India's economic life on modern and scientific lines. His theory of trusteeship in relation to regulation of property and his belief in a peaceful non-violent transformation proved to be a speed breaker in India's march towards communism or radical socialism. Being essentially a religious man and a sympathiser of poor and down-trodden, he could never reconcile himself to the doctrine of class war and violent methods for establishment of new social and political order. On the basis of his experiences in the struggles in South Africa as well as in India, he was highly convinced that the poor and oppressed could not meet the mighty forces of rulers and exploiters with violence.

A political revolution is not enough because it brings about changes at the top level of organisation. A change to be real must be in the very nature of man a realisation on the part of the individual to follow his *swadharma,* his basic nature, the will to develop in him the desire to be a human being first and last, to imbibe non-violence in thought, deed and word. Gandhi believed in the change not for the sake of change but for the sake of *Sarvodaya.* He, therefore, suggested that change must be peaceful, natural and self-adjusting as opposed to violent and overturning change.

The communist critics of Gandhi have taken pains to trace out the influence of bourgeoisie on Gandhi during the period of struggle for freedom. Different people assessed Gandhi according to their own vested interests and prejudices as he was uncompromising on many ethical, political and social issues. As an ideology, Gandhism passed through two phases of development : One extending from about 1920 to 1940, and another developing in the subsequent period as fast changes were taking place after Quit India Movement and onward.

Gandhi's role in the struggle for freedom, in the eyes of the communist, safeguarded the interest of the capitalist class as a whole. To sum up, the communist evaluation of the Gandhi's role during the struggle for freedom tend to represent the whole concept of Gandhism as the supreme expression of the consciousness of the Indian bourgeoisie. The acceptance of the communists' thesis would not only downgrade the whole philosophy of Gandhi in the public estimation, but it would also subject the whole course of freedom struggle to a different direction. The communists viewed Gandhi's role from their own angle and since it did not suit their interest they decried him as an enemy of Marxist movement in the country.

Despite Gandhi's personal dislike for modern civilization, he never put a deliberate brake on the progressive idea in the country. Though he abhorred violent methods, Gandhi had a clear sympathy for the poor, down-trodden and economically and socially crippled. His *Satyagrah* in South Africa, Champaran, Kheda and Bardoli cannot be described as an attempt to safeguard the interest of the capitalists or bourgeoisie. When Gandhi found himself unable to regulate the exercises of his followers in reference to methods and techniques designed to be adopted in the freedom struggle, he voluntarily retired from the Congress politics. He gave up his Congress membership and declared, "I am a dead weight in the Congress now.[22] Gandhi's economic programmes like *Swadeshi* and his indigenous methods of production and cottage industries were not designed or intended to thwart socialist movement in the country, their chief aim was to instil self-confidence in the people of the country and to make the character of the national movement very broad based. The constructive programme of Gandhi was designed to provide an opportunity to the rank and file of the *Satyagrahi* army, in fact, to every individual to take some part in the work of socio-economic reconstruction of the country.

Gandhi claimed himself to be a great revolutionary. He cleared that he had no attraction for the peace of the grave and that he would rather have India resort to arms to defend honour than she would, in cowardly manner, become or remain a helpless witness to her dishonour. While analysing the revolutionary aspect of Gandhi, Chester Bowles, an American Ambassador in India, observes :

> "Gandhi was also a key to the revolution of our time of all the revolutionaries who have dominated this century's stage. Lenin, Mussolini, Hitler, Stalin and Mao, Gandhi alone offered hope for reform without destruction."[23]

A violent revolution can be successful only if the government is disorganised as it was in Russia. *Satyagrah,* on the other hand, depends for its success not on external conditions, but on the capacity of the resisters to suffer in love and without illwill. Circumstances testified to the credibility and strength of Gandhian non-violent revolution. Chester Bowles reiterates again,

> "I began to see Gandhians' revolt had not only overthrown an empire but had laid the foundations in the minds and habits of the people for democracy. A faith in the persuasion and democracy, and such a faith was very cornerstone of Gandhi's philosophy."[24]

Then to brand Gandhi as a revivalist is unjust and also in bad taste. In his programme for socio-economic reconstruction, Gandhi had evidently weakness for indigenous methods of production, but he did not altogether eliminate the modern culture. His attack on feudalism, superstition and social behaviour repugnant to the programmes for the progress of the country allayed the fears of his critics. The socialists in India claim that the Indian society cannot materially, socially and culturally advance to a higher level except on a socialist basis. Many parties in India subscribe to the goal of socialism, but most of them hardly know the historical road to the goal. The Congress shares the major view of a socialist philosophy, yet is a victim of political romanticism moving from Panchayati Raj to nationalisation. Socialist parties and forces are scattered and they have lost the appeal to the masses. Ideological crises are there. Personality cults are the dominant theme. The CPI and CPI(M) do not see eye to eye, both accusing each other for having sabotaged the Marxist movement in the country. Today, the ideological offsprings of the communist are not to be easily counted and they have resorted to violent and extremist activities being completely divorced from ideological commitment and true left orientation.

In the words of D.G. Tendulkar, socialism was a great doctrine. It did not admit of condemnation but utilise application. Gandhi accepted socialism as a part of his programme to do way with the social and economic inequalities. He strived to wash away tears from every eye and helplessness, fear and frustation from every heart. It is highly significant to note that Gandhi did not derive his concept of socialism from his studies of the writings of Marx, but it evolved out of his deeply religious outlook.

In order to make judicious evaluation of Gandhian socialism, the following propositions must be noted :

> "Gandhi's genius was essentially spiritual rather than intellectual. Gandhi was not an academician in a technical term. He did not write a thesis on socialism. He was a *Karmayogi,* a man of action, not a systematic philosopher like Marx and Engel. Naturally, he does not appear to be consistent. A practical idealist, as he was , it was not his concern to be systematic and uniform. At the time of writing, he says, "I never think of what I have said before. My aim is not to be consistent with my previous statements on a given question, but to be consistent with truth as it may present itself to me at a given movement."[25] This is why he maintained, "I would like to say to the diligent reader of my writings and to others who are interested in them that I am not at all concerned with appearing to be consistent. In my search after truth I have discovered many ideas and learnt many new things. What I am concerned with is my readiness to obey the call of truth—my God from moment to moment, and therefore when anybody finds inconsistency between any two

> writings of mine ... he would do well to choose the latter of the two on the same subject."[26]

In fact no great man, who has brought about a revolution in thoughts and activities, has been altogether free from contradictions. Prof. Lindsay in reply to such inconsistencies opines, "The original thinker is too much occupied in trying to express creative thought which is willing up in him to trouble himself about getting it all straightened out. These are always parts of his works which has taken over as they stood from other people. These are always bits of dead woods in great man's work. The really tidy and consistent thinkers are the average minded disciples who make a neat and orderly system out of their master's work in which the inconsistencies are explained away along with them. Fortunately, it is much easier to make a tidy pattern out of the dead wood than out of the growing shoots".[27] Gandhi claimed that he was a foremost socialist. Expressing his views on socialism he maintained, "Socialism is a beautiful word and so far as I am aware in socialism all the members of society are equal, none low, none high. In the individual body, the head is not high because it is the top of the body, nor are the soles low because they touch the earth. Even the limbs of individual body are equal so are the members of the society. This is socialism. In it, the prince and the peasant, the wealthy and the poor, the employer and the employee are all on the same level. There is no duality. It is all unity. Looking at the society all the world over there is nothing but duality or plurality. Unity is conspicuous by its absence. In the unity of my conception, there is perfect unity in the plurality of designs. In order to reach this stage we may not look on things philosophically and say that we need not make a move until all are converted to socialism. Without changing over life we may go on giving addresses, forming parties and hawk-like seize the same when it comes to our way. This is no socialism. His socialism is as pure as crystal. It, therefore, requires crystal like means to achieve it. Impure means results in an impure end. One cannot reach the truth by untruthfullness. Truthful conduct alone can reach truth. This blessed state is unattainable without perfect unity. Harbour impurity of mind or body and you have untruth and violence. Therefore, only truthful, non-violent and pure hearted socialists will be able to establish socialist society in India and the world.[28]

Some of important economic contents of Gandhian socialism have been discussed while dealing with the basic essence of *Sarvodaya* as expounded by Gandhi. On the basis of purusal of above facts following features of Gandhian socialism can be noted:

Gandhian socialism is a class in itself. It is unique in its internal qualities. It did not come as a result of his studies from the writings of eminent personalities like Marx and others, nor it was derived from the horror of capitalism, nor it was the outcome of the reactions against the prevailing faulty socio-economic set-up as was the case with saint Simon, Owen, Fourier. It came natural to him. It was the inevitable outcome of predominantly religious bent of his mind. He held that true socialism or communism did not come as a result of the misuse of capital, it is rather implicit in the *Shastras.*

The *Bhagwat Puran* is much more emphatic on the basis of principles of socialism as an equitable sharing of the blessings of God-where Narada tells Yudhisthira that, "one is entitled to take as much as is sufficient for fulfilling up the stomach, he who takes more than this is guilty of the theft and deserves to be punished."[29] *Gita* also proclaims that we may not own anything beyond our strict requirements but should share equally with all God's creatures the means of subsistence.[30]

Echoing in the same spirit, Gandhi says, "A thing not originally stolen must, nevertheless, be classified as stolen property, if we possess it without needing it.[31] Since possession implies a provision for future, it is inconsistent with the law of non-violence and truth. He, who has made truth and *Ahimsa* as the sole basis of his life, has faith in the providence of God that He would give him his daily bread. Ignorance of this law on our part has given rise to inequalities with all the miseries attendant upon them, believed Gandhi and declares, "If we retained possession only of what we needed, no one would be in want and all would live in contentment".[32]

One of the grounds on which Proudhon regarded, "Property as theft, is possession". Only that property is just which is shared by all not collectively and impersonally, but directly and individually.[33] The property, which as a matter of fact, belongs to the society as a whole, if possessed by some persons or groups without the sanction of the society, the occupier is considered to have committed the theft. Gandhi goes much farther and traces the motive which impels the occupier to possess the thing which, indeed, belonged to all.

Socialism in the real sense, says Gandhi, has been handed down to us by our ancestors who taught, "All land belongs to Gopal". Gopal stands for shepherd, it also means God Krishna. In the modern language, it means the state, people.[34] Land and property, of course,

Gandhi says, 'belongs to him who works for it'. He expressed socialism in the tone of Indian genius.

Gandhian socialism is unique too, on account of its being non-violent through and through. *Ahimsa* is, thus, essentially a positive force and means conscious suffering for the good cause rather than meek submission to the evil doer.[35] He believed that the sublime socialist goals of equality, liberty and fraternity could only spring out of love for humanity at large and not from violence, hatred, intrigues and vengeance. Hence, "truth and non-violence must incarnate in socialism". He adds, 'only truthful and pure-hearted socialist will be able to establish a socialist society in India and the world.'[36]

An equitable dispensation of nation's wealth is the key note of socialism. Gandhi believed that so long as the horrible distinction between the rich and the poor continues, the attainment of socialism will be a far cry, an impossibility.[37] He warns that unless haves voluntarily abdicate their riches and power for the common good, a violent revolution is a certainty.[38] Hence, the urgent need is to bring about economic equality that constitutes cornerstone of non-violent socialism. Here Gandhi offers the lasting solution for equitable distribution of wealth and income through the application of trusteeship doctrine. The theory of trusteeship comes very close to the ancient Hindu ideal. According to traditional Hindu view, "Property is a mandate held by its possessors for common use and benefit of commonwealth. Anyone if desires more without needing it commits theft and deserves punishment". *Gita* says that those who desire salvation should act like trustees.[39] *Ishopanishad* too proclaims enjoyment through renunciation.[40] Wealth belongs to all as such should be shared by all. No one is its sole legal authority.

Gandhi while agrees that the concentration of capital in the present set-up is the fruit of exploitation to a very large extent but if there is a choice between the individual and the state violence, he would prefer violence of individual to that of the state as the lesser of the two evils.[41] Because the state represents violence in the concentrated and organised form. The individual has a soul, but the state is a soulless machine. He, therefore, favours not the centralisation of powers in the hands of the state, but an extension of sense of trusteeship, since to him the violence of private ownership is less injurious than the violence of the state.[42] But in case it is unavoidable, he would support, "a minimum of state ownership, as a concession to human frailty. Trusteeship alone, thus, provides a possible escape from the dilemma, make man free and they become unequal, make them equal and they cease to be free.[43] Under the doctrine of trusteeship, the character of production will be determined by the social necessity and not by personal greed or whim. The criticisms advanced by Marxists are untenable as they base their analysis on the basis of class structure and inherent conflict which is stoutly refuted by Gandhi. His purpose, therefore, is to bring about change from within and to stir the necessity and usefulness of bread-labour and develop the feeling of humility, service and cooperation in place of hatred, class struggle and violence. Socialism begins with the first convert. Socialism in its essence is not a gospel of mechanical efficiency but a way of life.[44]

Here a brief comparative estimate of Marx and Gandhi is essential. Each is a path finder for humanity groping in darkness.[45] But wherein Marx sticks to violence, Gandhi sticks to non-violence in thoughts, words and deeds. Marx would coerce but Gandhi would persuade; Gandhi stands for the conversion and the inner purification, whereas Marx would bring about change in the outer structure of life without changing the inner conversion. Gandhi would aim at the revolution by agreement but Marx aims at a revolution by violence. The one is the apostle of truth and non-violence, whereas the other of violence and hatred. The fundamental difference between Gandhian and Marxian approaches lies in their different attitudes towards life and universe.[46] And all other differences, whether of ends and means or of ideas about political, social, economic or religious order arise from this basic difference.

On being asked, whether he could avoid class war, Gandhi reaffirmed, "I can, most decidedly, if the people will follow the non-violent method ... when people adopt it as a principle of conduct, class war becomes impossibility.[47] Similarly, Gandhi repudiates Marx's *Economic Interpretation of History.* Briefly stated the theory is that, "the driving force is not the thought and wills of men, but changes of climates, discoveries of raw materials, and the inventions of the new technical processes which determine the course of the history. Thus, even the activity of inventing or creating is not, as it appears to be a spontaneous mental activity, but function or byproduct of environmental circumstances.[48] Gandhi rejected the Marxian thesis and held that economic forces alone are not responsible for all changes in social set-up. According to Dr. Radhakrishnan, "The emphasis on the importance of the economic conditions is correct; the assertions that they are exclusive determinant of history is incorrect."[49] Thus

Marx is materialist, Gandhi an essentially spiritual genius. Marx advocates hatred and anger, Gandhi to compassion and to love. Marx adopted violence to right the wrong. Gandhi adhered to non-violent resistance and loving persuasion. Now sometimes question arises : Can Gandhi be characterised as a socialist? As a matter of fact, all depends what one takes the essence of socialism. Those who accept dialectical materialism, class antagonism and the economic interpretation of history as the essence of socialism, would easily reject his claim to be called a socialist. Obviously, he cannot be called a socialist in the Marxist sense of the term. Likewise, other brands of socialists will also reject his claims to be a socialist. Nevertheless, all does not end here. Gandhi himself has claimed to be a socialist. Those who regard him as a socialist do not accept Marxian tenets as the essence of socialism. State ownership of the means of production may not be accepted as the crux of the socialist faith. Socialisation at best is a means to an end and not an end in itself. Socialism as discussed here is a commonwealth of equal and free in which everyone is ensured without any discrimination fullest of opportunities for the development of one's personality. Socialism means the ends. In this sense Gandhi was a socialist and a socialist par excellence. He upheld the ideal of social justice and would strive to secure a more equitable distribution of national wealth. He was opposed to all exploitations, all injustices, all distinctions and discriminations between man and man and strives to put an end to them. His socialism is ethical and humanitarian.

To sum up, to determine whether or not Gandhi is a socialist, one has first to determine what is socialism. If it is sympathy and solidarity with the down-trodden sections of the society? Then Gandhi is certainly a socialist. If it is passion for social justice? Then nobody dares challenge his claim. Is it an economic means towards the free development of human personality? Then Gandhi has an assured place in the crusade. Is it a peaceful international society, free from exploitation and dominance of any kind? Thus who is as staunch a socialist as Gandhi. On the basis of comprehensive analysis of the existing situation and empirical experiences, a holistic view of the socialism is required and then Gandhi is rated as the confirmed socialist in thoughts, words and deeds. Some of important aspects of Gandhian socialism have been discussed while dealing with the basic essence of *Sarvodaya* as expounded by Gandhiji.

NOTES

1. Inaugural Address of Pt. Nehru at the *Seminar on Parliamentary Democracy*, 25.2.1958.
2. Speech of the Vice President, *Ibid.*
3. *Statesman*, 25.10.1976, p. 1, 28.10.1976, p. 1.
4. Barker, *Reflections on Government*, Paperback, pp. 192-93.
5. M.K. Gandhi, *India of My Dream*, pp. 9-10.
6. Onkar Sharad (1972): *Lohia*, U.B.S. Publishers Distributors, Delhi-6 pp. 65-67.
7. *Ibid.*, p. 94.
8. Shreeman Narayan (1960): *Principles of Gandhian Planning*, Kitab Mahal, Allahabad, pp. 127-28.
9. *Ibid.*, pp. 125-139.
10. Doke, J.J. (1909): M.K. Gandhi—An Indian Patriot in South Africa, London, *Indian Chronicles*, p. 48.
11. Desai, A.R. (1966): *Social Background of Indian Nationalism*, Popular Prakashan, Bombay, p. 48.
12. Mahatma Gandhi (1906): *Hind Swaraj*, Navjivan Publishing House, Ahmedabad, p. 60.
13. John Stretchy (1957): *Contemporary Capitalism*, Victor Gollanex, London, p. 276.
14. Huxley (1937): *Ends and Means*, London, p. 320.
15. V.P. Verma (1972): *The Political Philosophy of Mahatma Gandhi and Sarvodaya*, Luxmi Narayan, Agra, p. 86.
16. Joad, C.E.M., *Introduction to Modern Political Theory*, Oxford University Press, Madras, p. 40.
17. William Eienstein (1970): *Modern Political Thought*, Oxford University Press, New Delhi, p. 636.
18. G.D.H. Cole (1935): *A History of Socialist Thought*, Vol. I, McMillan, London, p. 11.
19. V. I. Lenin, *Collected Works*, Vol. 19, Progress Publishers, Moscow, p. 27.
20. Rajgopal (1964): *Bhartiya Rajniti*, Gyan Mandal, Banaras, 1964, p. 81.
21. M.K. Gandhi (1909): *Hind Swaraj*, Navjivan, Ahmedabad, p. 2.
22. B.R. Nanda (1962): *The Nehrus: Motilal and Jawaharlal*, George Allen Unwin, London, p. 201.
23. Rafiq Jakaria (Ed) (1969): A Study of Nehru, *Times of India Press*, Bombay, p. 17.
24. Chester Bowles (1970): Key to Revolution in Norman Consins *(Ed) Profile of Gandhi*, India Book Company, Delhi, p. 162.
25. *Harijan*, 30.9.1939.
26. *Harijan*, 24.4.1933.
27. Adopted from Mahadev Prasad, *Social Philosophy of Mahatma Gandhi*, 1958, p. 186.
28. *Harijan*, 30.7.1947.
29. *Bhagvat Puran*, Chapter-14, Verse-8.
30. Verse-12, Chapter-3.

31. Bharatan Kumarappa (1957): *Towards Non-Violent Socialism,* Navjivan, Ahmedabad, p. 2.
32. From Yervada Mandir, pp. 23-24.
33. Asoka Mehta, *Studies in Asian Socialism*, p. 66.
34. *Harijan*, 2.1.1937
35. *Young India*, 11.8.1920.
36. *Harijan*, 13.7.1947.
37. *Constructive Work*, Navjivan, Ahmedabad, 1961, p. 24.
38. *Trusteeship*, Compiled by Ravindra Kelkar, Navjivan, Ahmedabad, 1960, p. 15.
39. *The Story of My Experiment with Truth*, p. 222.
40. *Harijan,* 1.2.1924.
41. *Young India*, 26.11.1931.
42. N.K. Bose (1962): *Studies in Gandhism*, p. 54.
43. Pyarelal, *Towards New Horizon*, p. 89.
44. *Harijan,* 13.7.1947.
45. *Gandhi Marg,* Vol. 5, April 1961, p. 237.
46. K.G. Mashruwala, *Gandhi and Marx*, p. 40.
47. R.K. Prabhu (1952): Compiled, *Communism and Communists,* Navajivan, Ahmedabad, p. 9.
48. C.E.M. Joad, *Guide to the Philosophy of Morals and Politics,* p. 667.
49. Radhakrishnan, *Religion and Society*, p. 35.

11

Gandhi and Environment

Modern world is marked by environmental crisis, enveloping the individual, social, political and cultural life of man. Pursuit of materialism with all its emphasis on growth and development has led neither to individual happiness nor to social harmony and peace. Man lives in a state of inner-contradictions and outer disconnections being placed against man, society and nature. Problems of poverty and hunger, unemployment and inflation are assuming staggering proportion day by day. Threats of environmental pollution, depletion of scarce natural resources and deteriorating ecological balance loom wider than ever before. The world is today faced with catastrophic situation. Albest Schwetzer remarked, "It is clear now to everyone that the suicide of civilization is in progress". Some feel that if the present way continues there may be no one to write our obituary.[1]

It is in this background that Mahatma Gandhi's ideas have become relevant for the present ailing world. Gandhi is well known in history as a philosopher saint and political leader, we have so far failed to recognise him as a human ecologist and environmentalist. The concepts, environment and ecology, were not in vogue during the Mahatma's time, as they are today. But we find evidence of his serious concern on many occasions about environmental problems and their solutions. Gandhian concepts of ecology and environment are scatterd throughout his vast and voluminous literature, writings, speeches and letters. Here the objective is to find out the Gandhian ideas about sustainable development, and maintenance of nature and establishing human harmony with nature, put them in systematic order and examine their relevance as livable approach to life. Man and nature have always lived in harmony through centuries. The relationship and interplay between man and nature have been demonstrated by renowned ecologists, namely, Dale Tom Carter and Vernan Gill in the following words :

> "Man whether civilised or savage is a child of nature, he is not a master of nature. He must confirm his action to certain natural laws if he is to maintain his dominance over his environment. When he tries to circumvent the laws of nature, he usually destroy the natural environment that sustains him. And, when the environment deteriorates rapidly his civilization declines".[2]

From molten mass of fire we came into living beings, from living beings we have come to animals, from animals we came to human beings but man is not the crown of evolution. Man has to be surpassed. He has to preserve himself. The future is in our hand, it is not inevitable. There is no such things as historical determinism or mechanical necessity. The whole past tells us that there is hope for mankind if they are able to use their freedom, their responsibility in the right way. Future of man appears not merely as a succession of probable futures, but an array of possible futures and a conflict over preferable futures. But he has to put in efforts to convert certain possibles into probables in pursuit of an agreed preferables.

The nature sets limits. But has man always tried to cross that limit while the animals adapt themselves according to the environment. Man tries to modify the environment according to his requirement. This very requirement is at the heart of the problems humanity faces these days.

Environment has become a catchword of present era. Today, we are in the midst of a great debate over the problem of as how to protect the global environment which is being threatened by growing pollution, maintenance of ecology and exhaustion of non-renewable resources. Our preoccupation and obsession with materialistic concept of growth and technological advancement have given rise to serious concern for ecology and preservation of healthy environment. People are now highly concerned about 'greenhouse effect', depletion of ozone layer, deforestation, pollution of water, traffic congestion, noise pollution. These are causing both mental and physical health hazards.

Environment refers to the quantity and quality of natural resources, both renewable and non-renewable. It includes the ambient environment, which consists of landscape, water, air and the atmosphere, and is crucial determinant of human quality of life, as well as supporting human life. The state of the environment is a critical determinant of the quantity, quality and sustainability of human activities.[3]

The environmental economics follows neoclassical economics in having as its central concern the efficient allocation of scarce resources among competing uses. This branch of economics brings scarce environmental resources into mainstream economic analysis. It addresses issues of pollution control, efficient setting of emission standard, waste management and recycling the industrial activity of environmental externalities, the conservation of natural resources, the valuation of natural resources and so on. The objective of environmental economics is to identify policies which will move the economic system towards an efficient allocation of natural resources.

The environmental economics is distinct from ecological economics to the extent that it adheres more closely to conventional and neo-classical economics. That is, it emphasises the desirability of attaining environmental objective by means of using market mechanism. The interdependence between the environment and economy arises from the fact that the environment provides the raw materials for economic activity as well as directly providing welfare, and because the way in which the economy is managed impacts on the environment. Thus, environmental damage caused by economic activity will, in turn, affect both welfare and the performance of the economy.

Environment and energy resources can be thought of as a natural asset which provides valuable services to humans. For instance, ecological systems are responsible for providing clear air and water, scenic values, maintaining soil fertility, and regulating flows of water, as well as assimilating and processing wastes and regulating the world's climate. Environmental resources include stocks of exhaustible mineral resources. These resources perform many functions including provision of raw materials for production and the generation of energy.

Environmental sustainability can be defined as sustainability of the ecological services on which humans depend. These services include the provision of food and other raw materials and the ecological services required to support agricultural production including hydrological regulation, production and protection of soil, and the regulation of the climate. Environmental sustainability at a global scale includes maintaining the ecological stability of the global ecosystem for instance limiting the emissions of green house gases to levels which will not lead to catastrophic changes in the climate.[4]

With the increasing attention to these environmental and ecological problems, a new 'ism' is fast engulfing the world.

Eco-disaster, environmental degradation and the like have become the catchwords of the present era. The U.N. Rio de Janeiro (1992), the Global Forum (1992), the activities organised by the International Forum and a Draft Treaty on Global Warming in the Japanese City of Kyoto (1997) show that environment is on the agenda of international community. People in different parts of the world are trying to be more eco-friendly with the goal to save the earth. The global human concern and awareness to preserve environment make it pertinent to know environment as a concept.

Environment is what constitutes our existence. The term environment etymologically means surroundings and is generally used for an abstract concept. Surroundings may be natural or man-made and may be physical, chemical or biotic. The environment is thus a complex of many things encompassing an organism that interacts not only with the organism but also among themselves. As a result, it is difficult to isolate or alter any one of them without affecting other components. The growth behaviours of life of an organism are, therefore, influenced by the environment in which they live.[5]

Another environmentalist has explained environment in the following words : "Environment is not the atmosphere and other physical factors surrounding us but a complex of all the factors which not only affect one oganism, one time, but all organisms all the time."[6]

In broader sense, environment constitutes the various physical, mental, social, spiritual, educational, economic and intellectual aspects of whole humanity and when kept healthy and inspiring it promotes the progress and development that acts as saviour and is boon to mankind.[7] The air, water and land are, therefore, the basic components of environment. Their indiscriminate degradation poses a serious danger to environmental stability. The necessity to protect and improve such environmental stability has recently been recognised by all the developed and developing nations.

The Stockholm Declaration (1972) on human environment, said to be the *'Magna carta'* on human environment, proclaimed :

> "The natural resources of the earth, including air, water, land, flora and fauna are especially representative samples of natural eco-system, must be safeguarded for the benefit of present and future generation through careful planning and management, as appropriate. The state should take all possible steps to prevent pollution of seas by substances that are liable to create hazards to

human health, to farm, living resources and marine life to damage amenities or to interfere with other legitimate uses of seas. The man and environment must be spared against the nuclear weapons and all other means of mass destruction."[8]

As mankind has entered 21st century and it is being frequently talked and heard, the refrain that the world is perched uneasily on a 'powerkeg'. Indeed the 'overkill capacities of major powers', the growing threats of environmental degradation and ecological decay, the problem of rising population and poverty and impoverishment of the vast masses of people, especially in the Third World countries, all these end products of industrialism and high technology have taken mankind of such a formidable predicament that it seems well high impossible to return to a normal or rationally ordered life within a framework of modernity.

Gandhi has foreseen these problems in the beginning of the 20th century. He observed : It is not possible to conceive Gods inhabiting a land which is made hideous by the smoke and the din of mill chimneys and factories and whose roadways are traversed by rushing engines dragging numerous cars crowded with men who know not for the most what they are after.[9] In *Hind Swaraj,* Gandhi had characterised modern civilization as disease and a nine days wonder.[10] And even thirty years later in 1938 he said "after the thirty years which I have since passed, have been nothing to make me alter the views expounded in it". Earlier in 1927, he had forewarned the civilized West that "a time is coming when these, who are in the mad rush today of multiplying their wants, will retrace their steps and say what have we done"? Barely two weeks before his death in January 1948, Gandhi made the rather prophetic statement that this modern civilization is such that one has only to be patient, and it will be self-destroyed.[11]

Given the present balance of terror, with its plans for mutually assured destruction, who could doubt the terrible possibility of self-destruction of major power and with them perhaps the rest of the world too, by accident there are also ecological scenario portraying massive deluge like flooding as a result of the melting of the polar ice caps or emergence of a new ice age resulting from increase in the diversity of particular matter in the atmosphere due to atmospheric pollution.[12]

The Club of Rome has termed it as the predicament of mankind.[13] In a commentary on the report, "The Limit of Growth—A Report of Club of Rome," the executive committee of the club expresses this view :

> "We are convinced that realisation of the quantitative restraints of the world environment and the tragic consequences of an overshoot, it is essential to the initiation of new form of thinking that will lead to fundamental revision of human behaviour and by implication, of the entire fabric of the present day society ....We affirm finally that any deliberate attempts to reach a rational and enduring stage of equilibrium by planned measures, rather than by chance or catastrophe, must ultimately be founded on a basic change of values and goal at individual, national and world level."[14]

Alvin Toffler, in his best seller *Future Shock* has nicely described the inexorable price we are paying for degradation of environment and application of high technology:

> "Our technological power increases but the side effects and potential hazards also escalate, we risk thermo pollution of the ocean themselves, overheating them, destroying immeasurable quantities of marine life, perhaps even melting the pollar ice caps. On land we concentrate such large masses of population in such small urban technological islands that we threaten to use up that air's oxygen faster than it can be replaced, conjuring up the possibilities of new Saharas where cities are now through such destruction of natural ecology, we may literally in the words of biologist Barry Commoner be destroying this planet as a suitable place for human habitation".[15]

Similarly, the major findings of the Global 2000, Report to the President of United States of America, are :

> "If the present trend continues, the world 2000 will be more crowded, more polluted, less stable ecologically and more vulnerable to disruption than the world we live in now. Serious stresses involving population, resources and environment are clearly visible ahead."

Thus, the cumulative impact of this degrading environment and growth syndrome is now being felt like shock waves in rising disillusionment, thickening frustration and mounting fear. It would, therefore, be in a fitness of things to examine critical global concerns, chiefly pollution and environmental degradation, and to see whether and to what extent Gandhi offers an alternative to the larger problem of a peaceful world order.

Man and environment have always been in interaction depending on how mankind used the environment. From ancient Indian scripts, we get a myriad of examples which show that people used to live in harmony with nature. '*Van-Prastha'*, the last phase of life in Indian culture, is nothing but a change from the materialistic life to a non-materialistic one and to adjust and adopt the natural environment. India's cultural tradition inculcates the principle of reverence for all living objects, men, animals, trees and plants. If we look into various traditional *Pujas,* we will notice that nearly every tree is worshipped more particularly banyan, pipal, mango, bamboo, neem, etc. Cutting of green trees was considered sin, cow is worshipped as mother. Rivers are considered sacred. Even God's incarnations have been in the forms of the pig, the tortoise, the fish. Monkeys and bears were those who helped Lord Rama to fight the evil that Ravana was. Lord Krishna was named Gopal, the protector of cows.[16] There was absence of legislation but environmental stability was maintained to its maximum extent during the Vedic period to 18th century. With the emergence of British, imperialism and colonialism of Indian soil, the eco-balance started deteriorating. British imperialism came to India with its high technology, use of modern machines, factory life and modern life complexities. Gradually, Indian environment started getting disturbed. The British Government through Indian Penal Code (1860), Water Pollution and Atmospheric Pollution Code of Criminal Code 1898, Police Act, 1861, tried to maintain ecology and environment but their attempts failed as they were only an eyewash.

In post-independence period, the gravity of deteriorating ecology and environment was realised but no attempts were made till 1972, when United Nations Conference on Human Environment was held in Stockholm. In 1976, 42nd Amendment was done in the Indian Constitution committed to the protection of environment. Even in the Directive Principles of State Policy, Article 48A was included :

The state shall endeavour to protect and improve the environment and safeguard the forests and wildlife of the country. (Article 48A) By the same amendment is created a fundamental duty of every citizen under Article 51-A(g) :

"To protect and improve the natural environment including forests, lakes, rivers and wildlife and have compassion for living creatures."

The Indian Parliament has also enacted several statutes especially Water Prevention and Control of Pollution Act, 1974, Air (Prevention and Control of Pollution) Act, 1981, and the Environment (Protection) Act, 1986.

The courts have also pronounced judgements showing their grave concern for ecological balance and have also sounded a note of caution to the executive with warning if falls an deaf ears, the court would not remain silent.

It was the UN Conference on Human Environment, held in Stockholm (1972), which declared environment and related issues of pollution, ecological decay and resources depletion as matters of overwhelming global concerns. As a first step to deal with the problem, it set up United Nations Environmental Programme (UNEP) and latter established an expert group to study the impact of perspective environmental issues on policies and international development.[17]

The global environmental problems have two major dimensions, namely, resource depletion and environment pollution, which are together linked with modern industrial and agricultural production, population and poverty. Population of the world has exploded since the industrial revolution two centuries ago. What is more, bulk of the population is tending to migrate and settle in urban areas and engage in non-agricultural activities. Even in the Third World, according to Club of Rome estimate, over 60 per cent of the population will be living in cities by the end of this century.[18]

This shows that fewer hands will be engaged in agriculture and food production. This trend is not encouraging, Karl Marx once wrote, cultivation when progresses, spontaneously and is not consciously controlled ...leaves deserts behind it.[19] Thus, we find that while demand for food is growing, food production is on the decline.

It may be recalled in the environmental context that food production has also suffered from reckless deforestation which in turn leads to floods, soil erosion, silting up of rivers and eventually desertification. The hapless residents of UP and Bihar have experienced the worst type of natural calamities due to flood, heavy rain, soil erosion and landslides created by human muddling with natural balance in the name of development. The growth of demand for farmland and increased export of forest products to the affluent industrial countries have caused deforestation to the extent of 11 million hectares every year in the Third World countries. This has led to a large scale flooding, as the Brandt Commission Report has pointed out, in many countries notably in Bangladesh, Nigeria and Panama. In India, since 1947, 5300 sq km of forest area, larger than Punjab, has been lost.[20]

Thus deforestation, a substantial case of ecological disruption, arises largely from the need of modern industries in affluent countries or from "wasteful pattern of resources use for the conspicuous consumption by money elites everywhere."[21] In India, indiscriminate felling of trees is reducing the forest cover. In Orissa, denunciation of forest is causing deserification in the western region. The hilly region of Kumaun, which was once the scene of Jim Corbets legendary encounters with tigers and other ferocious animals, has been deforested by urban based contractors. This has generated the famous *Chipko* movement. This peaceful and non-violent movement has been inspired by Gandhian ideas and techniques and has caught global attention.

Soil fertility and earth's recuperative powers are also damaged in the long run by the excessive use of chemical fertilizers and pesticides. Pesticides and chemical fertilizers are also great pollutants. Excessive use of these chemicals and fertilizers tends to pollute the soil and some of it finds way into the cereal and other agricultural products. Thus, rendering them unfit for human and animal consumption.[22] Their persistent use in Japan is reported to have poisoned land and water surrounding major cities.[23]

In this scenario of increasing demand for food and diminishing production and availability of food for human consumption, the world may soon be inclined towards a condition of widespread hunger, famine or starvation, which may endanger global peace and cause irreparable damage to the quality of life everywhere. In Africa, about twenty-four countries have been in the grip of severe famine and hunger and "pockets of hunger exist in the United States."[24]

Along with food, the non-renewable mineral resources of the world are also fast getting depleted. According to the study undertaken by the United States National Academy of Science, the world mineral resources, like iron ore and tungston, may not last beyond two hundred years at the present rate of utilisation and consumption. The coal reserve may last only a century and oil may well disappear by the year 2050 or even earlier.[25] And no safe or viable substitute for these fast depleting resources has been discovered. Gandhian way is memorable in this context.

Air is one of the most important constituents of man's environment. It is calculated that a man inhales about 16 kg of air by weight. Therefore, pure and clean air is a prime necessity for survival and good health. But due to air pollution, our health and survivability have been endangered, especially in big cities and metropolitan centres. A complete definition of air pollution, according to India's Air (Prevention and Control) Pollution Act, 1981, is "air pollution means any solid, liquid or gaseous substance including noise present in the atmosphere in such concentrations that may or tend to be injurious to human beings or other living creatures or plants or property of environment."

Air pollution has attracted the attention throughout the world. Air pollution is the major cause of diseases in India. A World Bank Report reveals that every year 40,000 people die due to pollution-related problems. Another study by The Tata Energy Research Institute (TERI) mentions 62 cities in India are reeling under air pollution with 20 in dangerous category.

Water, like air, is an indispensable and precious natural resource on this planet. But due to industrialisation, urbanization and other development related activities, water resources have become highly polluted. Today, many of the rivers of the world receive millions of litres of sewage, domestic waste and industrial effluents. In India, all the 14 major rivers have become polluted. The holiest river of the country, the Ganges, has become highly polluted. All the big cities of North India with their industries dump their wastes and effluents into the Ganges. From only Kanpur, 270 million litres of untreated sewage and industrial effluents flow into it. Many of the ponds, smaller rivers and lakes have become darkened, smelly and choked with excessive growth of algae.[26]

Forests are a major factor of environment concern. According to Brewbaker (1984), the total forest area of the world in 1900 was nearly 70 m km^2 but in 1975 it was reduced to 28.9 m km^2. If this alarming trend continues, by the year 2000 the forest cover would be nearly 23.7 m km^2.

India has a total geographical area of 32,88,000 km^2. Out of this,

7,47,800 km^2 (22.74%) was occupied by the forest at the time of independence. But according to an assessment done in 1989, a loss of 18.39 per cent of the forest cover has disturbed the bio-economic environmental balance in India. Deforestation leads to soil erosion, loss of foodgrains, occurrence of droughts and threat to Himalayan eco-system. Thus afforestation has become a necessity. Plant more trees campaign was started by K.M. Munsi in the forties of the last century. Now, of course very late, social foresty, agro-forestry and movements like *Chipko,* Tehri Dam opposition, Narmada Bachao Andolan get international prominence.

Environmental chaos has threatened wildlife. Indian biological and botanical heritage are in perilous stage. T.N. Khoshoo says, "since the turn of century, nearly 132 plants species face extinction, 24 plant species are already extinct. One mammalian and three bird species have become extinct and 71, 47 and 15 species of mammals, birds and reptiles respectively have been declared threatened.[27] To preserve the wildlife and protect the environmental balance, eco-system stability is to be maintained at all costs.

In the area of energy, hydro-electric power, nuclear energy and solar energy are considered as good substitutes for coal and oil. But each of them has its limitation. Water resources are unevenly distributed in the world. As far as nuclear energy is concerned, it is hazardous source of energy and is fraught with the risk of accident and long-term exposure to radiation. The solar energy is still in the realm of experimentation, it is contingent on the evolution of a low-cost technology and a breakthrough in the techniques or method of storage. Thus, given the present urban industries and mechanised agricultural system and present consumption patterns, the world would be moving fast towards a severe depletion or exhaustion of its food resources, mineral and energy reserves which together should lead to impoverishment and degradation of human conditions.

The greatest and the deadliest pollution today is radio-active fallout from nuclear testing or from long-term storage and disposal of nuclear wastes. The effects are not limited to the present generation. The worst of all, there was the horrifying tragedy at Chernobyl in 1996.

It is widely and quite reasonably believed that the cumulative pollution of the atmosphere, land and water may in the long run interfere with the life support system. Some scientists have even predicted that our world may reach the "doomsday" on 14th November 2026 A.D.[28] There is no way to check the accuracy of a "doomsday" projection. Perhaps, its author has used the term to highlight the unmistakably tragic fate of the modern world which continues to disregard environment and ecological consideration in its craze for unlimited production and often wasteful production. It is, in essence, a counsel for restraint and even reversal over a period of time. Some of the best minds in the world have lately voiced their concern and seen in the present order the portents of impending danger of catastrophe which Gandhi foreseen nearly eighty years ago.[29]

Various dimensions of environmental degradation and serious concern for pollution in India and the world have been discussed in detail. It is only recently that thinkers all over the world are giving increasing attention to the problem of ecology, pollution and exhaustion of non-renewable resources. Gandhi was quite aware of this situation in the beginning of the 20th century.

Man must recognise the necessity of cooperating with the nature. He must temper his demands and use and conserve the natural living resources of their earth in a manner that alone can provide for the continuation of his civilization. The final answer is to be found only through comprehension of the enduring process of nature. The time for defiance is at end.[30]

It can be safely asserted that in a world devoid of other living creatures, man himself would die. All living things are interrelated, even the tiniest insects. It is a fact that animal life on the earth, its relationship, its preservation are wrapped up directly with our well-being. In human history, in the rise and fall of different civilizations, one factor was almost common to the decline of these civilizations and that was man's destruction of his living environment. It must be realised that in the long run life cannot be supported by artificial processes and science is incapable of providing for the continuity of human life by substituting its methods to those of nature. There would be no real hope for the future unless we are prepared to accept the concept that man like other living things is a part of biological scheme.

Our pre-occupation and obsession with materialistic concept of growth and technological advancement has given rise to serious problems of ecology and preservation of healthy environment. People are now highly concerned about green house effect, depletion of ozone layer, deforestation, pollution of water, traffic congestion, etc. These are creating health hazards, both physical and mental. The observation of Laing quoted in Turning Point is significant. A child born today in United Kingdom stands a ten times greater chance of being admitted to mental hospital than to university. This can be taken as an indication that we are driving our children mad more effectively than we are genuinely educating them. Perhaps, it is our way of educating them that is driving them mad.[31]

With increasing attention to these environmental and ecological degradation, efforts are being made to diagnose the causes and find technological and mechanical remedies. Several arguments are being advanced, more particularly for developing countries. Reasons advanced are :

(i) growing animal and human population that are making increasing demands on natural resources resulting in the exploitation of resources in an unsustainable manner,
(ii) general indifference of the industrial sector on aspect of environmental safety and protection leading to the spread of available air, water and soil pollution,
(iii) low level of environmental literacy,
(iv) a pattern of industrial, agricultural development and emerging consumption patterns that lead to energy mix in the country,
(v) indifference of central and state governments towards environmental problems for short term gains, and
(vi) poverty, undernutrition and high infant mortality coupled with widespread inequality and conspicuous consumption.

The world over, a lot of fuss is being created about these problems. There is no dearth of those whom we can easily define as shallow environmentalists. They want to meet the situation by more efficient control and management of natural environment. They essentially rely on the mechanical approach and think in terms of still better and more sophisticated machine. Really, it is self-defeating. They still refuse to realise that these problems are the outcome of the growth of technology beyond human control and an economic system which is unmindful of the ecological and social cost of excessive growth and technological development.

What is required is a radical change in our thinking. Real concern for ecological environment must advocate profound changes of the role of human beings in the planetary eco-system. It will require a new philosophical and religious awareness of oneness of all life and interdependence of multiple manifestations of nature. The philosophy of survival of the fittest based on competition struggle, destruction, exploitation of man and nature need to be replaced by the integrative and cooperative principles which should be essential aspects to organise living systems at all levels. These should be rooted in the deepest motivation which spring from moral and spiritual values. Nature has enough wisdom for us. We have only to be receptive to this wisdom offered to us through eco-system.

The solution ultimately lies in what Gandhi had suggested in changing the lifestyles, reversal of sense of value which encourage conspicuous and wasteful expenditure, small-scale industries, and a technology that assists and helps the individual and not overpowers him, and that teaches us to live in harmony with nature. We can destroy nature but we cannot recreate it.

When an interviewer asked that the material resources of the West have advanced out of proportion to its moral resources and something need to be done to bring them in a level with each other, Gandhi replied : "That is precisely what the *Charkha* is intended to do". On other occasion, Gandhi has observed: I cannot only imagine but I am working for a civilization in which possession of a car will be considered no merit and railway will find no place. It would not be for me an unhappy events if the world once more becomes as large as it used to be at one time...it is not an attempt to go to the so-called ignorant dark-ages. But it is an attempt to see beauty in voluntary simplicity, poverty, and slowness ...the modern craze for variety, for flying through the air, for multiplicity of wants, etc. have no fascination for me. They deaden the inner being in us.[32]

Again, Gandhi wrote :

> "High thinking is inconsistent with complicated material life based on high speed imposed on us by Mammon worship. All the graces of life are possible only when we learn the art of living nobly."[33]

Gandhi realised that the development of the world was not in right direction. Therefore, in one of his letters to Jawaharlal Nehru, he expressed his fear and suspicion about the future. He said :

> "It must not fear if the world today is going wrong way. It may be that India too will go that way and like the proverbial mouth burn itself eventually in the flame around which it dances more and more fiercely."[34]

The present situation is fraught with danger. In the wake of astounding advance of science and technology, and use of heavy machines in a big way, the problems not only remain unresolved but newer and newer problems beset mankind. While planning for peace, we have created a world of violence, acceleration of tension, conflicts and problematic environment. Poverty and hunger still prevail. While resources are being increasingly misutilised for mass production for consumption and material comforts, the world is faced with a situation of energy shortages, ecological imbalances, exhaustion of non-renewable resources, environmental pollution and highly sophisticated technology that is ignoring and undermining human values. Another major problem has been a feeling of helplessness.

The technological society has committed the plunder of world scarce resources. These supply the cheap materials for constructing the new industrial society, but have left a debt of destroyed and depleted resources to be paid by later generations. But how we are encroaching on the basic amenities of life, air, water and soil, now a new conservationist movement is needed to preserve the life itself.

Excessive technological growth has created an environment in which life has become physically and mentally unhealthy. Polluted air, noise pollution, traffic congestion, chemical contamination, radiation hazards and many other sources of physical and psychological stresses and strains have become part of everyday life for most of us. Ecological process has been damaged and disrupted that sustains our natural environment and the very basis of our existence.

Without a holistic approach to development and environment we have no hope of success or even of survival. The following remarks are very apt and pertinent to consider thé gravity of situation :

> "the rules of survival are as immutable as the laws of physics. There will be no pardons for us if we fail to obey and respond to the iron imperatives. We now recognise and understand, there may not even be anyone to write our obituary".[35]

Sustainable development is not a fixed state of harmony, but rather a process of change in which the exploitation of resources, the direction of investments, the orientation of technological development and institutional change are made consistent with future as well as present needs..[36]

Some of the mind boggling problems Gandhi mentioned are hereunder :

(i) Prevention of environment which is increasingly endangered by ever accelerating degradation and pollution, which might soon reach truly divesting and irreversible dimensions is now imperative.
(ii) Another major problem confronting mankind is sustainable exploitation of resources including food, energy and raw materials.
(iii) Prevention of war, which in the nuclear age will be last war.
(iv) Promoting human well-being in the widest sense, balancing advances of science and technology with human development and quality of work and life.

The present human civilization is trying to solve these problems. Reports like, "the Limits to Growth", "Small is Beautiful", Report of the World Commission on Ecology and Development and organisation of several non-governmental associations to safeguard environment and maintain balance are simply long-belated echoes of what Gandhi said in the beginning of the present century. He was dubbed as an idealist. But the idealist has become the only realist of the present age.

Human Survival and Gandhi

In nutshell, it can be said that the present ecological crisis is direct consequence of man's ability to rise to the level of understanding and responsibility demands by his new power role in the world. Findings of Schumacher and a host of other technologists and ecologists have reinforced the basic validity of Gandhi's approach. Considering these points time and again, one becomes progressively convinced that the present ecological crisis is a direct consequence of man's inability to rise to the level of understanding. The problem is within man not outside him, and so is any solution. And this is precisely what Gandhi emphasised. Human being will have to realise that a way of life that rapidly depletes the power of earth can only be called violent. Man's urgent task is to follow a non-violent way of life. It is a concept that needs to be widened to combat human dealing with living creature around him and with the limited and finite resources of nature.

It is clear that the development strategies in the majority of Third World countries borrowed from the affluent countries and based on high technology and capital-intensive industries, resource depletion and unmindful of distributive justice and the need for the amelioration of the conditions of the masses and high consumption and domination by a centralised and organised elite, are utterly incapable of delivering the goods. There is, therefore, an urgent need for a new alternative model of development conservation, production, labour-intensive production, equitable distribution. Such is the order of the society that Gandhi conceived.

The Delhi Declaration in November, 1986 was a welcome sign in this context. For it committed ... not only India but also a superpower to a world free from weapons of mass destruction, and a world without war, a non-violent world by solving problems such as environmental degradation, shortage of food, illiteracy and growth of population. Let us hope that as we moved into the 21st century, this perceptive Gandhian vision of a "non-violent eco-friendly world order", would spread to other areas of the world, not only at a verbal or declaration level but also into the concrete realm of personal, international action.[37]

There is no other avenue but man has to explore himself his goal and values as much as he seeks the world to change. There needs to be unending commitment to ensure that man will survive without falling into a state of worthless existence. More and more people all over the world should look for the ways to redirect ecological system as if people mattered.[38]

Today we are faced with a crisis of survival. Gandhian path and philosophy have answers to all the worries and anxieties of the modern world. The philosophy of Gandhi has been summarised beautifully by Schumacher in the following lines :

> "Towards smallness rather than giantism, towards simplification rather than growing complexities, towards capital-saving rather than labour-saving and towards non-violence, in a rather generalised sense."

The continuing multiplication of want associated with the spread of materialistic philosophy of life has brought the world to the brink of a major disaster. Success at any cost and wealth without limit is the plank of the present generation of the materialistic order which is impossible to be achieved for the masses. Thus Gandhian doctrine of limitation of wants becomes extremely significant for the survival of mankind.

NOTES

1. Quoted in J.S. Mathur's Preface, *Ailing World and Gandhian Alternative,* Bharatiya Vidya Bhawan, Bombay, 1997, p. IX.
2. Dale Tom and Carter Vernon Gill (1995): *Top Soil and Civilization*, Norman University of Oklahoma Press, p.6.
3. Pnayayotou, T. (1993): *Green Market, Economics of Sustainable Development*, Institute for Contemporary Studies Press, San Francisco.
4. Perman, R. (1996): *Natural Resources and Environmental Economics,* Longman, Harlow.
5. Anil Markandya, Rehat Perelet (Ed) (2001): *Dictionary of Environmental Economics,* Oxford University Press, New Delhi, pp. 86-87.
6. Agrawal, K.C. (1996): *Environmental Biology*, Agro-Botanical Publishers, Jaipur, p. 1.
7. Verma, B.L. (1988): *Man, Nature and Environmental Laws* (Ed.), By G.S. Nathawa, Shastri and Vyas, R.B.S.A. Publication, Jaipur, p.51.
8. Mathur J.S., *op. cit.*
9. Gangal, S.C. Gandhi and the Major World Problems, A Contemporary and Futuristic Perspective, *Gandhi Marg,* Vol. 9. No. 1, April 1997, p. 336.
10. *Ibid.*
11. Falk, Richard (1975): *A Study of Future Worlds,* New Delhi, p.108.
12. The Limits of Growth, A Report of the Club of Rome's Project on the Predicament of Mankind, Massachusetts Institute of Technology, 1972, p.17.
13. *Ibid.*, p.12.
14. Toffler, Alvin; *Future Shocks,* New York, A National General Library, 1971, p. 430.
15. Global Report to the President of the United States, Washington D.C. 1980, p. 39.
16. Quoted in Kinkri Devi *Vs* State, AIR 1988, HP. pp. 4, 8.
17. Gangal, S.C. *op. cit.,* p. 337.
18. Tinbergen, Jan (Co-ordinator) (1977): *Reshaping the International Order,* London p. 251.
19. Karl Marx & F. Engels (1995): *Selected Correspondence,* Moscow, p.202.
20. Thapa, Vijay Jung, Bring back the Wood, *India Today*, August 10, 1948.
21. Sachs, Ignancy: Human Development in Jan Tenbergen's *op.cit.* p. 285.
22. Mukherjee, T. N (1979): *Forward with Nature,* Bombay, p.17.
23. Knese, Allen. V. (1979): Development and Environment, *Third World Quarterly*, Vol. I, No. 1, London, p. 88.
24. Rao, V.K.R.V. (1982): Disarmament and Development, *Gandhi Marg,* May-June p. 431.
25. Falk, Richard, *A Study of Future World, op. cit.* p. 111.
26. Agrawal, K.C., *Environmental Biology, op.cit.* p. 430.

27. Khoshoo, T.N. (1986): *Environmental Priorities, India and Sustainable Development, Presidential Address,* ISCA, p. 224.
28. Tinbergen, Jan. *op.cit.* p. 237.
29. Gangan, S.C. *op.cit*. p. 342.
30. Quoted by Osboon, Fairfield. Our Plundered Planet Turning Point, p. 200.
31. *Ibid.* p. 201.
32. Lal, Pyare, *Last Phase,* Vol. 11. 1979, p.799.
33. *Ibid.*, p. 544.
34. Behn, Sarala, *South Link,* p. 9.
35. Prasad, Rajendra, *Legacy of Gandhi,* p. 99.
36. J.S. Mathur, *op.cit*., p. 19.
37. Gandhi, M.K. (1950): *Hindu Dharma,* Navajivan Publishing House, Ahmedabad, p. 70.
38. Schumacher, E.J. (1989): *Small is Beautiful, A Study of Economics as if People Mattered*, New York.

12

Overview

Now we have to see what is the real picture of our economy in the 21st century. Many things are said for publicity but real picture is not very satisfactory as far the conditions of masses are concerned. Recent reports from various sources such as Reserve Bank of India, the International Monetary Fund (IMF) and several merchant banks have come to the realisation that the Indian economy is poised for a 7 per cent growth has given rise to self-laudatory mood in certain quarters. But existing facts do not support this. According to them, India is shining. Furthermore, a recent article "Can India overtake China" in a prestigious U.S. Journal *Foreign Policy,* co-authored by Yashing Huang and Tarun Khanna, has put an additional gloss over it. Both belong to reputed institutions hence have impressive credentials. This article comes at a time when India's anticipated economic growth would come closest to that of China in more than a decade.

But we must not forget that 7 per cent growth comes after a year of 4.6 per cent preceded by performances of 5.7 per cent and 3.9 per cent which still shows the average growth rate to be in a low trajectory. But even if we accept that India is shining, how good is that shine? Very simply, the decade after the launch of the so-called reforms has not been very much better than the decade before it. GNP growth rate, for the post-reform period (1992-2001) crept up by a mere 0.2 to 5.9 per cent. With a performance like that it would be extremely difficult to make a case that the economic reforms or liberalisation have made much impact on the nation as a whole.

Of course, some have benefited. As the government told the Lok Sabha recently that there are no queues for telephone or gas connection. But India's teledensity a mere 3.2 per cent, and with just 58 million of the 180 million households with gas connection suggesting that most households with an income less than Rs. 80,000 per annum are without cheap and subsidised energy, hardly indicates any great spread of happiness. No queues for telephone, gas and even for Maruti cars and two wheelers is a good news. But certainly not enough to warrant an outpouring of self-congratulations, for it is indices for infant mortality (69 per thousand), life expectancy 65 years, literacy 65 per cent as well as energy consumption (a mere 379 kwh per capita) that make the reality.

The comparison of the first ten years of economic performances of India and China after reforms (1992-2001) for India and 1979-88 for China is instructive, China entered the first decade of the reforms as a fast developing and modernising country with an average decadel growth rate of 5.32 per cent. But more important than this was the performance of 1980 of reducing infant mortality to 42 per thousand, elevating life expectancy to 67 years, raising adult literary to 66 per cent. India by contrast had a better growth rate of 5.7 per cent in 1980s but came burdened with an infant mortality of 119 per thousand, life expectancy of 59.2 years, and adult literacy of 48.41 per cent. Many reasons have been advanced for China's relative advantage over India is a product of its pre-reform (pre-1979) groundwork rather than its post-reform redirection.

Yet another comparison will be more instructive. In 1978, at the inception of its reforms, China's per capita GDP (in constant 1995 US$) was $ 148 whereas that of India in the same year was $ 236. Seven years after it began its reform in 1986 caught up with India in per capita GDP. A term ($278 *vs* $273) and a decade after reforms in 1988 was comfortably ahead of India with a per capita GDP of $ 342 compared with India's $ 312. In the first post-reform decade, the Chinese economy grew at 10.1 per cent while the Indian economy grew at 5.7 per cent in the corresponding debate. Quite clearly that was India's lost decade.

But what did we achieve in the first decade of our reforms? In 1992, the first year of its reforms India's per capita GDP was $ 331. This grew to $ 477 in 2001. In the same period the Chinese per capita GDP surged from $ 426 to $ 878 in 2001. In the 1990s, China grew at the rate of 9.7 per cent while India grew at the rate of 5.9 per cent. Quite clearly, far from beginning to catch, we fell well behind.

It is true, both countries have transformed themselves after they embarked on the path of economic reforms but the transformations were entirely different. In 1980, the sectoral breakup of China's economy was as follows : agriculture 30 per cent, industry 49 per cent, and service 21 per cent. In 1990 that changed to agriculture 27 per cent, industry 42 per cent and services 31 per cent. In 2000 that picture transformed further. Agriculture fell to 16 per cent, industry grew to 51 per cent. While services steadied at 33 per cent. The growth of industry is to be noted which is quite remarkable. This was primarily made possible by overseas investment which amounted to $ 293 billion during the decade, which also created millions of new jobs. The share of FDI enterprises to total export rose from under 2 per cent in 1978 to 45.5 per cent in 1999. Today China accounts for 3.79 per cent of the world trade while India's share is just 0.93 per cent. Consequently, China's foreign exchange reserves have burgeoned to $ 383 billion while India's is $ 92 billion, now it has crossed $ 100 billion.

Indian picture makes for a study in contrast. The share of agriculture fell somewhat from 31 per cent in 1990 to 28 per cent in 2000. The share of industry too fell from 28 per cent to 26 per cent. Services grew from 41 per cent to 46 per cent. Softwares exports apart, the biggest contributive factor to the growth of India's services sectors has been the growth of public administration, which has been hounding at an average rate of 32.5 per cent each year from 1993-94 onward. In 2001, central, state and local government salaries together topped Rs. 167,715 crores. This kind of spending was not what Keynes had in mind when he advocated public spending to stimulate the economy. Quite clearly, China is an industrialising country whereas India seems to be entering the post-industrial phase without having industrialised. The challenge ahead of us is not catching up with China's growth rate which inevitably must slow down. When nations compete growth rates matter little if one is already well ahead, can we do what China did to us in 1986? Can we come abreast with it? To do that in 2020, we need to grow at 11.6 per cent and to do that long after most of us are gone in 2050. India must now grow at 8.9 per cent every year. Catching up with growth is not good enough. If that were the game we are already doing much better than the US, Europe and Japan. In India, contribution of agriculture to GDP has decreased substantially but dependence of population on this sector is almost static. This means economic conditions are further deteriorating.[1]

The latest publicity of performance of Indian economy is quite attractive as well as assuring. India is shining and there is an all pervasive feel good factor in the country. But in reality, average citizen is not very comfortable with macroeconomic management of the situation. The questions are still being asked as to why there are still poor people in India when Government of India is sitting on a pile of $ 105 billion foreign exchange. Jobless youth wants to know why the government is not able to provide them with jobs if the economy is doing so well. The villagers want to know if they can summon a doctor using that brand new cellphone. A vast continent sized economy has its problems, the problems of diversities. India is a country where very rich people of the world live, it also houses more than 268 million of the poorest of the poor. India has vast middle class with those living on the fringe of poverty. With these stark realities it is well nigh impossible for every Indian to see a shining future all at once. There are cases of affluence in the vast desert of poverty, hunger and helplessness.

Despite increase in economic growth during the last decade of liberalisation, employment growth has been tardy. It is also called "jobless growth". Highlighting "economic gains and social challenges", the Asian Development Bank in its latest economic bulletin on India has pointed out that the services sector was the fastest growing and the largest sector in the economy accounting for 26 per cent of the total employment. But employment in this sector declined from 3.1 per cent during 1987-93 to 2 per cent during 1993-99. In the agriculture sector, which now accounts for only 22 per cent of the total output of the economy, there has been no growth of employment.

As a consequence, while the GDP growth has now risen to over seven per cent, overall employment was growing at less than one per cent, the phenomenon is described as jobless growth, the ADB said. Thus the resultant increase in open unemployment and under-employment poses a major challenge for India. Indicators of development of social sector is equally disappointing.

Disparities are persistent across gender, regions and different social groups which are undermining social cohesion. The juvenile sex ratio has recorded sharp decline, highlighting the vulnerable status of the girl child and women. There is also accentuation of regional disparities with the Southern and Western regions doing much better than the Northern and Eastern regions. Human poverty indices based on health, literacy, income and social exclusion factors place some states on the top rung while others are on the lowest rung.

Even India occupies a very low position in the world in terms of human development indices. It is placed below the many African and Latin American countries.

Going further on the social challenges, the report points out that rural-urban and gender disparities continue to exist between and within the states. Significant inequalities also exist in the distribution of interpersonal consumption and levels of living, even within the states.

The studies revealed that the intensity of poverty was the highest among the landless wage earners, marginal farmers, scheduled castes and scheduled tribes, and indigenous population. These are the areas where India does not shine. This scenario has added significance of Gandhian economic doctrines.

With the appearance of Gandhi on the political stage, and with the revolt of Indian masses under his leadership, Indian history witnessed the dawn of a new era. Gandhi's clarion call for freedom is indicative of a new landmark in the history of mankind's great political struggles because of the entirely new and novel techniques.

Gandhi's works and deeds literally flew all over the subcontinent and embraced every aspect of individual as well as of society. He was all embracing and comprehensive in his vision, his mission and his approach to the problems confronting mankind all over the world. There was no sense of imposition or infliction. It was persuasion from the beginning to the end and yet the strength behind persuasion was unthinkable. In the words of Nehru: "The little man of poor physique had something of steel in him, something rock like... There was royalty and kingliness in him which compelled a willing obeisance from others."[2]

It was Gandhi's task to unify India and he accomplished it. And this was done by him through the unique combination of religion, philosophy and new politics. For him, philosophy is a way of life first and a way of thought next. His life systematised his plan of work and expressed it in practice, not exactly in theory. Philosophy of life reflected itself in life that has become self-conscious, and his self-consciousness expresses itself now and then as a theory of his practice.

Toynbee sums up Gandhi's motive for entering politics in the following words: " Gandhi's objective was to raise the spiritual level of life in spiritual slum, the slough of politics. Gandhi waded into the slough, showed the slough can be purified and remained personally uncontaminated by his immersion in it. This gives the measure both Gandhi's own spiritual stature and of the magnitude of his service to mankind at a turning point in human history."[3]

Einstein has paid him a rich tribute: "A leader of his people, unsupported by any outward authority; a politician whose success rests not upon craft nor mastery of technical devices, but simply on the convincing power of personality, or victorious fighter who has always scorned the use of force, a man of wisdom and humility; endowed with resolve and inflexible consistency, who has devoted all his strength to uplifting of his people and the betterment of their lot; a man who has confronted the brutality of Europe with the dignity of the simple human being, and thus at all times risen superior. Generations to come, it may be, will scarcely believe that such a one ever in 'flesh and blood' walked upon this earth.[4]

Gandhiji was deeply and essentially a religious man. My patrotism is subervient to my religion, he said. All that we see in this universe is pervaded by God. Renounce it and enjoy. Do not covet anybody's wealth or possession. He pinned all his faith to *Satyagrah,* as a weapon for fighting for freedom, and the final goal for individual action to be strong not with the strength of the brute but with the strength of the spark of God. In Gandhi's words :

> "I am not a visionary. I claim to be a practical idealist. The religion of non-violence is not meant merely for *Rishis* and saints. It is meant for common people as well. Non-violence is the law of the species as violence is the law of the brute. The spirit lies dormant in the brute and he knows no law but that of physical might. The dignity of man requires obedience to a higher law—to the strength of the spirit. I have, therefore, ventured to place before India the ancient law of self-sacrifice. For *Satyagrah* and its offshoots, non-cooperation and civil resistance are nothing but new names for the law of suffering. Non-violence in its dynamic conditions means conscious suffering. It does not mean submission to the will of the evil doer, but it means putting one's whole soul against the will of the tyrant working under this way of our being, it is possible for a single individual to defy the whole might of an unjust empire to save his honour, his religion, his soul and lay the foundation for that empire's fall or its regeneration."[5]

Under the backdrop of these fundamental philosophical foundations that Gandhi's ideas, actions, and various forms of *Satyagrah* and movement can be understood and judged in proper perspective and with certain degree of objectivity and relevance in the existing situation.

Gandhi's views on development were radical and far reaching. He was not satisfied with mere political freedom of the country. It had "little value if it did not herald the era of the common man". He considered India completely independent when the masses feel that they can improve their lot by their own efforts and can shape their destiny the way they like. He had a very clear vision of the development of villages which is the base of the economy. Gandhi wrote: "I am convinced that if India is to attain true freedom and through India the world also, then sooner or later the fact must be recognised that people will have to live in villages not in towns, in huts not in palaces. I hold that without truth and non-violence there can be nothing but destruction for humanity. I must not fear if the world today is going the wrong way. It is my bounden duty upto my last breath to try to protect India and through India the entire world from such a doom.[6]

Gandhi further asserted that man should rest content with his real needs and become self-sufficient. The old should be reclothed and refashioned in the light of modern science. He also said that the ideal village of his dream would contain intelligent human beings who would not live in dirt and darkness and as free men and women they would be completely free from diseases of virulent type while no one will be idle, no one will wallow in luxury. Everyone would have to contribute manual labour for the good of the others while such a village would not rule out modern facilities such as railways, post and telegraph and the like.

A sound system of the cconomy was, for Gandhi, the hallmark of true development. The system of economy, as he held, incorporated intensive, small-scale and diversified farming supported by co-operative endeavours. This type of farming is opposed to mechanised large-scale and collective farming whereas development of cottage crafts will be a help and compensatory to agriculture. The economy is to be cattle-based where law of return is observed. Whereas, on the other hand, a proper balance has to be established between animal, human and plant life, both human and animal are to be protected against competition of the machinery, on the other. His contemporaries failed to guage the significace of his suggestions. They critised and condemned him as 'unprogressive' steeped in pre-scientific medievalism and a retrograde going back to bullock cart mentality cowdung era. But both amazingly and instructively the recent advances in agronomy, biology, health and hygiene, dietitics and other important aspects of human development have not only supported and sanctioned what Gandhi upheld but have also re-emphasised his stand with added vigour.

The idea of *Swadeshi* is an inalienable part of Gandhi's scheme of development and progress. This concept is in utter contrast to the negative though prevalent concepts of 'getting rich quickly' with new and powerful and transfer of capital across regional or political boundaries. The brazen exploitation and plunder that the powerful nations of the world perpetrated upon the less powerful and, therefore, unfortunate nations especially during the hey day of colonial and imperial power is dark chapter in the history of mankind. The Western nations thus achieved tremendous prosperity and power with concomitant depletion of resources of the weaker nations. It is significant law of nature that if food and raw materials produced in one region are consumed in a distantly located one, its balance and equilibrium is disturbed. Only regional self-sufficiency, therefore, can lay the foundations of an economy of permanence.

The common belief that machines increase the productive efficiency is erroneous. The craze for cheapness squanders the natural resources at a faster rate and their depletion of natural resources cannot be compensated or regenerated at will. By running after cheapness and mass production, man is first deprived of the benefits of natural life, fresh air, sunshine and fresh and wholesome foods by concentrating them in small specific areas. Biological costs turn to be much heavier as spurt is provided to social unrest, class conflicts and antagonism and mental health. Thus the illusion of prosperity and cheapness goes on perpetuating peril to our own existence. Production, therefore, should be meant for man and not vice versa. But "where money and mechanism are given free play", he warned, "capital exploits the labour of a few to multiply itself, but the sum total of the labour of the crores, wisely utilised, automatically increases the wealth of the crores".[7] In his scheme of capital-labour production relationship, production is envisaged to become a source of life, joy and freedom and none of these is to be dominated by money values.

The anxiety at the uppermost of minds of the people who are believers in the efficacy of mechanical production is that in case man reverts back to the use of home made things and cooperative way of living, their standard of living will be lowered. But contrary to this, people will live in better contact with nature and the needs of many will not be sacrificed to the privileges of the few or for the so-called national prosperity and progress. This way of life will enable even the commonest to be the maker of his destiny and have an equal opportunity to attain the best in life. High standard of living and modern life style have brought alarming results in terms of physical illness and mental maladjustment in Europe and America. The huge sale of tranquilising drugs and happiness pills are the best testimony to the prevailing situation in the West.

Gandhi had clearly perceived that freedom and independence must go hand in hand and hence his emphasis on spiritual values. It implied an utter simplification of the pattern of living and recognising society on the basis of small, autonomous and manageable units in which rural communities would weild effective political power by becoming self-sufficient concerning their basic needs. This self-sufficiency in basic needs was to him the hallmark of proper development. In his *My Ideal of Village Swaraj,* he underlines his basic ideas of man's development in small, independent communities. He says :

> "It is a complete republic, independent of its neighbour for its own vital wants, and yet interdependent for many others in which dependence is a necessity. As far as possible, every activity will be conducted on a cooperative basis. The government of village will be conducted by the Panchayat of five persons annually elected by the adult villagers possessing minimum prescribed qualifications. Here there is a perfact democracy based upon individual freedom. The law of non-violence rules him and his government. He and his village are able to defy the might of a world. The law governing busy villager is that he will suffer death in the defence of his and his villagers' honour."[8]

His ideas of interdependence and mutual willing help are at once majestic and revolutionary. He says, "In this structure composed of innumerable villages, there will be ever-widening and never ascending circles." Life will not be a pyramid with the apex sustained by the bottom. But it will be an oceanic circle the whole becomes one life composed of individuals sharing majesty of the oceanic circle of which they are integral units.[9] Such a society will be highly cultured and would be animated by an inexorable and inviolable belief in God, i.e. a self-existing, all knowing, living force.

A legitimate question regarding technological choice is very important in Gandhian scheme of things. Gandhi himself was once asked about his view for industrialising India. He said he was definitely in favour of industrialisation, but his pattern was different from the current one. Asked about the place of machine in his scheme of industrialisation, he said "I would prize every invention of science made for the benefit of all."[10] Any machinery that helped individuals and lightened the burden of the millions of cottages was welcome to him. Scientific truth and discoveries were not the instruments of greed in the hands of few. The guiding principle would always be that the introduction of costly and complicated machines or processes must not impair the self-sufficiency of the community and they would be within the mental reach and comprehension of people. The machines should further be within their financial capacity to own individually and collectively.[11]

The dignity of labour is of prime concern for Gandhi. To him manual labour was neither primitive nor barbaric as it is thought by many modern intellectuals. Bread labour is the law of life binding upon all. Gandhi maintained if all worked for their bread, distinction of rank would be obliterated and what ever rich remained would be better advised to work as trustees for their property and not squander it for foolish and partisan ends. Intelligent bread labour is also the highest form of social service. If everybody lives by the sweat of his brow the earth will become a paradise.[12]

Gandhi often said that organisation is the crux of non-violence. To what extent non-violence put into practice is reflected by the very working of an organisation and the way it is constituted. As such planning is a very important items of Gandhian social organisation and is directly related to man's all-sided development. It takes into consideration the latest development which majority of the mankind finds itself faced with. The development may be upto as follows :

(1) World as well as Indian population exceeds the present available resources of food for adequate human consumption and pace of population growth is much faster than the development of new resource. The result has been that vast millions are either facing starvation or are on the verge of it.

(2) As food has priority over other things, agriculture assumes greater importance than either industry or comforts and covenience.

(3) It is now no more possible to exploit raw materials of which much came from lands inhabited by coloured races. In the past, the exploitation was possible only through violence which is being gradually rendered obsolete through world development and growing consciousness of man in every climate and country.

(4) Changes such as social, economic, political and educational are taking every new stride and, therefore, minds and hearts of poor people everywhere are clamouring for justice, opportunity, self-respect and human dignity.

(5) Conditions in India are widely different from those of the West not only in terms of a large peasantry in proportion to her population but also in terms of poverty, health, energy, initiative, self-confidence, courage and hope. With these factors in view, India needs an altogether different treatment in comparison to its counterparts in the West.

Thus, simple living and high thinking comes to be the very foundation and essence of Gandhian planning. The chief aim of socio-economic organisation and also of planning is neither multiplication of wants nor accumulation of comforts and luxuries although minimum standard of living assured to all is never ruled out. Gandhi said in 1946 : "I believe that independent India can only discharge her duty towards a groaning world by adopting simple and ennobled life by developing her thousands of cottages and living at peace with the world. High thinking is inconsistent with complicated material life based on high speed imposed on us by Mammon Worship. All the graces of life are possible only when we learn the art of living nobly."[13]

Even before Gandhi, many scholors and political activists have raised the issues of decline of village industries and handicrafts due to deliberate policy of the Britishers. But Gandhi was not willing to be a helpless spectator of the decline of rural industries. For him, it was not enough to express through agitations and demonstrations the urgency for the uplift of the village people. He, therefore, outlined his constructive programme primarily with the motive of discovering a self-reliant process of development within the villager as the starting point of rural regeneration. The educated townsman, on the other hand, was keen to accelerate industrial development on the Western model of creating greater wealth, employment and progress. Social education was the key note of Gandhiji's constructive programme.

Gandhi was never prepared to accept legitimacy of institutionalised injustice, whether economic or social. He personally aligned himself with the lowest of the low, with the poorest of the poor. He projected an image of himself as the unfailing friend of the friendless of the village poor and dumb millions who were crushed by centuries of social injustice and economic inequality. Gandhi thought if we depended upon the British or requested them to find work for the unemployed, it would be construed as an invitation to them to stay on and continue with goodwork of helping the poor whom we were unable to support on our own initiative and resourcefulness. It was almost an indirect admission of the necessity of British rule. It was for this reason that he launched the Khadi and Village Industries programme. In his view, the spinning wheel and his programme of Khadi spun and woven in the villages was a token of our determination not to depend upon on alien government. In the words of Nehru, Khadi became "livery of Indian freedom". Thus all his programme for villages reflected a steady spirit of self-reliance.

In post-independent India, national planning shifted the initiative of development to the centre and state governments. Whereas Gandhi's contructive programme strove to transfer initiative and responsibility to the village people themselves. All post-freedom rural development schemes are initiated by the centre through the state governments, thus using every programme to increase the dependence of the free citizens on the state and keep them at the mercy of government administrative agencies which finally resulted in 'Mai-Baap Sarkar Culture' just opposed to what Gandhi intended.

In the opinion of Achyut Patvardhan, India is a land of peasant-owners and peasant-ownership is the norm of new face of post-independence rural India. The second factor essential for abolishing rural poverty, we must achieve a zero rate of growth of population. If we do not want poverty, we must achieve a zero rate of growth of population. For preventing fragmentation and sub-division of holding, it is most important as it is obvious that poverty cannot be abolished unless India's population can be curbed. We must not forget that the striking increase in urban population is the direct consequence of the rural poor migrating to the towns in search of employment. In Bombay alone, nearly 4.5 million people are slum dwellers and they are forced to lead a sub-human life.

Gandhi, therefore, pleaded for decentralised village industries relying chiefly on local resources, a voluntary limitations of wants and leading place in society for basic communities where people have a sense of simple communion with one another. This is a model for universal application. The whole world can adopt it without fear of over-stepping limits of global resources and in conformity with the deeper needs of human nature. As a model, it may look idealistic and rather too removed from current reality. But Gandhi believes that human society as a whole must start moving in this direction as a corrective to the dreadful imbalance that has been growing within it.

The crisis of our time is multidimensional and it takes different forms in different parts of the world. Yet it has significant common features. Chief among them are militarism which dies hard and a pernicious proneness tall forms of violence, consumerism and a vain pursuit of spiritually exhausting and campetitive pleasures, and finally, ecological imbalance and predatory attitude towards nature. These provide a test of relevance for a social philosophy today.

In addition to the arms race between the East and West, the world is divided between the Rich North and the Poor South. The logic of the development policy with its emphasis on industrialisation has promoted infrastucture in these countries that encourages a miniscule minority to live luxuriously in a sea of mass poverty where malnutrition, hunger and lack of shelter and medicare are the rule. The UNICEF estimates that thousands of children die everyday for lack of food in a world where production and supply far outstrip the subsistence demand. The process of development divides the country into dual societies of rich and poor. The dynamics of a dual society and compulsions of international relations between rich and poor countries help bring to power authoritarian government that rule by a police state mentality, and where the institutions that are created to uphold law and order are themselves involved in neutralising or murdering their own citizens or, to use a contemporary euphemism, making people "disappear". Many countries in the South thus are in a state of turmoil on the edge of a violent revolution—successful or otherwise.

In the name of greater affluence for the rich and more development for the poor countries, the existing world order is involved in the extraction of ever-increasing non-renewable resources to the point of reaching the every limits of our planet. We are witnessing not only increasing strategic shortage on the horizon but also compelling important changes in the methods of production and nature of consumption. Shortages of oil and consequent soaring prices are clear manifestations. Other problems such as top soil and its erosion, acid rain, deforestation, overfishing, and grassland loss are being noticed everywhere which will have their impacts. In the near future, the impacts are likely to become both more visible and more detrimental. The unfortunate situation with these basic resources is that by the time their limits become more clearly visible, it may be already too late for any remedial action. Some even think that it may be beyond repair and lead to serious calamities. This is creating various kinds of instablities in the economics and world order.

Such instabilities of the existing international order tell us much about economic and political health of various countries rich or poor, belonging to the East or West. In the rich countries, quality of life is deteriorating even if standard of living has phenomenally improved. The value of family life and other social values are breaking down. A substantial number of children have never lived with both the parents. The adult life is marked by anxiety and job stress. Work for a large majority of workers is both stressful and meaningless. Old age is full of loneliness. Life has, no doubt, been prolonged, but life style in many places has become more like a nightmare. Crime has become so common that minor crimes are not even cared or taken notice by the police.

In the poor countries, poverty stares into our face. The size of the poor population is unbelievable large. A visit to big cities in the South, e.g. Calcutta, Delhi, Karachi, Cairo, Mexico, etc. introduces to the visitors begging and starving children as also mutilated bodies, dying old people, and people living on the street without any amenities of shelter, food, medicine, etc. At the same time, the government of those countries boast of growth in GNP, new industries, advanced technologies, and more and better higher education and research. All these analyses, estimates and other evidences point to the fact that this poverty is on the increase both in terms of absolute numbers and in terms of proportions to total population.

The growth in poverty, deterioration in the quality of life, instability in the international order, depletion of non-renewable global resources, disappearances of people and production of weapons of mass destruction have been rationalised by the policies of economic growth models face the situation, they very wilfully and deliberately ignore these realities and they again typically argue for an accelerated rate of economic growth and development. The public, on the other hand, recognising that the future is uncertain and quality of life is deteriorating, is losing faith in such policies not only in policies but also in the ideas and conceptual frameworks from which these policies follow. The science in general and economic science in particular is no longer sacrosanct. The high priests of both of them are losing their authority and in reality science of economics is in crisis. When a science is in crisis, it begins to question its own philosophical assumptions and methods and begins a search for alternative paradigm. The main reason for the crisis is that modern economics has no philosophy whatsoever.

This crisis is confirmed when Gandhi spoke in Allahabad in 1936 on "Does Economic Progress Clash with Real Progress"? He warned the audience explaining the nature of existing crisis. In the major part of his address, Gandhi first argued that material advance has a strong tendency to lead to moral decay. You cannot serve God and Mammon is an economic truth of the highest value. We have to make a choice. Western nations are groaning under the heels of monster-God of materialism. Concluding his address, he admonished his audience, "Let us seek first the kingdom of God and His righteousness, and the irrevocable promise is that everything will be added onto us. These are real economics. May you or I treasure them and enforce them in our daily life".

An examination of his lecture clearly points out to what he knew rather than what he did not know. He was interested in the scope and method of economic science as the economist generally understand it. Rather he worked for a whole lifetime on articulating the principle of an alternative and more real human economics centring on the very themes, outlined in his lecture: the lack of correlation between material expansion and genuine process, the need for an economics-cum-ethics that will enable more growth and dignity for all, the fallacy of seeking happiness in individual acquisitive behaviour, and the need for encouraging people to seek a life rich in self-esteem and genuine meaning. It is our contention and firm belief that Gandhi's legacy offers a new set of economic strategies and policies that may one day come to be seen as a promising rival to the accepted doctrines that have prevailed through the centuries.

A normative economics of Gandhian style, that intertwines economics and ethics into one inseparable whole, reflects a vertical and multidimensional image of man where both material and spiritual forces need to embrace each other in the human quest for unity and wholeness. The integrated and holistic perspective in economics boils down to this simple injunction; never advocate actions or policies that lead to material advancement at the cost of social, moral or spiritual impoverishment. Instead, the economist as the holistic economist should ascertain that the organisational principles and policies enable, possibly even encourage, a high overall quality of life for all.

Once it is recognised that the public good is at times not secured by maximising of private self-interest, but by self-restraint or even self-sacrifice, Adam Smith's invisible hand loses much of its glamour. At the same time, economists are pushed to entertaining new thoughts on what kind of action does lead to social welfare.

Sarvodaya is a full-fledged alternative to the utilitarian goal of using an existing resources base for output of goods available for consumption. Rather it seeks to develop resources to enable a decent life for everyone. Unlike Rawl's Theory of Justice (1971) to Gandhi, on the other hand, pure justice is never attained by fear, but is inspired by fellow-feeling or compassion for another and that way of justice which has no place in its for fellow feeling or compassion is known as Satanic or modern justice. *Sarvodaya,* the welfare of all, indicated by the well-being of the poor can be seen as a shift away from an economics based on individual desires and wants towards an economics of human needs. We all have an inborn need to be whole and we need a holistic economics to acknowledge this and enable us to work towards that end. Ideas of truth and justice have to be realised.

The conventional development strategy states that development is to occur by means of capital-intensive technologies replacing the traditional labour-intensive activities and with it the gradual elimination of the limited exchange systems of the traditional village economics. This was assumed on the basis of long-term efficiency of productive resources. Here Gandhian perspective differs radically and sheds much additional light on the problem. Gandhi foresaw the central and ever-worsening problem of the stagnation and decay of the traditional sector resulting directly from such modernistic and the singleminded stress on urban, capital-intensive development. By what is today known as the "backwash effect", much of the indigenous skills and crafts get destroyed by the new market competition of mass-produced consumer goods. Structural unemployment is rather a consequence of excessively capital-intensive development adopted by the Third World countries. Gandhi advocated appropriate technology as distinct from the conventional stress on least-cost technology. He outlined several conditions that make a technology appropriate, i.e. both non-violent and non-exploitative. E. F. Schumacher argued very ardently in favour of appropriate technology in his celebrated book *Small is Beautiful.*

In order to tackle the problem of acquisitive culture of the modern society and to emancipate the mankind from mad rat race for affluence, Gandhi stated the basic principles of his organisation. These principles were:

(a) no one has any right over property which is a social phenomenon;
(b) state ownership of property leads to concentration of economic and political power in the hands of bureaucracy

which has the monopoly of violence and hence is an antithesis of trusteeship;

(c) trusteeship is by definition a communitarian system, a kind of general cooperation of efforts and resources;

(d) trusteeship is a system of social self-management and a kind of socialist democracy from below; and

(e) trusteeship is based on the Gandhian theory of labour.

Even Marxists have come round to the view that nationalisation is a necessary but not a sufficient conditions for having a humanist and non-alienated society. Gandhi made it clear that without eliminating the component of alienation from politics there should be no elimination from elsewhere. In other words, politics for him was inseparable from other social and economic activities. The revolutionary minority had to be highly politically conscious, morally exemplary and sensitive and fully capable of understanding and undertaking the practice of *Satyagrah.*

Gandhi did not postulate any economic plan in the sense it is understood in the present context. Still the economic ideas of Gandhiji constitute the Gandhian plan, which envisages (i) a self-contained economy with emphasis on village industries based on simple machinery aiming of maximisation production and productivity by indigenous resources and not on mechanisation of economic production as in modern industrialism, (ii) equitable distribution of return and material surpluses not by any coercive law but on imbibing a spirit of metaphysics and economic ethics particularly infusing a sense of trusteeship in the category of "haves" on a distinction between the idea of possession and possessiveness, and (iii) striking a balance between capitalist, bourgeoisie and state capitalism.

Basic tenets of Gandhian economics are amply contained in five year plans of India, for example, First Five Year Plan envisaged for "a fuller utilisation of idle manpower in the country to be a major objective," through improvement of agriculture and development of cottage and small scale industries.[14] The Second Five Year Plan provided for rebuilding rural India to lay the foundation of industrial progress and to secure to the greatest extent possible opportunities to weaker and underprivileged sections of our people aiming at a socialist pattern of society.[15] The Third Plan upheld the objective of self-sufficiency in foodgrains and greater equality of opportunity and reduction in the disparities in income and wealth and even distribution of economic power.[16] The Fourth Plan was more realistic and emphasised on self-reliant economy and the importance of the institution of Panchayati Raj and form of cooperatives.[17]

Theoretically, these are the objectives but the lack of sincerity, commitment and conviction on the part of the planners priority was distorted and real objectives hijacked at the level of implementation to suit the vested interest of politicians, bureaucrats and powerful lobbies in the country. The consequence is obvious before the nation. Gandhi is worshipped and adored whereas Gandhian principles and ideas are sidetracked, ignored and sometimes vilified as well.

The problems confronted by mankind in general and India in particular are complex and alarming and all the strategies to tackle them fail as they are based on erroneous notions and assumptions that problems created by technology can be solved by higher level of technology which proved to be elusive and deceptive. The consequence is multiplication of problem and aggravation of the crisis. Safety and security of mankind are threatened and mankind is in peril. There is increasing awareness that Gandhian doctrine can offer durable solution. Whether it is a question of production or distribution of wealth, peace and security, Gandhi offers alternative which if adopted can rid the society of its ills. Poverty, unemployment, disparity and deprivation of the masses have been discussed in depth and sustainable solutions have been given in terms of self-sufficiency, trusteeship, non-possession, bread labour and *Sarvodaya* which take care of the poorest of the poor which as termed as *Antyodaya.*

Limitation of wants and inculcation of self-disciple in life is *sine qua non* of civilised society which offers opportunity to every member. Gandhi realised that tears from every eye have to be wiped out if society is to developer and prosper. He further asserted that was the constructive programme and said:

> "A violent and bloody revolution is a certainty one day unless there is voluntary abdication of the riches and the power that riches give and sharing them for the common good".

Similar views were also expressed by B.R. Ambedkar on 26th January 1950 when he declared:

> "We have entered into life of contradiction. We shall have equality in politics and inequality in social and economic life. How long to continue this contradiction? If equality is denied in social and economic life, political democracy will be in peril."

This view is also shared by J.F. Kennedy when he publicly announced that if you could not help the poor who were in majority you could not protect the rich who were in minority. This is quite compatible with Gandhian doctrine of trusteeship, *Sarvodaya* and non-possession.

One of the greatest sons of Mother India, Swami Vivekanand emphatically and strongly opined :

> "So long as millions live in hunger and ignorance, I hold every man a traitor who, having been educated at their expence, pays not the least heed to them."

He was a saint hence he expressed his views in emphatic and strong language to warn the mankind from imminent disaster. The saner advice of saints and *Rishis* have been ignored at the cost of inviting troubles for mankind which is on the brink of disaster. Thus Gandhi offers holistic approach and comprehensive socio-economic, political and spiritual framework for the final emancipation of mankind, if heeded in time. Even person like F.D. Roosevelt's thinking is consistent with Gandhian thought when he says, "the test of our progress is not whether we add more to the abundance of these who have much it is whether we provide enough for those who have little."

Now the irresistible conclusion is that creation of wealth is the main concern of economics while it ignores the fact that man is the central concern. Man is a rational social being hence he may not be treated only as a bundle of self-interest, desires and personal felicity. Man also possesses heart and soul which transcends material acquisition and physical pleasure. Material acquisition may help in fulfilling the basic needs of survival but it may stultify the heart and soul beyond a point. When man is treated as a central concern, economic activities must revolve round the man and not vice versa. In this context, search for material well-being will not solve the purpose of life which is more important than mere survival.

People live in society and have obligations to each other. Hence, human welfare is obtained and maintained through social actions. Society is based on moral foundation, hence people and society have to act morally and behave rationally. Social relationships are patterned and structured on ethics, morality, love, respect and mutual consideration for each other. Economic man is kept out of the ambit of these considerations which is neither desirable nor conducive for harmonious social order. Due to innovation and technological breakthrough there have been perceptible changes in the material conditions of the society. The attitude and perception of the people have also changed. Under the changed scenario, there is greater awareness of the wider social phenomenon which necessitates the search for alternative paradigms of development. The existing theories and models have failed to meet the challenges posed by development itself. It has become imperative to bridge the gap and that is possible and feasible only if we succeed in evolving alternative paradigms of development. Here Gandhi offers the alternative in terms of human economics combined with ethics. Gandhi seems to be the last hope. His ideas, thoughts and practices assure the mankind to get new lease of life. Material needs must be compatible with the spiritual needs. *Artha* and *Karma* should be subordinated to the *Dharma* and this is what Gandhi prescribes.

Madhav Govind Ranade was the first person to term "Indian Economics", to mean systematic treatment of Indian economic problems. Gandhiji strongly supported this view, "India has got to develop her own economics, her own policy, her own method of dealing, with her industries and everything else".[18] An economic doctrine that would relegate the individual to the background and provide for an artificial picture of growth and delusive plenty of the society is abhorred under Gandhian economic philosophy.

Gandhi could realise that it was the amelioration of the villages that was the basic economic need, hence all emphasis was laid on villages where 85 per cent of population lived and earned their livelihood in a starkly uncongenial condition. The spinning wheel or *charkha* and *khadi* were held to be epitome of economic doctrine and were believed to be the panacea for economic ills of the country. *Khadi,* according to Gandhi, represents three basic factors of economic development and these symbolise (i) self-help, dignity of labour and employment potential, (ii) utilisation and husbanding of indigenous resources, and (iii) self-contained economy. Besides, charkha and khadi were held to carry the message of not only of economics but an ideal of simple life and high thinking and it is a living against the modern craze of material affluence which knows no bounds of satiety. The whole gamut of the Gandhian concept of economics rests on this ideal of strengthening of village economy.

Thus one may be tempted to conclude that Gandhian economics is tantamount to an economics of non-violence. Gandhi left for us a guide to non-violent economic action :

> I give you a talisman. Whenever you are in doubt or when self becomes too much for you, apply the following test. Recall the face of the poorest and weakest man whom you have seen, and ask yourself if the step you contemplate is going to be of any use to him. Will he gain anything by it? Will it restore him to a control over his own life and destiny? In other words, will it lead to *Swaraj* for the hungry and spiritually starving millions? Then, you will find your doubt and yourself melting away.

In view of the growing violence in any form, parasitism and multiplicity of social conflicts, no method other than *Satyagrah* is going to serve us and save us from final disaster in the long run.

REFERENCES

1. Mohan Guruswamy, Abhishek Kaul and Vishal Handa (2003), Is India Really Shining? *The Hindu*, Dec. 03, Delhi, p. 8.
2. Jawaharlal Nehru, *Soul of India*, pp. 313-14.
3. Quoted Durant, Our Oriental Heritage, New York, 1995, p. 129.
4. A Day of Thoughts from Mahatma Gandhi, Mac Millan, 1951, p. 4.
5. M.K. Gandhi (1961) *Non-Violence in Peace and War*, Vol. I, Ahmedabad, Navjivan Publishing, pp. 4-5.
6. Pyare Lal (1958) *Mahatma Gandhi—The Last Phase*, Vol. II, Navajivan Publishing House, Ahmedabad, p. 543.
7. Pyare Lal (1998) *Mahatma Gandhi—The Last Phase*, Navajivan Publishing House, Ahmedabad, p. 569.
8. *Harijan*, 26.07.1946.
9. *Harijan*, 28.07.1946.
10. *Harijan*, 27.07.1935, p. 146.
11. Pyare Lal, *Mahatma Gandhi—The Last Phase*, Vol. II, p. 583.
12. *Harijan*, 02.03.1947, p. 477.
13. S.N. Agrawal (1960) *Principles of Gandhian Planning*, Kitab Mahal, Allahabad, p. 65.
14. The First Five Year Plan, Govt. of India, p. 30.
15. The Second Five Year Plan, Govt. of India, XIII.
16. The Third Five Year Plan, Govt. of India, p. 48.
17. The Fourth Plan (Final Draft), pp. 27-28.
18. *Speeches and Writings of Mahatma Gandhi*, G. A. Satesan & Coi (4th Edition), p. 844.

Bibliography

A. Das, *Foundation of Gandhian Economics,* New Delhi, Publishers, 1979.

Albert Hirschman, *The Passions and Interest,* Princedom University Press, 1978.

A. Hirschman, *The Strategy of Economics Development,* London, 1976.

Alexander Gerschenkron, *The Economic Backwardness in Historical Perspective,* London, 1983.

A. Maddison, *Economic Progress and Policy in Developing Countries,* New York, 1970.

A.M. Haq, Welfare Criteria in Gandhian Economics, in Ramesh Diwan and Mark Lutz, (Eds) *Essays in Gandhian Economics,* Gandhi Peace Foundation, Delhi, 1985.

Alfred Mansel, Revolution and Counter-Revolution, *Encyclopedia of Social Science.* Vol. XIII.

Ashok Mehta, *Studies in Asian Socialism.*

Anil Markandya, Rehat Perelet (Eds), *Dictionary of Environment,* New Delhi, Oxford University Press, 2001.

A.K. Sen, *Social Welfare and Collective Choice.* San Fancisco, 1970.

A.K. Sen, *Choice of Techniques on Economic Inequality,* New Delhi, Oxford University Press, 1973.

Adam Smith, *An Enquiry into the Nature and Causes of Wealth of Nations,* 1976.

Ajit Singh, Liberalisation and Stock Market and the Market for Capital Control in Isher Ahluwalia and I.M.D Little (Eds) *India's Economic Reforms and Development,* Delhi, 1998.

Achut Patwardan, quoted in Bhagwan Das Kela, in *Rajya Vyavastha Sarvodaya Ki Drishtee.*

Alan Richardson, *Religion in Contemporary Debate,* 1956.

Alvin Toffler, *Future Shocks,* A National General Company, New York, 1971.

A.C. Bhatia, *The Gandhian Economy in what Gandhi has done for India,* Lahore. Ilami, 1946.

A. Chakravarthy, *Mahatma Gandhi and the Modern Word,* Calcutta Book House, 1945.

A.K. Dasgupta, *Economics of Austerity,* Shastri Memorial Lecutre, Banaras Hindu University, Oxford University, 1974.

Bipan Chandra, *India After Independence,* New Delhi, Penguin Books, 1999.

Bhahatosh Dutta, *Indian Economic Thought,* New Delhi, Tata McGraw Hill, 1980.

B. Heggins, *Economic Development,* London, 1964.

Behim Behari, *Gandhian Economic Philosophy,* Bombay, Vora & Co., 1963.

B.N. Ganguli, *Gandhi's Social Philosophy,* Delhi, Vikas Publishing House, 1973.

Bimal Prasad (Ed), A Revolutionary Quest, *Selected Writings of Jayaprakash Narayan,* Delhi, 1980.

Bhagwat Puran, Chap. 14, Skand 7, Verse 728.

Bertrand Russel, *Political Ideals,* London, 1946.

Brij Narayan, *Economic Structure of Free India,* Building from Below, All India Khadi and Village Industries Board, Bombay, 1955.

Bharatan Kumarappa, *Capitalism, Socialism and Villagism,* Sarva Seva Sangh Prakashan, Varanasi, 1965.

B.R. Nanda, *Gandhi and His Critics,* Oxford University Press, Delhi, 1985.

C.B. Shukla, *Gandhi's Veiws of Life,* Delhi, 1981.

C.D. Desmukh, *Economic Development in India 1946-56, A Personal Retrospect,* Bombay, Asia Publishing House, 1957.

C.E.M Joad, *Guide to Philosophy of Morals and Politics,* London, 1954.

C.H. Hanumantha Rao, Agriculture Policy and Performance in Bimal Jalan (Ed) *The Indian Economy,* Delhi, 1992.

C. Rangarajan, Development, Inflation and Monetary Policy in Isher. J. Ahluwlia and I.M.D. Little (Eds) *India's Economic Reforms and Development : Essays for Manmohan Sigh,* Delhi, 1998.

——, *Collected Works of Mahatma Gandhi*, Vol. 1968. Publication Division, G.O.I, 1959.

Charles Taylor, The Concept of Man, B.N. Ganguli Memorial Lecture, C.S.D.S. Delhi, March 1981.

D.M. Dutta, "Philosophical Basis of Social Revolution", Proceeding of Indian Philosophical Congress.

Durant, *Our Oriental Heritage,* New York, 1995.

Diwan and Gidwani, Element of Gandian Economics in Essays in *Gandhian Economics,* Gandhi Peace Foundation, Delhi.

David Drekson, *Alternative Technology,* Fontana, 1974.

Devid Hume, *A Treatise on Human Nature,* Book I Part IV Section 6.

Dale Tom and Carter Vernon Gill, *Top Soil and Civilisation,* Norman University of Oklahoma Press, 1995.

David Ricardo, *The Principles of Political Economy and Taxation,* 1917.

Dadabhoi Naoroji, *Poverty and Un-British Rule in India,* Publication Division, Delhi, 1961.

Economic Survey, Government of India, 1996.

Economic Survey, Government of India 1998-99.

Economic Survey, Government of India 1997.

E.F. Schumacher, *Forework, Equality Through Trusteeship and Full Employment,* Bombay, Bharatiya Vidya Bhawan, Second Edition, 1978; Small is Beautiful.

E.F. Schumacher, *Future is Manageable,* New Delhi, Impex India, 1978.

Erich Fromm, *Beyond Chains of Illusions,* New York, 1965.

Ellen Meiksins Wood, Mind and Politics, *An Approach to the Meaning of Liberal and Socialist Indivisualism,* California, Berkeley University, 1972.

Erik H. Erikson, *Childhood and Society,* Paladin, 1977.

Eric Roll, *History of Economic Thought,* 1953.

Fred Hirsch, *Social Limits to Growth,* London 1977.

Fritjof Capro, *The Tao of Physics : Exploration of Parallels between Modern Physics and Modern Mysticism,* Shambhala, Boulder Publiscations, 1983.

Gunnar Myrdal, *Asian Drama,* Penguin Books.

G.R. Madan, *Economic Thinking in India,* Delhi, S. Chand and Co., 1966.

Gandhi—Autobiography Chap. XVIII, 1943.

Gandhi's Paraphrase of Unto This Last, 1951.

Geoffrey OStergaard, *Non-Violent Revolution in India,* New Delhi, 1985.

Global report to the President of the United States, Washington, D.C. 1980.

Gerald M. Mier and Robert E. Baldwin, Economic Development, London, John Wiley and Sons, 1926.

G.N. Dhawan, *Political Philosophy of Mahatma Gandhi,* Ahmedabad, Navajivan, 1946.

Harvey Leibenstein, Economic Backwardness and Economic Growth, Studies in *the Theory of Economic Development,* 1957.

Henrich Zimme, *Philosophy of India,* Princeton University Press, 1951.

Huxley, *Science, Liberty and Peace,* London, Chatto and Windus, 1950.

I.M.D. Little, *Critique of Welfare Economics.*

I.H. Rima, *Development of Economic Analysis,* Chicago, 1972.

J.A. Schumpeter, *Ten Great Economists.*

J.A. Schumpeter, *Theory of Economic Development.*

J.A. Schumpeter, *Capitalism, Socialism and Democracy.*

Jhingon, *Theory of Economic Development.*

J.K. Meade, A New Classical Theory of Economic Growth.

J.D. Sethi, Foreword, *Essays in Gandhian Economics,* (Ed) Ramesh Diwan & Mark Lutz, Gandhi Peace Foundation, New Delhi.

J.D. Sethi, *Gandhi Today,* Delhi, Vikas Publishing House, 1978.

Jayaprakash Narayan, *Socialism, Sarvodaya and Democracy.*

J.M. Keynes, *General Theory of Employment, Interest and Money.*

J.K. Mehta, *Gandhian Thought,* Allahabad.

J.K. Mehta, Advanced Economics.

John Dewey, *Individualism : Old and New,* New York, Capricorn Books 1982.

J.B. Kripalani, Philosophical Basis of Revolution, Proceedings of Indian Philosophical Congress.

J.B. Kripalani, Gandhi : *His Life and Thought,* Publication Division, 1951.

Jine Grasso, Jay Corrin and Michael Kart, *Modernization and Revolution in China.* M. 7 Shape, New York, 1997.

J.S. Mathur, Preface, *Ailing World and Gandhian Alternative,* Bhartiya Vidya Bhawan, Bombay, 1997.

Jawaharlal Nehru, *Soul of India.*

Joan Rohinson, *An Essay on Marxian Economics,* London, McMillan, 1949.

J.C. Kumarappa, *Gandhian Economic Thought,* Bombay, Vora & Co., 1951.

John Lewis, P. John, *Quest Crisis in India, Economic Development and American Policy,* Bombay, Asia Publishing House, 1963.

K.G. Mashruwala, *Gandhi and Marx.*

Karl Marx, *Economic and Philosophic Manuscript,* Moscow, 1961, Kapital.

Karl Marx, F. Engels and V.I. Lenin, *On Historical Materialism,* Moscow.

K.N. Raj, *Indian Economic Growth Performance and Prospects,* New Delhi, 1962.

Kenneth K. Boulding, *Why did Gandhi Fail and His Relevance for our Times,* Bhartiya Vidya Bhawan, Bombay.

K.C. Agrawal, *Environmental Biology,* Agra, Botanical Publishers, 1996.

K.S. Bharati, *Thoughts of Gandhi and Vinoba,* Concept Publishing Co., Delhi, 1995.

Louis Fisher, *Gandhi : His life and Message for the World,* New York 1954.

Mahatma Gandhi, *Socialism of my Concept,* Bhartiya Vidya Bhawan, Bombay, 1966.

Quoted in Pyarelal Mahatma Gandhi—The Last Phase, Navajivan, Ahemedabad, 1958.

M.K. Gandhi—*Ashram Observances in Action,* Navajian, Ahmedabad, 1959.

——, *The Story of My Experiment with Truth,* Navajivan, Ahmedabed, 1966.

——, *India of My Dream,* (Ed) by P.K. Prabhu, Bombay, 1947.

——, *All Men are Brothers,* New York, and Columbia University Press, 1958.

——, *Hind Sivaraj,* 1946.

——, *Sarvodaya : Welfare of All,* Navajivan, Ahemedabad 1954.

——, *Non-Violence in Peace and War,* Vol. I Navajivan, Ahmedabad, 1961.

——, *From Yergvada Mandir,* Navajivan, Ahmedabad, 1926.

——, *From Yergvada Mandir,* Navajivan, Ahmedabad, 1945.

——, *Constructive Programme : Its Meaning and Place,* Navajivan, Ahmedabad, 1970.

——, *Khadi : Why and How?* Navajivan, Ahmedabad, 1959.

——, *My Socialism,* compiled by R.K. Prabhu, Navajivan, Ahmedabad, 1949.

Marx and Engles, *Communist Manifesto.*

M.N. Roy, *India in Transition,* Nachiketa, Bombay, 1971.

Marshall, *Principles of Economics,* McMillan & Co., London, 1949.

M.R. Masani, *The Communist Party of India : A Short Story,* Bharatiya Vidya Bhawan, Bombay, 1967.

M.L. Sharma, *Gandhi as a Socialist,* Deep & Deep Publishing Co., Delhi, 1980.

Myrdal, *Asian Drama, An Enquiry into the Poverty of Nahanas,* 3 Vols., New York, 1968.

Myrdal, *The Challenge of World Poverty,* Penguin Books, 1970.

M.L. Dantwala, *Decentralized Economic Order,* Kashi, Sarva Seva Sangh, 1961.

M.L. Dantwala, *Gandhism Recosidered,* Bombay, Padma Prakashan, 1945.

N.R. Sarkar, Presidential Speech, FICCI, Annual Report, New Delhi, 1934.

N. Kaldor, *Essays on Value and Distribution,* 1960.

N.K. Bose, *Selection from Gandhi,* Navajivan, Ahmedabad, 1948.

N.K. Bose, *Studies in Gandhism.*

Namboodripad E.M.S., *The Mahatma and the Ism.* Peoples Publishing House, New Delhi, 1959.

N. Raghunathan, *Srimad Bhagwat,* Vigneshwar Publishing House, Madras, Vol. I, 1946.

Onkar Sharad, *Lohia Ke Vichar,* Lok Bharati Prakashan, Allahabad, 1969.

P.A. Samuelson, *Foundation of Economic Analysis,* Harvard University Press, 1947.

P.G. Prondhan, *What is Property?* London, 1840.

Pyarelal, *Towards New Horizon.*

Pyarelal, Mahatma Gandhi: The Last Phase, Vol. II Navajivan, Ahmedabad, 1958.

P.C. Ghosh, *Mahatma Gandhi: As I Saw Him,* Delhi, S. Chand & Co., 1968.

Prayayoto, T. Green Market, Economics of Sustainable Development, Institute for Contemporary Study Press, San Francisco, 1993.

P.A. Wadia, The Gandhian Approach to Economic, in *Social and Political Ideas of Mahatma Gandhi,* Oxford University Press, 1949.

R.F. Harrod Towards Dynamics in Economic Essays; Second Essay in Dymamic Economics, *Economic Journal.*

Ramesh Diwan and Mark Lutz, Introduction, *Essays in Gandhian Economic.*

Ramesh Diwan and Mark Lutz, *Gandhi,* Peace Foundation, Delhi.

Ramesh Diwan and Mark Lutz, *In Relevance of Gandhian Econonics* (Ed) D.S. Awasthi.

Ramesh Diwan and Mark Lutz, *The Economics of Love, An Attempt of Gandhian Economics.*

R.H. Tawney, *The Acquisitive Society,* New York, Har Court, Brace and Company, 1921.

R.K. Prabhu, *Communism and Communists,* Navajivan, Ahmedabad, 1952.

Rajendra Prasad, *Legacy of Gandhi.*

Rajendra Prasad, *At the Feet of Mahatma Gandhi,* Allied, Bombay. 1961.

Radhakrishnan, *Religion and Society.*

Ruskin, *Unto This Last,* Paraphrased by M.K. Gandhi, Navajivan, Ahmedabad, 1989.

Ramashray Roy, *Self and Society, A Study in Gandhian Thought,* Sage Publication, New Delhi, 1985.

R.P. Dutta, *India Today.* Peoples Publishing House, Bombay, 1949.

Richard Falk, *A Study of Future World,* Delhi, 1975.

Raghavan Iyer, *Moral and Political Thought of Mahatma Gandhi,* Delhi, Oxford Univerisity Press, 1981.

R. Perman, *Natural Resources and Environmental Economics,* Harlow, Longman, 1996.

Rashmi Sharma, *Gandhian Economics, A Humane Approach,* Deep & Deep Publication. New Delhi, 1997.

Suresh D. Tendulkar, Indian Economic Policy Reform and Poverty, An Assessment in AbuJuwalia & Little (Eds), *India's Economic Reforms 1991-2001,* Oxford University Press, 1996.

S. Narayan, *Selected Works of Mahatma Gandhi,* Vol. 5, 1968.

Swami Rama, *The Book of Wisdom, Isopanishad,* Illinois, North West Yoga Centre, 1972.

Suresh Ram (Ed) *Towards Total Revolution,* Thanjavur, 1968.

S.N. Agrawal, *Principles of Gandhian Planning,* Kitab Mahal, Allahabad, 1960.

Schumacher, *Roots of Economic Growth,* Gandhian Institute of Studay, Varanasi, 1962.

Shastri S. Gupta, *The Economic Philosophy of Mahatma Gandhi,* Ashok Publishing House, Delhi, 1976.

Sandip Chauhan, *Demand for New International Economic Order,* M.D. Publications, Delhi.

Sugata Das Gupta, Towards a Post Development Era: Essay in *Poverty, Welfare and Development,* Mittal Publications, Delhi.

S.N. Jha, *A Critical Study of Gandhian Economic Thought,* Agra, Laxmi Narain Agrawal, 1961.

Tarlok Singh, *Poverty and Social Change,* Calcutta, Longmans, 1945.

Tibor Scitovsky, *The Jobless Economy,* New York, Oxford University Press, 1976.

Tacques Maritaina (Ed) *Challenges and Renewals, Selected Reading,* University of Notre Dame Press, 1966.

Thakur Das Bung, *Kranti Ki Pukar.* The Limits to Growth, A Report of the Club of Rome's Project on the Predicament of Mankind, Massachusetts Institute of Technology, 1972.

Tom Tinbergen, (Coordinator), *Reshaping International Order,* London, 1977.

The First Five Year Plan, Government of India, New Delhi.

The Second Five Year Plan, Government of India, New Delhi.

The Third Five Year Plan, Government of India, New Delhi.

The Fourth Five Year Plan, (Final Draft), Government of India, New Delhi.

Toynbee Arnold, *Study of History,* Thames and Hudson, London, 1977.

T.N. Khoshoo, Environment Priorities, India and Sustainable Development Perspective, Address. I.S.C.A, 1986.

T.K.N. Unnithan, *Gandhi and Free India,* Holland, 1956.

T.K.N. Unnithan, *Gandhi and Social Change,* Rawat Publication, Jaipur, 1979.

Venkata Raman, *Nagarjuna's Philosophy,* Motilal Banarsi Dass, 1978.

Victor Hugo, *Dictionary of Thought.*

Vishwaath Tandon (Ed), *Eelection of Vinoba,* Varanasi, 1981.

V.P. Verma, *Political Philosophy of Mahatma Gandhi and Sarvodaya,* Laxmi Narayan Agrawal, Agra, 1981.

V.K.R.V. Rao, *Gandhin Alternative to Western Socialism,* Bhartiya Vidya Bhawan, Bombay, 1970.

V.I. Lenin, *Leftwing Communism; An Infantile Disorder,* Novosti Press, Moscow.

V.I. Lenin, *Selected Works.* Vol. II.

V.T. Patel, *Studies on Gandhi,* Delhi, Sterling Pubishers, 1983.

Vera Anstey, *Economic Development of India,* London, Longmans, 1952.

Vaikunth L. Mehta, *Decentralized Economic Development,* Khadi and Village Industires Commission, Bombay 1964.

Vrajendra Raj Mehta, *Beyond Marxism: Towards an Alternative Perspective,* Manohar, New Delhi, 1960.

W.W. Rostow, *The Stages of Economic Growth,* 1960.

W.W. Rostow, World Commission on Environment And Development, Our Common Future, Oxford University Press, 1987.

W.A. Lewis, *Theory of Economic Growth,* London, George Allen and Unwin, 1955.

Journal

A.M. Huq, Welfare criteria in Gandhian Economics, *Gandhi Marg,* January-1977.

A.Bergson, On the concept of Social Welfare, *Quarterly Journal of Economics.*

Amrit Bazar Patrika, Calcutta - 17.09.1933

Amrit Bazar Patrika, Calcutta - 2.8.1934

Bhoodan, *English Weekly,* 19.03.1958

D. Seers, The meaning of Development, *International Development Review,* Vol.II, 1969

D. Jorgenson, The Development of Dual Economy, *Economic Journal,* 1971.

Sugata Dasgupta, Towards a Counter -Civilization, *Gandhi Marg,* Gandhi Peace Foundation, New Delhi-1973

Arnold Edwin, The Songs celestial, quoted in *Young India,* 20 October,1921

M.K. Gandhi, *Young India,* 23 March, 1921.

S.C. Gangal, Gandhi and the Major World Problems, A contemporarya Futuristic perspective, *Gandhi Marg,* Vol. 9, No. 1, 1997.

Harijan - 13.03.1946

Harijan - 18.08.1940

Harijan - 02-01-1937

Harijan - 31-01-1946

Harijan - 31-03-1946

Harijan - 30-07-1947

John Fei and Gustav Ranis, A Theory of Economic Development, *A.ER.*Vol.51, Sept.,1984.

Knese Allen, Development and Environment, *Third World Quarterly* Vol.I No.I London 1979

L.C. Thanu, Relevance of Gandhian Thought to Economic Growth, *Gandhi Marg,* Feb,1986.

Modern Review, October 1935

M.K. Gandhi, Towards a Non-violent Socialism, *Harijan,* September 1947.

Mohan Guruswamy, Abhishek Kaul and Vishal Handa, Is India shining, *The Hindu,* Delhi December, 2003.

Mahalanobis P.C., Some observations on the Process of Growth of National Income, *Sankhya,* September, 1953.

Ramesh Diwan, The Economics of Love, An Attempt at Gandhian Economics, *Gandhi Marg,* Vol. XIV. No.2 June,1982.

Ramesh Diwan, Trusteeship and Decentralisation, *Gandhi Marg,* January, 1980.

Ramesh Diwan, Mahatma Gandhi and Economics of Exploitation, *Journal of Social Science,* 1903.

V.K.R.V. Rao, Disarmament and Development, *Gandhi Marg,* May-June 1982.

S.K. Nath, Are Formal Criteria Required? *Economic Journal,* September 1964.

The Hindu, Delhi 10.02.2003.

The Hindu, Delhi 02-07-2001.

The Modern Review, July 1935.

The London Times, 13th October, 1968.

Vinoba Bhave, Bhoodan, *English Weekly,* June,1956.

Young India, 11-08-1925.

Young India, 03-09-1925.

Young India, 17-05-1926.

Young India, 26-11-1926.

Young India, 08-08-1929.

Young India, 26-11-1931.

A.M. Huq, Investment Criteria in Gandhian Economics, *Gandhi Marg,* May 1986.

A. Agrawal, Politics of Environment, *Gandhi Marg,* Vol. 87, 1986.

Index